DATE DUE

NO 19 98			
JE 7 98			
DE 15 99			
DE 10 01			
FE 1 03			
AP 20			
AG 9 07			
FE 10 10			

DEMCO 38-296

COMMON WOMEN

Common Women

*Prostitution and Sexuality
in Medieval England*

RUTH MAZO KARRAS

New York   Oxford
Oxford University Press
1996

Oxford   New York
Athens   Auckland   Bangkok   Bombay
Calcutta   Cape Town   Dar es Salaam   Delhi
Florence   Hong Kong   Istanbul   Karachi
Kuala Lampur   Madras   Madrid   Melbourne
Mexico City   Nairobi   Paris   Singapore
Taipei   Tokyo   Toronto

and associated companies in
Berlin   Ibadan

Published by Oxford University Press, Inc.
198 Madison Avenue, New York, New York 10016

Oxford is a registered trademark of Oxford University Press

Library of Congress Cataloging-in-Publication Data
Karras, Ruth Mazo, 1957—
    Common women : prostitution and sexuality in Medieval England/
    Ruth Mazo Karras.
        p.   cm. — (Studies in the history of sexuality)
    Includes bibliographical references and index.
    ISBN 0-19-506242-6
    1. Prostitution—England—History.   2. Prostitutes—England—
Social conditions.   3. England—Social conditions—1066–1485.
I. Title.   II. Series.
HQ186.A5K37   1996
306.74'0942—dc20   96-19801

1   3   5   7   9   8   6   4   2

Printed in the United States of America
on acid-free paper

For C.G.K.

Acknowledgments

During the years this work took to complete, I have enjoyed both practical and intangible support from a plethora of institutions and people—and have incurred many debts. It is my pleasure to thank the staffs of the libraries and archives whose collections I consulted. *In Britain:* The Bodleian Library; Borthwick Institute for Historical Research; British Library, Manuscript Students' Room; Canterbury Cathedral, City, and Diocesan Record Office; Corporation of London Records Office; Devon Record Office; Essex Record Office; Greater London Record Office; Guildhall Library Department of Manuscripts; Kent Archives Office; King's Lynn Borough Archives; Lincolnshire Archives Office; Public Record Office; Lambeth Palace Library; Norfolk Record Office; Nottingham Record Office; Southampton City Records Office; Suffolk Record Office; Westminster Abbey Muniments Room; Warburg Institute; York Minster Library. *In the United States:* Family History Library of the Church of Jesus Christ of Latter-Day Saints, Broomall, Pa.; Free Library of Philadelphia, Rare Book Department; Huntington Library; Index of Christian Art, Princeton University; Van Pelt Library, University of Pennsylvania, Rare Book Room.

Financial support for research visits to Britain was provided by grants from the American Philosophical Society, the National Endowment for the Humanities Travel to Collections program, and the Research Foundation of the University of Pennsylvania. During the trips I enjoyed the generous hospitality of Iain Phillips and of Jeff Mazo and Georgina Clark-Mazo.

The year during which the writing of the book was completed was funded by a fellowship from the National Endowment for the Humanities (Grant no. FA–31489–93), and spent as a Member of the School of Historical Studies, Institute for Advanced Study, Princeton. I owe special thanks to James Hilty, then chair of the Department of History, and Carolyn Adams, dean of the School of Arts and Sciences, Temple University, for making this leave possible.

Some of the material in the second chapter originally appeared in my article "The Regulation of Brothels in Later Medieval England" (*Signs: Journal of Women in Culture and Society* 14, no. 2 [1989] © 1989 by The University of Chicago). Some of the material in the sixth chapter originally appeared in "Holy Harlots: Prostitute Saints in Medieval Legend" (*Journal of the History of Sexuality* 1, no. 1 [1990] © 1990 by The University of Chicago). Permission to reprint this material is gratefully acknowledged.

My initial interest in this subject was kindled by John Boswell, who continued to be a mentor and an inspiration for nearly two decades. This book makes no pretensions to either the broad scope or the direct contemporary impact of his work, but I hope that it follows in his scholarly tradition. I wish he had lived to read it.

Many other individuals also provided intellectual support and counsel. Those who have given advice or shared their own unpublished work include: Caroline Barron, Judith Bennett, Martha Carlin, Jeremy Goldberg, Monica Green, Jeffrey Hamburger, Richard Helmholz, Derek Keene, Maryanne Kowaleski, Sheila Lindenbaum, Marjorie McIntosh, Mavis Mate, John Post, Robert Stacey, and John Van Engen. A number of people read chapters in their areas of expertise and saved me from many errors (although those that remain are, of course, my own): David Boyd, Richard Helmholz, Janet Senderowitz Loengard, Mavis Mate, Dan Sherman, Paul Strohm, Heather Swanson, Robert Swanson, and Siegfried Wenzel (who was also generous with loans of microfilm). Judith Bennett, Judith Brown, Richard Dunn, Barbara Hanawalt, Paul Hyams, Christopher Karras, Joel Kaye, Lynn Hollen Lees, E. Ann Matter, Edward M. Peters, Guido Ruggiero, Hugh Thomas, and John Van Engen all read drafts of the entire manuscript and provided very helpful comments. In particular, Judith Bennett, Ann Matter, and Ed Peters have supported this project at every stage and in many ways, for which they have my deep gratitude.

As is customary, my family comes last but not least. Nicola Karras cheerfully accompanied me on several research trips and tolerated my absence on others; Elena Karras was a latecomer to this project but cooperated in allowing me the time to finish it; and Christopher Karras admirably fulfilled the roles of editor, computer consultant, traveling companion, temporarily single parent, and much more.

Contents

COMMON WOMEN

Introduction

Common Women, Prostitutes, and Whores

A "common woman" in medieval England was one who had many sex partners, often for money. Any woman not under the dominion of one man—husband, father, master—ran the risk that her independent behavior would lead to her being labeled a whore. Medieval society attempted to control such women by treating them as though they belonged to men in common (though they were not legally property). These women were also "common" in another sense: they were working women trying to make a living. Yet, though taking money for sex characterized their behavior, what defined their nature in the eyes of their contemporaries was their indiscriminate sexuality.

Since sex constitutes an important way in which men and women relate to one another, the history of sexuality forms a significant part of the history of gender relations. Norms about sexuality govern, and are governed by, gender roles, and behavior deemed inappropriate for one gender is often denigrated as immoral. The history of sexuality is also peculiarly relevant to women's history. Sexuality is an important part of the way society constructs masculinity as well as femininity, but in medieval culture women were more closely connected than men with the body and sexuality, and their sexual behavior identified and defined them much more than was usually the case with men.[1] Attitudes toward sexuality were intimately tied to the structure of the family and the economy.[2] "Common women," whores, or prostitutes, as women entirely defined by their sexuality, provide the extreme case that helps define views of feminine sexuality in general.[3] Money, power, and sexuality were closely intertwined in the Middle Ages, as they are today, and prostitution was a key point of contact.

In recent years, as the history of sexuality has become a respectable subdiscipline, both feminist and nonfeminist scholarship on prostitution has begun to explore the fundamental questions of the place of sexuality in human societies and its determination by economic, political, and religious structures.[4] This book is concerned both with the practice of commercial prostitution in medieval English society and with the way the idea of prostitution affected the construction of feminine sexuality. I argue that prostitution deeply affected gender relations because its existence fostered the connection of feminine sexuality with venality and sin, and thereby justified the control of all women.

This work explores how various people and groups in medieval culture (preachers, lawmakers, prostitutes themselves, their customers, and their neighbors) understood what it meant to be a whore. It examines the role of commerce and of sexuality in these understandings, and shows how prostitutes lived and what societal and individual factors led them to take up the sex trade.

Chapter 1, "Prostitution and the Law," deals with legal understandings of prostitution: how the various jurisdictions (towns and the church) regulated whores and what they thought they were regulating. As we shall see, medieval law understood prostitution as a commercial enterprise that women engaged in for money; but this understanding coexisted with a more general notion of the whore as a sexually immoral woman. Chapter 2, "Brothels, Licit and Illicit," examines the institution of the brothel, especially in those jurisdictions where it was legal. I discuss the nature and purpose of institutionalized brothels and the regulation of illicit brothels, both of which served to keep women sexually available to men while keeping the women themselves under strict control.

The next two chapters examine the experiences of women who engaged in sex for money. Chapter 3, "Becoming a Prostitute," describes the broad economic and demographic conditions influencing women's options and choices and the factors that influenced or coerced individual women to become prostitutes. Prostitution was a choice made within an economic structure that did not favor women; coercion, whether by individuals or by economic necessity, was not unusual. In chapter 4, "The Sex Trade in Practice," I turn to the mechanics of prostitution, tracing the lives of some of the women involved (both prostitutes and procurers), and describing modes of operation and types of clients. This discussion demonstrates the great diversity within the trade and the adaptability of its practitioners, whether casual or professional.

The last two chapters place medieval English prostitution in its cultural context. Chapter 5, "Marriage, Sexuality, and Marginality," discusses the degree to which prostitutes were accepted within society. I consider the institution of marriage among the nonelite and the relation of other sexual practices to it. This chapter also discusses the commodification of feminine sexuality in general, both within marriage and without, especially as expressed through secular literature, and concludes that in one sense at least, prostitution fit into a broader practice of purchasing sexual access to women. This did not, however, make prostitutes socially acceptable. Even though on a local, individual basis they might not be ostracized from their communities, the very resemblance of their trade to the sexual exchange found elsewhere in the culture necessitated the marginalization of some women so that others might be considered respectable. The role of the church in the development of this discourse about feminine sexuality and money is discussed in chapter 6, "Saints and Sinners," which analyzes misogynist literature generally and the representation of prostitutes in particular to show that whores formed a subset within a widespread association of women with venality and lustfulness. Medieval society recognized the existence of professional prostitutes, but because of this association found it easy to equate other women with them.

Because of their position on the margins of society and their high visibility, prostitutes assumed a significance for medieval culture out of proportion to their numbers.[5] Prostitution was central to medieval culture because people believed that it offered a necessary outlet for masculine sex drives which, unrelieved, would undermine the social order, and because it represented in the most extreme and dramatic way tendencies that were characteristic of feminine sexuality. The attitudes of the church, town authorities, customers, and other women toward prostitutes tell us a great deal about attitudes toward women generally. And an understanding of the experiences of women in the sex trade helps reveal how women responded to prevailing economic conditions—constraints as well as opportunities—making choices for themselves within a system over which they had little control.

Late medieval England presents a particularly interesting moment in the history of prostitution. Commercial prostitution itself is not a by-product of capitalism, for it was certainly present in ancient Rome as well as in the Middle Ages; but its prominence in the culture was a by-product of urbanization and the growth of a commercial economy in the High and late Middle Ages.[6] This book roughly covers the period between the Black Death (1348–49) and the end of the fifteenth century, although I have occasionally used earlier and later evidence as well. This was a period not of decadence but certainly of change. It was a time first of demographic stagnation and then of growth as population recovered from the ravages of the plague. English trade was shifting from the export of wool (raw material) to the export of cloth (manufactured goods); the rural economy was moving from serfdom to a copyhold system; and the land began to be enclosed for grazing sheep, leading to the displacement of the rural population. The Hundred Years' War and the Wars of the Roses kept the aristocracy, and hence the landowners, in turmoil. The period also produced the great works of Middle English literature by Chaucer, Langland, Gower, and others; by the end of the fifteenth century, printing and wider literacy were bringing these texts, as well as a large quantity of devotional literature, to a larger public than ever before. The church, retrenching against the Lollard threat, boasted few great spiritual or political leaders; but this was a time of intense piety among the laity, many of whom banded together to found chantries and provide for their souls in the hereafter.

Women's as well as men's lives changed with the social, economic, and religious developments of the late Middle Ages, but there were also significant continuities in the situation of women. In some ways women had more in common with one another than with men of their own social milieu. As in most of medieval Europe, there were few independent women. Women went from being daughters to wives, and only in widowhood could they control even that property they themselves owned. In many English towns, borough customs granted women a certain measure of economic independence: even if married they could trade as *femmes soles*, meaning that they were responsible for their own debts and could enter into contracts like single women. Even so, a woman's identity usually came through her husband.[7] And not all of these economically active women were prosperous. They were helping to support their families in an environment that did not allow them very many options. Their work tended to be less skilled and less well paid than that of men. Prostitution was one of the few careers open to them, and prostitutes, who in at least some parts of the profession could control their own working conditions, may have been less exploited than certain textile workers or domestic servants.

Most medieval people expected to marry and would have seen reproduction as a major social obligation. Among the nobility and gentry, and perhaps the wealthier townspeople, families chose husbands for their daughters. A few steps down the economic ladder both women and men may have had more influence in arranging their own marriages, since financial considerations did not play such a large role (the dowry did not become as important in medieval England as, for example, in Italy). Even so, family interests were still paramount. In a marriage based on considerations other than the feelings of the parties for each other, spouses might not find the same sexual satisfaction that people in the modern West have come to expect. Yet they were not supposed to seek that satisfaction elsewhere; all sex outside of marriage was considered sinful. The medieval church's teaching on sexuality was complex, but the fundamental notion was that sexual pleasure was basically wicked—tolerable between spouses (if nothing was done to impede procreation), but no more. At the same time, it was seen as a natural drive, both for women, who were thought more lustful than men, and for men, whose premarital or extramarital exploits tended to be tolerated in practice though condemned from the pulpit.

In this situation, where the sex drive was accepted as natural and at the same time proscribed, the medieval institution of prostitution developed. It was considered a necessary evil; many medieval writers followed Saint Augustine in arguing that if a man had to commit unnatural (nonprocreative) sex acts, it was preferable to commit them with an already corrupt woman rather than corrupt his wife. The medieval world adopted a hydraulic model of masculine sexuality: people believed that pressure builds up and has to be released through a safety valve (marriage or prostitution), or eventually the dam will burst and men will commit seduction, rape, adultery, and sodomy.[8]

Although the view of prostitution as a safety valve was not consistent with the medieval medical theory that accorded women a stronger sex drive than men, many European towns nonetheless adopted the ideology of "necessary evil," permitting and regulating prostitution both within and outside their walls. Municipal brothels were not as common in England as they were elsewhere in Europe, but England, too, combined toleration with marginalization. Prostitutes had their place in society, though not a respected one.

Prostitution was necessary to the functioning of society because it was central to the construction of gender in medieval culture.

Scholars have approached medieval prostitution from a variety of perspectives.[9] Sociologists have tended to discuss modern prostitution in the context of deviance and crime. Much creative and interesting work on medieval prostitution in the last few years has made use of the related but more complex notion of marginality.[10] But we must not lose sight of the fact that marginality, like criminality, is culturally constructed and relative. Prostitutes are marginal only if the society places them on the margin. The process of marginalization—the way a society delimits and excludes prostitutes—is worth studying; marginal status cannot simply be treated as a given.

Studies of modern prostitution have often focused on the role of the state.[11] Whether it prohibited or regulated prostitution, governmental authority shaped the experiences of the women involved. A similar focus on the role of authority can help explain the institutionalization of prostitution in medieval Europe.[12] For the modern period another extremely fruitful area of study has been the activity of moral reformers, male and female, and their interactions with prostitutes and with the state. Prostitution provided a focus for nineteenth-century feminism, albeit a feminism that revealed its class-based attitudes.[13] Although the impact of moral reformers on the enactment and enforcement of prostitution laws can be documented for some regions in the Middle Ages, these reformers were exclusively male and clerical.[14] There were no medieval Josephine Butlers taking the woman's perspective.

Some recent work on medieval prostitution has examined the issue from a demographic perspective, focusing on the late age of marriage for men and accepting the medieval model of the brothel as a safety valve for masculine sexual energy that otherwise would find its outlet in violence against the property of other men.[15] Masculine demand, however, is not in itself sufficient to explain the existence of prostitution.[16] The prevalence of unmarried men leads to prostitution only within a culture that privileges masculine heterosexual desire. Only because of the gendered structure of power in medieval culture could women be made into prostitutes to meet the perceived demand—"made into prostitutes" in that they were forced into the job by violence, deception, or lack of attractive alternatives, as well as in that they behaved in a certain way to fill men's needs and then were stigmatized for that behavior by being defined as whores.

Writing about prostitution poses in a pressing way a question that faces any historian of women: whether to emphasize oppression or empowerment. Stressing the patriarchal nature of medieval (or any other) society tends to cast women as helpless victims. If we look at the sources left to us, which come from the church and the legal system, we do indeed see a nearly unremitting misogyny and oppression, but this may not reflect the way women actually lived their lives and viewed themselves. Recent work has questioned the thoroughgoing misogyny of medieval religion.[17] The nature of the sources, however, makes women's interpretation of their religion more accessible than their interpretation of their own daily lives. We can avoid casting women as victims by working from the logical assumption that they made decisions about participation in the work force and marriage,[18] but this is largely an a priori assumption and is not based on evidence about women's attitudes and feelings.

But placing too much emphasis on women as agents can lead to the obliteration of the oppressive context in which they exercised agency, and to putting the responsibility for their straitened economic circumstances or their sexual objectification on women themselves.[19] Focusing on the positive aspects of women's history—their achievements, their efforts to subvert or overturn patriarchy, and their significance in the economy, the community, and the family—may be a more inspiring way of writing history than focusing on the negative and casting woman as the eternal victim. But overemphasizing the positive obscures the fact that the history of women has been a long uphill struggle in which progress has hardly been continuous. Sometimes women *are* victims. The only solution is to find a balance between the history of oppression and the history of achievement—as Judith Zinsser and Bonnie Anderson put it in their history of women in Europe, between "traditions subordinating women" and "traditions empowering women."[20]

In the history of prostitution, the tension between subordination and empowerment is particularly acute. Some historical scholars have chosen the empowerment route, depicting prostitution almost exclusively as work chosen by its practitioners. Luise White, in her study of prostitution in colonial Nairobi, argues that historians have too readily accepted the viewpoint of reformers, who see prostitutes as exploited by the privileging of the sexual needs of middle-class men. She argues that the historiography has produced "a literature that speaks of women's victimization and not women's actions." If women are not held responsible for becoming prostitutes, then they cannot be held responsible for using their earnings from prostitution to buy property or establish themselves in a trade.[21] White treats prostitution as work and the different forms it took as labor forms determined not by sociocultural factors but by economic strategies. Similarly, Marilynn Wood Hill, writing on prostitution in nineteenth-century New York, focuses on "the positive appeal and rewards of prostitution" for its practitioners, suggesting that those who see prostitution as invariably degrading and exploitative are influenced by residual Victorian prejudices.[22] Both these scholars are careful to acknowledge that prostitution could be a dangerous career and that prostitutes were occasionally the victims of violence; but the thrust of their arguments is that women chose prostitution for rational economic reasons and were not dissatisfied with their choice.[23]

The argument from women's agency is compelling and appealing: it has the advantage of keeping the history focused on how the women themselves experienced prostitution.[24] Yet, while recognizing the importance of the economic opportunities prostitution may have provided for women, we must not lose sight of the reasons why this was the case. The choice of prostitution as a career is not made in a vacuum; it is a choice among available alternatives. If prostitution was the best money-making opportunity open to women, that was because other options were closed to them. Neither does the profitability of prostitution develop in a vacuum; it is a function of demand, which contains a large cultural component. If prostitution was a good economic opportunity for women, that was because the sexual norms of the culture created a demand among men for nonmarital or extramarital sex.

Treating prostitution simply as a form of labor also obscures the nature of the labor. If a society finds a particular type of work degrading, it will consider the practitioners of that type of work degraded, even if they themselves do not share that view. Very few if any societies have treated prostitution neutrally as work; it has always had implications for the status of the women involved which derive from its sexual nature. Perhaps in an ideal society neither a supply of nor a demand for prostitutes would exist; or else prostitution might be a service occupation with good working conditions, as respected as any other. But we do not live in such a society. Prostitution exists today because women are objectified sexually, and because it is considered more permissible for men than for women to have purely sexual experiences. The same was true in the Middle Ages.

So the demand for prostitution cannot be considered in strictly economic terms. It also depends on the meanings prostitution has in the given society. One of the best studies of prostitution and its meanings is Judith Walkowitz's work on Victorian Britain. Walkowitz shows how prostitution became a battleground for contesting (among other things) the validity of the sexual double standard, the role of the state in the regulation of personal behavior, and the relation of middle- and working-class morality.[25] She is far from neglecting the experiences of prostitutes themselves, but she recognizes that prostitution had a social meaning beyond those experiences. A view of prostitution as just another form of labor loses sight of that meaning.

This book attempts to steer between the danger of portraying prostitutes as victims by concentrating too much on how others saw them and the danger of decontextualizing them by concentrating too much on their agency. It attempts to bridge the gap between social and cultural history, or between reality or experience and representation.[26] The life of a prostitute in medieval England was affected both by the economic and demographic situation in which she found herself, and by the way the various discourses of the law, religious preaching, and imaginative literature treated her. The story of prostitution is not that of individual lives but of the larger social and discursive relations in which those lives were embedded. Indeed, the prostitutes themselves understood their own experience within these contexts.[27] Neither the records of practice (which are themselves affected by ideology) nor the records of ideology (which are themselves affected by social practice) tell the whole story. Medieval social historians have relied largely on legal records, with literary texts for anecdotal support and illustration. To understand what it meant to a society to classify women as prostitutes, it is necessary to look at law and literature not just for illustration but for an understanding of how these kinds of texts were used to create the identity of the prostitute.

The foregoing brief discussion of approaches to the history of prostitution presupposes that there is some agreed-upon institution or practice in the historical record that we can identify as "prostitution." This is the assumption implicit in the phrase "the oldest profession": prostitution has always been around; we just have to describe the form it took at a particular time. This view universalizes what our society sees as the defining feature of prostitution by treating all instances of the exchange of sex for money as different cases of the same thing.

Not all cultures, however, distinguish among material, status-related, reproductive, and emotional reasons for engaging in sex, and not all exchanges of sex for money are the same. A system in which all young women must once engage in sex for pay with a stranger as an act of worship is different from one in which slaves are sold into brothels, and a priestess who stands in for a goddess in fertility rites is different from a drug addict who offers sex in return for her next fix.[28] In some societies—medieval Europe, for example—it was not the exchange of money, nor even multiple partners, but the public and indiscriminate availability of a woman's body that was the defining feature of prostitution. It does not make much sense, then, to say that women with multiple sex partners were prostitutes if they took money but not otherwise; that is not a distinction that medieval people would have made. The concept of social construction (often applied to gender, race, and sexual orientation) is useful here. The modern Western notion of a prostitute as a woman who takes money for sex is a creation of particular understandings of sexuality and money. It is not a category that is automatically meaningful in any other culture. Behavior may be similar, but the meanings placed on it and the labels it incurs are very different depending on the context.[29]

A more useful project than tracing prostitution through history as though it were a single, clearly identifiable institution is to examine how a given society comes to classify certain women as sexually deviant. The circumstances under which men will pay for sexual services, as well as the way a society treats the women (or occasionally men) who provide those services, reveal a great deal about gender relations in a particular culture. If we are not simply to impose modern categories on the medieval world, we must look at medieval sexuality in medieval terms. The problem is compounded, of course, by the question of translation. Neither the word "prostitute" nor any cognate form appears as a noun in any of the English, Latin, or French sources used for this book, although it occasionally appears, in Latin, as a verb.[30] The question thus becomes not What did people mean when they called someone a prostitute? but What terms should we translate as "prostitute"?

Medieval writers did not take particular care to define the terms that we would especially like to see defined. Unlike modern law, which must describe in very specific terms the behavior prohibited, medieval law often assumed a general understanding.[31] It is important that in the process of translation we do not assume a priori that women who were called "meretrix," "common woman," "putain," "femme de mauvaise vie," "strumpet," and so forth were the same thing as what we today call a prostitute. Some writers recognized that the terms in question were used in a variety of ways. Thomas of Chobham, the early thirteenth-century theologian, for example, cited different meanings of *meretrix*, including a woman who has sex outside of marriage, a woman who has sex with many men, a woman who denies herself to none, a woman whose sin is public, and a woman who sells herself.[32] Simply to translate the term as "prostitute" omits much of the medieval way of looking at things. Yet if we analyze all our modern categories out of existence, we are left without a language to talk about the past. Since this book is written neither in Latin nor in Middle English, I find it more helpful to translate terms than simply to adopt the term used in any given source and leave it up to the reader to figure out what it means.

In order to get around problems of translation without assuming an equation between medieval and modern categories, I have chosen a strategy of dual terminology. "Prostitute" and "prostitution" are used according to a modern definition to refer to the exchange of specific sex acts for money (as opposed to concubinage, which may involve the long-term exchange of sexual access for financial support).[33] Medieval writers do not necessarily mean "one who exchanges specific sex acts for money" when they use words such as *meretrix* (the most common Latin word that is generally translated as "prostitute").[34] So, to distinguish the medieval understanding from the modern concept, I shall translate *meretrix* as "whore," the modern English form of one (arguably the closest) Middle English equivalent. I have also translated a variety of other Latin and French terms, meaning roughly the same thing, as "whore." When dealing with a Middle English text, I have simply modernized the terms used, unless no modern equivalent exists, in which case I have also used "whore." Similarly, I translate *pronuba* and its equivalents (which could mean roughly the equivalent of "procurer," "pimp," "go-between," or "madam") as "bawd," the modern version of the nearest Middle English equivalent.

The meaning of "whore" and "bawd," as I use them, is deliberately imprecise; the terms represent medieval categories whose meaning we do not assume in advance. The terms *meretrix* and *putain* (a French equivalent), like "whore" in modern American English, could be used in a technical sense or could refer more generally to any woman who engaged in nonmarital sex, even with only one man. The choice of a word with a wide semantic field to translate *meretrix* allows us to note when it seems to be used as the equivalent of "prostitute," without assuming such a correspondence in all instances.[35]

Throughout the various medieval ways of talking about sexual behavior —the legal, the literary, the didactic—runs a tension between money and lust. Sometimes the whore is represented as someone who primarily seeks money—what we think of as a prostitute—and sometimes primarily as a woman of loose morals. This tension meant that the loose woman, or any woman out of place, sexually or otherwise, could be conflated with the commercial prostitute. It is only partly a modern perspective that makes us see these two groups as separate, somehow unnaturally shoehorned into the same category by medieval culture. To medieval people they were both separate and indistinguishable: separate because medieval culture did have a concept of a prostitute as a wage earner, yet indistinguishable because exactly the same terms used to talk about the prostitute were used of any woman whose sexual behavior was considered wanton.

The questions a historian asks are inevitably the result of the concerns of her own time, although the answers ought to be phrased in terms of the concerns of the society under study. This book asks questions both about prostitution—the exchange of sex for money—and about whoredom, that is, the way society understood feminine sexuality as expressed outside of marriage. It is concerned in part with the distance, or lack of distance, between medieval English people's ways of understanding sexuality and our own. In the Middle Ages people did not have a concept of sexuality as such, but they did have a variety of discourses about sex.[36] They understood that certain people practiced certain types of sexual behavior, and while they identified people by behavior rather than by desire or orientation, they still used what we can identify as their sexuality to categorize them. The whore was one of those completely identified by her sexuality.

Prostitution and the Law

This chapter approaches medieval understandings of feminine sexuality by looking at what different jurisdictions thought they were regulating when they legislated about whoredom, and how and why they attempted to control it. Law is one of the most powerful means any society has at its disposal to control behavior. This is not only because legislation can prohibit particular acts (with greater or lesser degrees of effectiveness), but also because simply by establishing what kind of behavior is deviant, it asserts power over those who practice that behavior. Law does not emerge on its own; society creates it, and law reflects that society's needs, assumptions, and mores. By being enshrined in the law, these assumptions and mores become increasingly clear, tangible, and entrenched. Whereas attitudes and conventions may evolve on their own, law requires formal action if it is to change. It provides a fixed, codified point, usually presented in carefully chosen language, to which people can refer.

Laws about whoredom are thus powerful tools for delimiting appropriate feminine behavior. Whatever opprobrium society chooses to heap on anyone labeled a whore gains force when it is backed by legal clout. In medieval English law, however, neither prostitution nor whoredom was ever formally defined. There were no official registers of prostitutes as there were, for example, under the Contagious Diseases Acts of the 1860s. The application of the legal category "whore" to women other than commercial prostitutes blurred the boundaries between the latter group and deviant women generally, just as the Contagious Diseases Acts functioned to control not only prostitutes but all poor women through the involuntary registration as a prostitute of any woman the authorities deemed immoral.[1]

This chapter treats in turn the regulation of prostitution in towns (by both borough and manorial courts), in rural areas (by manorial courts), and under ecclesiastical jurisdiction.[2] The last was concerned with moral issues, which varied less between urban and rural communities than did issues of public order. Borough charters gave towns the right to police themselves according to their own customs. Each town generally had one type of court—Wardmote, Mayor's Tourn, Leet Court, Mickletourn—whose purview included commercial offenses (selling goods at too high a price, for example), assaults, nuisances (such as blocking streets), and sometimes minor breaches of the peace and moral offenses. Manorial courts, in which a lord (an individual or an ecclesiastical institution) exercised private jurisdiction, could be urban or rural, and held sessions called leets or views of frankpledge at which they fined tenants for the same sorts of offenses.

Church courts, in their disciplinary capacity, also dealt with sexual behavior and its regulation, prosecuting offenses such as adultery, fornication, whoredom, bawdry, and occasionally incest and sodomy. Disciplinary or "ex officio" cases included other matters besides the sexual—from failure to pay tithes to heresy—but cases involving sex made up the bulk of the disciplinary business of the church courts.[3] By discussing the theory and practice of the law in the various jurisdictions that dealt with prostitution, I show in this chapter that regulation was aimed not at abolishing commercial prostitution but at keeping it accessible while keeping its practitioners in their place.

Urban Regulation

Commercial prostitution tends to be largely an urban phenomenon because of the relative anonymity of city life and because the concentration of population creates the demand for a wide variety of services. Town governments in later medieval England took responsibility for the regulation of various occupations and pastimes, and prostitution was one of the matters with which they concerned themselves.[4] Unlike most modern legislation about prostitution, which outlaws specific acts (loitering, solicitation), medieval English urban legislation criminalized or regulated whores without ever defining precisely what the term meant. Whoredom was a status rather than a specific set of behaviors. Some towns simply outlawed whores, although this was never particularly effective. Some tolerated them de facto if not de jure. And three jurisdictions followed the European pattern of regulating and even institutionalizing prostitution; these officially condoned brothels are discussed in chapter 2.

In the many English towns that prohibited whores from operating within their walls, the language of the prohibitions implies that they were directed against habitual promiscuity, which medieval people would have expected often to be connected with the exchange of money. Their application, however, could also be more general. The laws may have been occasioned by a perception that the sex trade disturbed the social order. Yet, since prosecution was based on common fame or identification by a jury of presentment drawn from the district, any woman who had a bad reputation was at risk of being classified as a whore. Medieval legislation focused on the woman's classification, not on the particular acts she committed, so any woman whose neighbors chose to identify her that way could fall under the law.[5]

Laws prohibiting prostitution, though common, were never particularly effective. In London reiterated prohibitions against whores reflected the failure of legislation and policing. At least as early as 1277, the city prohibited any "whore of a brothel" from living within the walls, a prohibition against organized prostitution rather than general immorality. In 1310 Edward II ordered the mayor and sheriff of London to abolish brothels, which were harboring thieves and murderers.[6] Other legislation, however, focused on immoral women generally. The *Liber Albus*, a fifteenth-century compilation of London's customary law containing material that may go back to the thirteenth century, noted that thieves and other malefactors were harbored in the houses of "women of evil life," and provided that "henceforth no whore shall stay within the walls of the city. And if any henceforth shall be found dwelling within the walls of the city, let her be put in prison for forty days." Wardmotes were to expel any whore, "woman of evil life," or bawd from the ward.[7]

The *Liber Albus* also provided vivid public punishments for bawds and whores, which other records indicate were actually practiced.[8] Those convicted of bawdry had their hair cut or head shaved and were conducted to the pillory "with minstrelsy"; a second offense entailed ten days in prison as well, and a third offense meant banishment from the city. A common whore was "taken from the prison to Aldgate, with a striped hood, and a white rod in her hand, and from there taken with minstrelsy to the thew [a pillory for women], and there the cause is proclaimed; and from there through Cheap and Newgate, then to Cock's Lane, to remain there." A second offense required the whore to remain on the thew, and a third required the cutting of her hair and banishment from the city. The punishments for other sexual offenses (adultery and clerical unchastity) involved similar elements.[9] The striped hood is specified in a number of towns, and the white rod was a symbol of prostitution in hagiography as well as law.[10]

The use of public shame as a deterrent might imply that the law was directed more at the part-time or casual prostitute, or the sexually active woman who risked classification as a whore, than at the professional prostitute, for whom shame might not be a consideration. The same is true of the punishment for bawdry, which may have been intended to discourage the casual go-between. The records tell us that women were actually punished in this manner but do not tell us exactly what they did to incur the label of whore that led to their prosecution. In the cases of those punished as bawds, their offenses were sometimes specified as the procurement of young women (discussed in chapter 3).

In the fourteenth century the city of London tried at least to segregate whores, prohibiting them the city except for one street (Cock's Lane), banishing them to the area of the stews or bathhouses in Southwark, outside the city proper, and punishing them with the forfeiture of their hoods and upper garments. The justification for this 1393 ordinance was to prevent crime and the disruption of public order: "Whereas many and divers affrays, broils, and dissensions, have arisen in times past, and many men have been slain and murdered, by reason of the frequent resort of, and consorting with, common whores, at taverns, brewhouses of hucksters, and other places of ill-fame, within the said city, and the suburbs thereof. . . ."[11] The ordinance may have been directed mainly against professional prostitutes, but any woman frequenting taverns could have fallen under it.

Repeated attempts to remove whores from the city show the ineffectiveness of this legislation. Around 1439 the aldermen complained: "[N]ow of late days many persons in this city be found defiled in the detestable sin of lechery as in adultery, fornication commonly practiced, and many diverse persons also are common nourishers, promoters, and provokers of the same sins to the displeasure of almighty God and against the laws of this city, good customs and usages. . . ." Once again the language about adultery and fornication is inclusive enough to cover far more than just professional prostitutes. Because "the sharpness of punishment in old times ordained" was not enforced, the aldermen now provided that every "common strumpet," after being paraded through the town, was to be expelled from the city. On the second offense she was to "lose her outermost garment," and on the third she was to be banished forever. In addition, a fine of forty shillings was imposed on any citizen renting a house "to any such misliving woman."[12] The terms were not defined; a "strumpet" was anyone convicted as such upon presentment by her Wardmote inquest.

Another ordinance of the late fifteenth century, once again banning whores, reiterated the town fathers' moral outrage, although as before outrage was not translated into a serious campaign against vice. The preamble once again illustrates the fear not only of crime but also of uncontrolled feminine lust, not necessarily restricted to commercialized sex:

> For to eschew the stinking and horrible sin of lechery, the which daily grows and is practiced more than it has been in days past, by the means of strumpets, misguided and idle women daily vagrant and walking about by the streets and lanes of this city of London and suburbs of the same and also repairing to taverns and other private places of the said city, provoking many other persons unto the said sin of lechery, whereby many people, as well men as women, being of themselves well-disposed, daily fall to the said mischievous and horrible sin, to the great displeasure of almighty God and disturbance and breaking of the peace of our sovereign Lord the King and of the politic guiding of the aforesaid city. . . .[13]

In 1510 and again in 1520 the aldermen had once again to be reminded to make their Wardmote inquests inquire "specially of vagabonds, common bawds, and common women," the juxtaposition implying that lack of rootedness and stability was at least part of the problem, and in 1543 they were still agreeing that "the good and laudable ancient laws, acts, and ordinances theretofore made and devised for the punishment of harlots and bawds of the stews and other common women and women of incontinent life" needed to be carried out.[14] In these later pieces of legislation there are a few references to stewhouses and brothels, but the main thrust is against the immoral women, including not just prostitutes but any of "incontinent life."

None of the legislation expressed any concern with whether or not the women demanded or accepted money. Any woman deemed "misguided," "ill-disposed," or "common" fell under the legislation. A large number of those convicted under these laws were no doubt professional prostitutes, but not all. The case of Margaret Hopper, convicted as a whore for committing adultery with two men, one over a seven-year period, indicates that the net was cast wider.[15] The few cases in the city's plea rolls that mention whores clearly make sex with multiple partners the key: "Emmota Coltastatur, Margaret Poule, Margaret Clerk, Agnes Kyghley, and Margaret Cambridge . . . committed fornication with William Payne, and afterwards consorted with divers other unknown men, because of which the said Emmota, Margaret, Agnes, and Margaret are common whores."[16] These women were probably commercial prostitutes; but to accuse someone of whoredom, it was not necessary to allege that she had taken money.

Labeling and shaming the sexually deviant woman and banishing her from town were constants in the legislation of medieval London but not so prominent in practice. The legislation could be confusing and conflicting; even a single customary, the Liber Albus, included contradictory provisions (see p. 21). At the most basic level of local government, the concern seems to have been more with preserving public order than with shaming women: the scanty surviving records of the London Wardmotes include more presentments for harboring strumpets or women of ill fame (along with presentments of night-walkers, vagabonds, receivers of stolen goods, and the like) than for actually being a whore.[17] The bulk of Wardmote presentments for sexual offenses that found their way into the records of the city's central government, particularly in the fifteenth century, were for fornication and adultery by priests—not because priests committed these offenses more often than anyone else but more likely because of resentment against them, and particularly against their adultery with women of the parish, although technically it was not the secular courts' business to enforce vows of chastity.[18]

The aldermen concerned themselves with those who profited from the sex trade as well as with the whores themselves. In 1417 the council recognized that brothels still existed within the city. These were stews or bathhouses, which in the Middle Ages had the reputation of being more than just somewhere to get clean. Once again, the justification for council action was the social disorder, crime, and corruption of honest women caused by the brothels:

Whereas heretofore many grievances, abominations, damages, disturbances, murders, homicides, larcenies, and other common nuisances, have oftentimes ensued and befallen in the [c]ity of London, and the suburbs thereof, by reason and cause of the common resort, harbouring, and sojourning, which lewd men and women, of bad and evil life, have in the stews belonging to men and women in the [c]ity and suburbs aforesaid; insomuch that—a thing to be lamented—divers men and women have been of late slain, spoiled, and robbed . . . and, what is even worse, from one day to another, the wives, sons, daughters, apprentices and servants, of the reputable men of the [c]ity, are oftentimes subtly, by the false imagining, colouring, and covin, as well of those who keep the said stews, as of others for a little money, drawn and enticed thereto; and there they, as well as other persons, both regular [i.e., monastic] and secular, are permitted to do and carry on the illicit works of their lewd flesh. . . .[19]

On this occasion the solution was a ban not on whores but on stews, except that households might have their own individual stews for cleanliness. Instead of punishing the whore, the new law was intended to hit brothelkeepers in their purses. This legislation was enforced, at least at first.[20] After 1428, however, the provision was relaxed; citizens were allowed to keep bathhouses upon posting a bond that they would be "honest stews."[21] In 1475 it was necessary again to admonish keepers of stews that they could not harbor men and women in the bathhouse at night.[22] The council also attempted to punish any landlord who received tenants "of evil and vicious life,"[23] a broad concept that could cover all kinds of criminals and other offenders. Both the legislation against keeping stews and that against harboring sinful tenants were directed not at the prostitutes themselves but at those who profited from the trade.

A number of English towns besides London formally banned whores from the town. A York ordinance of 1301 provided that "if any common whore keeps a brothel and resides in the said city, let her be taken and committed to prison for a day and a night. And let the bailiff who takes her have the upper beam and the door of the building in which she lodged. Nevertheless, he who rented his houses to whores in this manner shall lose the rent of those houses for one term."[24] Here the subject of the ban was not the whore herself but the brothel, and in that sense it was a specific behavior, not the condition of being a whore, that the law prohibited. The ecclesiastical court records from York nonetheless provide ample evidence that this ordinance did not keep prostitutes from the town. In 1482 the aldermen agreed "that the common women and other misgoverned women shall inhabit them in the suburbs without the walls of this city and not within." Again, although not carefully observed, this law recognized that prostitution was inevitable and attempted to make it unobtrusive, but the inclusion of "other misgoverned women" widened its purview beyond the brothel.[25]

Bristol customs recorded in 1344 prohibited lepers or common women— again categories of persons rather than behavior—from remaining within the town.[26] King's Lynn banned brothels in the fifteenth century and excluded common women from inns, which were probably the most frequent meeting places for prostitutes and their customers. Leicester provided in 1467 "that no brothel be held within this town, bawdry nor bawd dwelling, but . . . that they be voided at the first warning on pain of imprisonment and fine and ransom to the King." Rochester, in a sixteenth-century book of customs whose contents probably originated much earlier, ordered its jury of presentment to identify "all such persons as be common chiders, ribalds of their tongues, common strumpets, bawds, or any other otherwise misruled, or harbor any vagabonds or misruled persons to the annoyance of their neighbors," placing sexually uncontrolled women in a more general category of disorderly people. Norwich apparently also expelled whores from the town: although its ordinances do not survive, a case from 1312–13 presented a man for attacking the bailiffs and attempting to rescue some "common whores" they were leading out of town. Winchester also had a provision for banishment, but it had little effect and was replaced in the fifteenth century by a system of fines.[27]

Some other towns deliberately imitated London's punishment of prostitutes. The town council of early sixteenth-century Gloucester, concerned about the reputation of the town, "the which is too abominably spoken of in all England and Wales of the vicious living of divers persons, spiritual as well as temporal, with too excessive a number of common strumpets and bawds dwelling in every ward of the said town," ordained that a pillory be set up in the marketplace "as it is done in the worshipful city of London and in the town of Bristol." All "abominable queans," roughly a synonym for whores, "living viciously to the open fame and knowledge of the community," were to be taken in a cart from ward to ward "with such solemnities that belongeth for them to have," including a striped hood and a paper sign.[28] In Exeter in 1525 the council ordered "that Joan Luter shall be carried about the city in a cart with a ray [striped] hood upon her head . . . according to the punishment of such lewd persons in the city of old time used and accustomed, and afterwards immediately to be banished from the city."[29] That this had not in fact been the old custom is indicated by the fourteenth- and fifteenth-century court rolls from Exeter, which show prostitutes repeatedly fined; it may well have been borrowed from London or elsewhere. Shame punishment was spreading, and its application was based on "common fame" or reputation. To be known to her neighbors as a whore meant that a woman would be treated the same way as a commercial prostitute.

The university towns of Oxford and Cambridge found the sexual interaction of students with women of the town a problem, and responded with a categorization of immoral women that once again included more than commercial prostitutes. In 1317 and 1327 the king required the local authorities of Cambridge to banish whores at the request of the chancellor of the university, and in 1459 the chancellor himself received the power to banish them. The chancellor of Oxford in 1461 was authorized "to banish from a circumference of ten miles around the said University all bawds, whores, and incontinent women." The distinction between "incontinent women" and "whores" makes it likely that here the latter meant professionals. The chancellor of Oxford also enforced penalties of imprisonment, fines, and the pillory against whores; in 1453 Margaret Curtys was placed on the pillory "for her great, notorious, and long-continued whoredom, since there was no hope or presumption that she would desist from committing this wicked sin."[30]

Coventry went farther than these towns, attempting both to punish those who rented to prostitutes and to prevent immorality. Single women, prohibited from living by themselves, had no legal choice but to enter domestic service. There could be no more direct demonstration of the use of the concept of the whore to control the behavior of all women. In 1492 the Leet reiterated a 1445 fine for anyone keeping or sheltering bawds or common women, with the addition "that no single woman, being in good health and strong in body to labor within the age of fifty years take or keep from henceforth house or chambers by herself; nor that they take any chamber with any other person, but that they go to service till they be married." The women could be fined six shillings eightpence for a first offense and imprisoned for the second. In 1495 any single woman under the age of forty was ordered to take a room with an honest person who should answer for her, or else become a servant. Apparently some who considered this law harsh sought the mayor's intercession for an exemption: in 1493 the Leet ordained "that if any person speak or entreat for the favoring of any misliving woman to the Mayor . . . which is known for a harlot, he shall lose twenty shillings."[31] Citizens were thus discouraged from speaking up on behalf of any woman with a bad reputation: once damned as a whore, she had no way out. The threat of whoredom justified controlling the behavior of all unmarried women.

English towns that attempted to outlaw prostitution during the later Middle Ages adopted one or both of two tactics: outlawing and banishing brothels, or punishing whores (including those practicing on a casual basis or noncommercially). Towns did not punish men for visiting prostitutes. It was the presence of whores that was held to disrupt the social order, even though it was men who created the demand and who committed most of the crimes with which the authorities tended to associate prostitution.

Other towns chose a different strategy, regulating prostitution while tolerating it de facto. As modern experience suggests, arresting and fining prostitutes does not stop prostitution; it just harasses the practitioners, who then return to the street to make the money to pay the fines. Medieval people were as capable as we of recognizing the ineffectuality of fines in eradicating the institution, particularly repeated fines levied against the same individuals.[32] Perhaps eradication was not their aim; jurisdictions may formally outlaw a practice while tacitly and implicitly tolerating it. Those laws that fined whores or restricted their behavior (in terms of what clothing they could wear or where they could live or work) tolerated their presence in fact if not in theory, and may be considered regulatory. Regulation was directed particularly against the money-making aspect of prostitution. Legislation strictly prescribed what a whore might or must wear in part out of a need to set boundaries between decent and indecent women, but also because of the temptation women might feel when they saw what ill-gotten gains could purchase.

Repeated fining of whores was similar to repeated fines for commercial offenses such as brewing or baking "against the assize" (ostensibly the fines were for poor quality or short measure, but all practitioners were fined; the assize of bread and ale had become in effect a licensing mechanism). The net might still be cast wide enough to catch women who did not take money for sex, or who did not do so on a regular basis, but a primary focus of this particular strategy, as with so much of medieval urban legislation, was the regulation and de facto taxation of commercial enterprise, and only secondarily if at all the eradication of offenses. Although the regulating and taxing of prostitutes may have been occasioned by fiscal needs, however, it also functioned to control women, marking them as whores by their clothing or their court appearances.

Although sumptuary legislation stigmatized whores and gave the authorities license to harass them, it implicitly recognized their occupation and the fact that they were likely to continue practicing it. The London legislation prohibiting whores from dressing like "good and noble dames and damsels" was a model for the rest of the kingdom. A prohibition on whores' wearing furred hoods had appeared in the Liber Albus, along with the laws banishing whores.[33] In 1351 the council passed an ordinance against "common lewd women" wearing fur or "noble lining." They were instead to wear ray (striped) hoods, unlined. The ordinance complained that these women had "now of late from time to time assumed the fashion of being clad and attired in the manner and dress of good and noble dames and damsels of the realm." The remedy would allow "all folk, natives and strangers, . . . [to] have knowledge of what rank they are."[34] A law from 1382 provided "that all common whores, and all women commonly reputed as such, should have and use hoods of ray only. . . . And if any one should be found doing to the contrary thereof, she was to be taken and brought to the Compter, and the Sheriffs were to have the coloured hoods [or fur]. . . ."[35] By allowing the sheriffs to keep the expensive garments, and by making the statute apply to anyone "commonly reputed" a whore, the city fathers provided the maximum incentive for the officials to harass women. The attempt to stigmatize sexual misbehavior may have been a step toward abolishing it; the Liber Albus provision, after all, had accompanied the requirement that all whores be banned from the city. But to regulate an activity while at the same time banning it casts into serious question the sincerity of the ban.

The problem that the sumptuary laws actually addressed was that of women out of place, pretending to be what they were not. The initial purpose of the restrictions on whores' clothing was not to protect respectable women from harassment by distinguishing them from whores but to force women to dress according to degree. In the late thirteenth century the council had prohibited any woman of the town from wearing a furred hood "except ladies who wear furred capes the hoods of which wear fur such as they wish." The legislation was occasioned by "brewsters, nurses, servants, and women of disreputable character" who had begun to wear furred hoods "after the manner of reputable ladies."[36] In terms of the type of clothing permitted to them, servants and whores were in the same category: they should not pass themselves off as better than they were. By the following century this restriction had been limited to whores, but it still had the same sort of class significance. Although prostitutes were the only group formally forbidden in the later legislation to wear furred hoods, they are not likely to have been the only women not wearing them, since most women would have been too poor to afford fur. The effect of the rule was thus to identify prostitutes with the women of the lower classes rather than with bourgeois or noble women, even if they could approach the latter in economic status.

Most prostitutes, of course, would not have been rich enough to acquire the accoutrements of status, but some—more likely concubines or mistresses—may have been, and, as in later periods, prostitutes may have used conspicuous dress as a means of advertisement. By the sixteenth century, the ordinances about dress seem to have been entirely disregarded (if indeed they were ever enforced to any great degree). In 1538 the Wardmote inquests were complaining about "the evil example for the gorgeous apparel of the common women of the stews, to the great temptation of young maidens, wives, and apprentices."[37] Again, the concern here was not to distinguish prostitutes from honest women in order that wives and daughters not be harassed (as was the case in some European towns), but to prevent prostitutes from dressing so well that those wives and daughters would want to imitate them. Family men probably feared not so much the temptation for the women to become prostitutes as the temptation for them to demand such elaborate clothing from their husbands or fathers.

The striped hood was widely adopted as a sign of prostitution, possibly owing to parliamentary legislation.[38] Such an identifying mark implies that prostitutes were tolerated, if grudgingly, although, as the example of London shows, such a regulation on whores' clothing could illogically coexist with a prohibition on whoredom. Bristol too proclaimed in the fourteenth century, "Let no whore walk in the town without a striped hood," at a time when whores were prohibited from living in the town. Another, undated, ordinance compromised, requiring "that no common woman come within the town but abide still at the gates and that they wear a striped hood,"[39] permitting them in the suburbs so long as they wore identifying clothing. In Great Yarmouth we find several cases of whores accused of "breaking the proclamation, not going about in striped hoods."[40] Yet other women in that town were fined merely for being whores. A prohibition on whores may have coexisted with a regulation on dress here too; more likely the presentments of whores were intended not to prohibit but rather to fine and license. In Hull the town itself provided hoods to "common women" in 1444–45, and in fact rented the town walls and the foreland to them.[41] This strategy approached that of the institutionalized prostitution found in Sandwich, Southampton, and Southwark (discussed in chapter 2).

In other jurisdictions the regulation of prostitution involved fining whores. Although one could argue that these jurisdictions were attempting to banish whores and the fines were punishments for those who refused to leave, repeated fining of the same women and the context in which the court records list these fines, alongside fines for other commercial offenses, indicate that the tactic was in some cases really a sort of licensing fee. Several London suburbs, which did not have borough status but were manors belonging to various ecclesiastical institutions, fined whores in this manner. The London legislation of 1393 had attempted to ban prostitution in the suburbs as well, but in most of them the city had no jurisdiction. In Southwark, just across the Thames, there were officially condoned stews or brothels in the liberty of the bishop of Winchester. Some of the other suburbs, while they did not welcome prostitutes with such open arms, were apparently more hospitable than the city itself. In manors such as East Smithfield, Westminster, Walworth, and Southwark (outside the bishop of Winchester's lordship), whores and bawds were repeatedly presented and fined.[42] It is not clear whether in these cases the fines were meant to discourage prostitution or whether they were meant to allow the lord to share in the profits of the trade. Most likely they were halfhearted attempts at eradication, combined with large dollops of regulation including both harassment and fiscal intent.

In other towns the purpose of the fines was clearly fiscal. Winchelsea, one of the Cinque Ports of Kent, banished whores outside the walls but made provision for regular quarterly payment of fines. The customs ordered that "no common woman dwell in any street of the town, but in the outermost part of the town, upon pain of losing and paying every quarter to the town as long as she abides therein six shillings and eightpence . . . and that no common woman be found walking in the town after curfew on pain of three shillings fourpence, and that she wear no hood within the town on pain of losing it."[43] The provision for quarterly payment indicates that the prohibition was directed at the professional prostitute and was regulatory in intent, allowing the authorities to keep track of all the prostitutes while labeling and demarcating them. Even when the fines were lower, they may have been a fiscal expedient for the town. In Exeter, for example, as in many other places, the presentments of whores were included among those for commercial offenses, and the latter certainly functioned more as licensing fees than as attempts to prevent the practices.[44] In Winchester the fines instituted in the fifteenth century were in the same amounts as those for minor sanitary offenses.[45] As directed against the commercial prostitute, the fines may be considered parallel to the fines for brewers and the like; but women who were not commercial prostitutes, or who were so only on the most casual basis, could also be included.

Women's sexual behavior in medieval society was controlled by many mechanisms, both legal and informal. Families monitored their daughters' activities, although not always successfully. Neighbors observed and gossiped, and this gossip might develop into accusations in the church courts.[46] The church shaped behavior not only through the disciplinary measures of its courts but also through the confessional, where its teachings could be individualized and enforced. Secular law, however, did not have much to say about most varieties of illicit sexual behavior, except on a few occasions such as the treatment of adultery as well as whoredom in London's *Liber Albus*. The one area of sexuality with which the law did deal consistently was whoredom, and here the trend was to regulate the women involved, generally in such a way that the law could be applied to a wide range of behavior. The banishment, public shaming, or labeling of whores thus threatened to reach any woman whose sexual behavior did not conform to public norms.[47] In three English towns the regulation of prostitution was taken to its extreme in the establishment of municipally run or seigneurially sanctioned brothels (see chapter 2).

Rural Prostitution

Within rural society, as one would expect, there was less commercial prostitution than in towns. The availability of such services may even have been one of the factors that drew men to towns. The more thoroughly monetized economy of the towns may also have played a role. The economy of the countryside was by no means a natural one; villagers marketed their produce and crafts for cash. But women were perhaps less active in the economy than in the towns, where they could trade on their own account as *femmes soles*.[48] The village whore may typically have exchanged sexual favors for goods other than cash. When Absolon, Chaucer's clerk in "The Miller's Tale," wishes to seduce Alison, he tries to woo her with gifts:

> He sent her sweet wine, mead, and spiced ale
> And cakes, piping hot out of the embers;
> And, because she was from town, he offered money
> For some folk will be won for riches,
> And some for blows, and some for gentility.
> (ll. 3378–80)[49]

Absolon sees gifts as the way to win a woman's love and money as an appropriate gift for a woman of the town. The implication is not necessarily that the sexual favors of all townswomen could be bought with cash, but rather that cash would most readily buy a townswoman.

There was certainly plenty of illicit sex going on in the villages. The *Fasciculus Morum*, a fourteenth-century moral text, assumed that villages would have brothels.[50] A village might not provide enough clients to support full-time prostitutes, so part-time or casual work may have been the rule. Given that the broader medieval understanding of "whore" extended beyond the professional prostitute, one would expect to find legal records dealing with village whoredom. But in fact this turns out generally not to be the case.

Presentments for prostitution are few and far between (though not nonexistent) in manorial court records, the material that survives from medieval villages. The courts leet or views of frankpledge in these records contain the same sorts of presentments for offenses such as assault or brewing against the assize which one finds in the towns, but only rarely for whoredom (though the numbers for moral offenses increased by the end of the fifteenth century).[51] At Kingston upon Thames in 1434, for example, Marion Butcher was accused of being a whore and keeping a tavern; she was presented again as a "dishonest woman, that is, a strumpet" along with two others in 1437.[52] In 1322, on the manor of Elton, Emma Sabbe was fined for being "a fornicatress, and common."[53] These cases are isolated examples in long runs of court rolls. The Battle Abbey manorial court records report the case of Agnes Petyt, or "Little Agnes," presented repeatedly in the late fifteenth century for procuring and keeping a "suspect house"; the fine was so small that it was "evidently more a license fee than a disincentive."[54] But a "suspect house" did not have to be a brothel, and the women its proprietress procured did not have to be prostitutes. Indeed, there are many other examples from manorial courts of people presented as procurers or bawds unaccompanied by any presentments for whoredom. Where prostitutes do appear, it is often on a manor near an urban area (as with Whitstones, a suburb of Worcester, which had quite a number of brothels in the mid-fifteenth century), or on a main road to London, like Ingatestone in Kent.[55]

Absence of prosecutions for whoredom does not, of course, mean absence of prostitutes; but we are concerned here with the treatment of prostitutes under the law, and village authorities do not seem to have been very concerned with them. To give some idea of overall numbers of accusations, an examination of every manorial court roll in Public Record Office class SC2 for two arbitrarily selected years, 1425 and 1475, reveals not a single presentment for whoredom except in the urban manors of Walworth and East Smithfield, both just outside London.[56] Given the haphazard survival of records, the absence of whores from those that remain does not mean that none were ever presented; but such presentments were clearly far from ubiquitous.[57] Perhaps prostitutes were present in such small numbers as neither to be perceived as causing a disturbance of the peace nor to present a significant source of revenue for the lord. Some of the women charged with leyrwite, the payment a villein owed her lord if she fornicated, may, of course, have been commercially active.[58]

In any case, prostitution does not seem to have been a major problem in the eyes of those who constituted the manorial courts; it may have become one by the end of the fifteenth century as people became more concerned with social order. Rural prostitution or whoredom also fell under the jurisdiction of church courts, particularly archdeacons' courts.[59] Perhaps the manorial authorities generally preferred to leave the policing of morals to the church courts (although they did levy leyrwite and childwite for fornication), or perhaps church courts were more effective at asserting their jurisdiction in the countryside than in the towns, where there was an active local government to challenge their monopoly.

Ecclesiastical Jurisdiction

It was the church courts that dealt with moral offenses (along with cases involving marriage and testaments), according to canon or church law.[60] The procedure in these cases involved compurgation. A defendant who denied her guilt had to purge herself by bringing a certain number of people known to be of good character to swear that they believed she was telling the truth. If she failed to do so, she could be punished. The punishments consisted of public expiations such as processions around the church, which could be commuted to monetary payments.

Ecclesiastical jurisdiction over prostitution overlapped with that of the towns, as the career of Mariona Wood of London illustrates. Wood was presented as a harlot in the Wardmote of Portsoken in 1479 and 1481, then in church court for fornication, adultery, whoredom, and bawdry on various occasions until 1496. Excommunication did not stop her; the ecclesiastical court system based on shame punishments may not have had much effect on hardened sinners. Because the Wardmote records survive only for Portsoken, we do not know whether she fell afoul of the civic authorities elsewhere as well, but the mayor and aldermen never expelled her from the city.[61] Prostitutes came under the spiritual jurisdiction of the bishop in whose diocese they lived, so women who worked occasionally in the stews of Southwark, sanctioned by the bishop of Winchester (see chapter 2), could be prosecuted for it in the bishop of London's court.[62]

In dealing with such offenses, the church courts were far less concerned than the secular courts with preserving public order and far more concerned with preserving moral order. But public order was involved, at least to the extent that the women brought before the courts for whoredom were those who had bothered their neighbors. The church courts received their information about moral offenses either from professional informers, who would have gotten much of their information from neighbors' gossip, or (especially in the case of visitations and episcopal inspection tours) from church-wardens or other members of the community. Indeed, Chaucer in his "Friar's Tale" depicts bawds telling the summoner what sexual liaisons they have arranged and "wenches" informing on the men they have had sex with.[63]

"Common fame," or reputation, was often the basis for prosecution; being thought of as a whore could be as damaging as actually being a prostitute. Even neighbors' informal statements about a person's morals might lead to prosecution. The neighbor could be punished for defamation, but not before the defamation had brought the offending behavior to the attention of the court. For example, in a pair of London cases Mariona Crayforth was presented for defaming Mariona Bulbere, calling her a "sterling whore"—perhaps a whore who charged a sterling, or silver penny, but more likely a whore to an Easterling (German merchant)—and the latter Mariona was presented as a bawd and "sterling whore" on the testimony of the former.[64] In 1505 in Buckinghamshire "Alice Everston was publicly defamed by a certain William Nash, publicly calling her a strong and great whore," and this defamation was taken as a formal accusation, with Everston treated as the defendant.[65] It was often women who defamed other women for sexual offenses, and thus helped determine who would be prosecuted. In a sample of records from the London church courts dating from 1489 to 1490, for example, of 160 defamations of women for sexual offenses, 87 were by women, 18 by couples, and 55 by men.[66]

Those whom the church courts deemed whores did not necessarily have to be commercial prostitutes. According to the canon law it was not financial exchange that made a woman a whore. Gratian's *Decretum*, a basic canon law textbook, followed Saint Jerome in emphasizing indiscriminate availability rather than the exchange of sex for pay. Later canonists attempted to define exactly what constituted whoredom, whether in terms of publicity or in terms of numbers, with Johannes Teutonicus suggesting numbers of lovers ranging from forty to twenty-three thousand. Even canon lawyers, however, recognized that while money was not the crucial defining factor, among those whom they did consider whores, financial exchange was customary.[67]

In court practice the fact of payment, although not a necessary part of the crime, could be taken as evidence that a woman was a whore. In the London Commissary Court, Margaret Weston was accused of this offense "by the token that she received a penny for her labor," Joan Burdon "by the token of a payment of six pennyweights." The wife of Denis Copeland was a "whore by the token that she came from the brothel." Yet Cecilia the servant of William Barnaby was accused of being a whore "by the token that the neighbors found her with a certain priest," without any mention of money.[68] Joan Cromp of Stratford was also accused of being a whore for having sex with her servant eighteen times in one week, paying twopence a time. Both Cromp and her husband were also accused of quarreling with and defaming their neighbors, so she was clearly the sort of unpopular person about whom such a story might circulate whether it was true or not. Nonetheless, that she was accused as a whore makes it clear that taking money did not constitute the essence of whoredom.[69]

We are not justified in concluding that every time the church court records identify someone as a whore she was actually a professional prostitute, especially since only a small percentage were ever convicted, and many of the prosecutions may have been maliciously instigated.[70] In some cases the accusation involved numbers of partners. Katherine Saunder, for example, was accused of adultery with a long list of men; the scribe then made an interlinear note that she was also accused as a common whore. Perhaps the second accusation was an afterthought based on the number of men she supposedly had sex with.[71] Yet a woman could be accused of adultery with seven men but not called a whore.[72] In some cases a woman was called a whore simply because she was a priest's partner, even if it was a long-term relationship in which she bore him children.[73]

In short, a woman was considered a whore when her behavior scandalized the authorities in some way. The church courts were acting along the lines suggested by Thomas of Chobham, who declared that a whore is a woman who either has sex with many men or has sex for money, but the sin must be public: "If someone sells herself in secret, she is not called a whore."[74] Mariona Wood was accused, in the same year but in separate accusations, of fornication, adultery, and whoredom; the charge of whoredom in this case and others probably was due not to specific acts but to reputation or common fame.[75] When the bishop of Lincoln's visitation found that "Joan Sothyll of Poynton was impregnated by Thomas Sturdy of Poynton, and the same Joan is reputed as a common whore," the community was relying on a generally bad reputation as to sexual morals rather than on any specific act of prostitution.[76] Accusations of whoredom "especially with" a particular man probably meant that the behavior was more notorious than an accusation of fornication would imply, although they could also mean that a woman had multiple partners and the named man was simply the customer with whom the informer had observed her.

The fact that a woman had been presented for or convicted of a sexual offense in a city court could constitute evidence of whoredom before a church court. Elizabeth Kirkeby was accused of being a "common whore, and especially with William Barber, by the token that they were previously imprisoned in the Compter [the London sheriff's prison]." It was very common for a woman to be accused in the church courts as an "indicted whore," meaning that she had been indicted in the temporal courts, whose records do not survive.[77] Although many women were accused by both jurisdictions, sexual behavior did not have to be illegal according to the temporal authorities for it to be censurable in the church courts. Even though the bishop of Winchester (as landlord) condoned the stews of Southwark, when men from the diocese of London visited, the bishop of London had responsibility, and the courts punished the visits, as with James Barber, accused of committing adultery with two women there.[78]

Outside London the label "whore" was not as common; instead the church courts more often accused women of specific acts of adultery or fornication. Occasionally these women may have been commercial prostitutes: for example, Joan James of the diocese of Lincoln was accused of "incontinence with divers vagabonds staying at her house at night."[79] Only a few women were actually called whores in the York court records.[80] But quite a number were accused of fornication with multiple men, and over a period of years. One accusation of fornication cannot be taken as evidence that a woman was a prostitute or even that she had more than one partner; people living together in a stable relationship, who could not marry because of some impediment, could be accused of fornication, as could people the validity of whose marriage was in some doubt, as well as unmarried people carrying on a sexual relationship that they may not have wanted to solemnize. Even two or three different accusations of fornication may only be the result of gossip or a bad reputation. When a woman was accused at a single court session of fornication with nine different men, though, we may assume that she was, if not a professional, at least what medieval society would have considered a whore.[81] When a woman repeatedly presented for fornication was punished but not the man, we can assume that she was treated differently because she was a professional. In addition, the number of compurgators required would vary depending on how egregious the woman's behavior was. Yet the York court seems to have been much more interested in judging the specific act committed by the accused than in pinning the label "whore" on her.

In addition to accusations of whoredom in disciplinary (ex officio) proceedings, the church courts also dealt with cases in which the term "whore" had a very wide range of meaning, covering all sexual infractions. In these cases it was used not in a technical legal sense but in witnesses' testimony. This can give us some idea of what the term meant in common speech. When Joan Kirkeby claimed that she was married to Henry Helwys, who in turn asserted that he was married to Alice Newton, witnesses testified that Henry had reproached Alice with being "his whore and not his wife" because he had previously contracted with Joan.[82] He was not asserting that she was a prostitute or that she was promiscuous; he simply meant that she was engaged in an illicit sexual relationship. The term "whore" also appears in defamation cases, which were handled by church courts and which often involved sexual insults. The court usually recorded the exact words of defamation spoken, and they were usually given in English even when the rest of the record was in Latin. In London the most common defamatory words were "whore," "thief," and "bawd," but there were often details and variations.[83] The percentage of defamations that were sexual in nature was higher in London than elsewhere, which may indicate either the greater prevalence of sexual offenses in London or the greater concern of Londoners with them.[84]

Where the term "whore" was used as an insult rather than as an accusation, the defamatory speaker often did not mean specifically to denote that the woman was a common prostitute; the term was more generally derogatory. A woman who said to another, "Art thou not ashamed, thou abominable whore, to be a Spaniard's harlot," did not necessarily mean that the latter accepted money for sex. Numerous defamation cases involve such language: "calling her in English harlot and whore and saying that she lived in adultery with Thomas Thewetes and he impregnated her," or "calling her in English harlot, and . . . that she lived in fornication with her husband before marriage was solemnized between them," or "calling her a common whore and that she had a child before she was married."[85] Joan Read's neighbor, who said "that the husband of the said Joan was a fool for believing any of the words or sayings of the said Joan his wife, because Joan is a common whore and lay at the Stews side to commit adultery and while Joan was there a silver dish worth ten pounds was stolen, for the redemption of which the said Joan gave the bawd of that house at the Stews side a piece of velvet, and also in order that the said bawd would keep his counsel," did not understand "whore" in a strictly commercial sense.[86] In one fourteenth-century defamation case from York, the complaint alleged that John Warde had called Alice Pepinell a whore; the testimony of the witnesses indicated that what he had actually said was "that a certain sir John, chaplain of Ronchcliff, knew her carnally," which she took as an accusation of whoredom.[87] A woman who called another "wedded-man whore" or "wedded-man strumpet" was probably slandering her with having sex with a married man, not with being a prostitute who specialized in married men.

A "monkwhore" or "friarwhore" could be the mistress of a member of a religious order, although she might also be a prostitute who catered particularly to these groups, which in an ecclesiastical city like York composed a significant portion of the potential client population.[88] The extremely common accusation "priest's whore" generally seems to have referred to a woman who lived with a priest as his wife. The church had been arguing for centuries that such a woman was a whore, and the public seems to have adopted this point of view, or at least adopted its language as an insult.[89] But one woman who called another "whore and bawd" and charged "that she got all the goods she has in uncleanliness" clearly had exchange in mind, and one who called another "strong whore of Stews side" or said that "she was as common as any woman in a brothel" was also implying professional prostitution, even if it was only as an insult and not a direct accusation.[90]

The fact that so many people were accused in court—especially in London—of having defamed others with sexual slanders indicates that people took their reputations seriously. Several scholars have argued that the increase in the number of sexual defamation cases in the sixteenth century, in various parts of the country, suggests that people were becoming more concerned about their sexual reputation at that time.[91] It certainly indicates that people did not just shrug off insults but treated them as though they might affect other people's opinions.[92] Bringing such a court case accomplished something other than simply giving greater publicity to the defamation: winning the case would have been expected to vindicate the plaintiff in the eyes of her peers.

Since the church court records provide evidence of the term "whore" referring to women ranging from the professional prostitute to the priest's partner to the woman who had sex with her husband before they were married, we might say that prostitutes were a subset of whores. But there was no technical term for distinguishing prostitutes from whores in general. Anyone accused of being a whore—anyone whose sexual behavior was offensive to her neighbors, especially female ones—could be placed by her neighbors' insults or by court action in the same category as the commercial prostitute.

Law, Morality, and Gender

Although different approaches to prostitution developed in different jurisdictions and from different sets of circumstances and pressures, all the tactics for dealing with the problem (as people of the time saw it) grew up within fundamentally the same cultural milieu. It is therefore legitimate to ask what the various approaches have in common, and what the body of law about prostitution reveals about the society that wrote it.

Moral considerations, especially about male sexual behavior, were significantly absent in the justifications for legislating against or regulating prostitution. Stated grounds are not necessarily the only motives behind the legislation, but they do reveal the impression the drafters wished to convey about the purpose of the ordinances. And as far as the community was concerned, it was social, not moral, disruption that the customs were intended to forestall. The various proclamations from London proper and elsewhere were more concerned with preventing crime and preserving public order, and with protecting women who were not prostitutes from sexual advances, than with upholding the morals of the community as a whole. The other sorts of leisure activities banned within London proper—archery, bowling, tennis, dice—indicate a wish to control activities that might provoke quarrels and riots or attract crime rather than those that might be deemed immoral.[93] Prostitution fell into this category as well. The laws and regulations collectively betray a complete lack of interest in inhibiting male sexual gratification. The ecclesiastical courts, which charged men as well as women with moral infractions in a fairly evenhanded manner, present a different picture. But even here the penalties were light, and men were charged with specific acts rather than with labels of opprobrium (although a few were called bawds).

The distinctive clothing required of the prostitutes, and the repeated fining of prostitutes in towns where prostitution was technically illegal, served the same labeling function as did the official brothels in England and elsewhere. Respectable women could be protected if another group of women was set aside as fair game. But identifying, controlling, and shaming the prostitute was not required just for the sake of the nonprostitute (or the man to whom she belonged); it was also necessary for the social order. The prostitute could pursue her trade at the price of being labeled a whore, a label that (as the defamation cases indicate) had serious consequences, and that also automatically granted both local secular and church authorities rights over her. Any woman who violated the norms of feminine sexual behavior ran the risk of incurring the same label.

The use of punishments involving public shame (in both civic and church courts) and the efforts to distinguish whores from respectable or honest women reflect the fact that women's honor depended entirely on their sexual reputation. The emphasis on honor in medieval English culture does not come through as strongly from the sources as in other medieval or early modern societies, for example Renaissance Italy.[94] Nevertheless, the way the law treated whores indicates that feminine honor and reputation were important and, we may infer, reflected on the honor and reputation of husbands and fathers as well. The extent to which prostitutes themselves accepted the label as dishonorable or felt shame about their profession, and the extent to which people among whom the prostitutes lived accepted the law's valuation, is discussed further in chapter 5.

Brothels, Licit and Illicit

Prostitutes practiced their trade in a wide variety of ways, but perhaps the most prominent, because the most formal and institutionalized, was in the brothel. Brothels could range from private dwellings used on a casual, ad hoc basis to enterprises established by municipal legislation. We know much more about the latter, which were few in number, than the former, which were numerous. The officially sanctioned brothels can tell us a great deal about how the authorities viewed the functions of prostitution. And because these brothels lasted longer than the more casual ones, the records that refer to them provide information about the actual practice of brothel prostitution. Institutionalized brothels were more the rule elsewhere in Europe than in England, but those places in England that established them followed some of the same patterns and used the brothels to make prostitutes available to men in a controlled and orderly manner.

European Practice

A number of towns in Continental Europe—in France, Germany, Italy, and Spain—had municipally owned or licensed brothels during the medieval and early modern periods.[1] The official rationale for the establishment and regulation of brothels accorded with church doctrine in treating prostitutes as degraded and defiled but tolerating their activity because of masculine demand. Municipal authorities licensed or sponsored the brothels not to protect the prostitutes or their customers but to maintain social order. Recent research agrees that across Europe the authorities saw regulated brothels as a foundation of the social order, releasing tensions that would otherwise lead to sodomy, rape, and seduction. In Florence the proclaimed purpose of institutionalization was to boost a declining birthrate by turning men away from homosexual practices. By initiating men into the pleasures of heterosexual intercourse, the prostitutes would supposedly inspire in them a desire to marry. The town of Dijon provided young men with opportunities for fornication with prostitutes as a remedy for an epidemic of rape which threatened the power of the governing elite. In German towns the purpose of the brothel was to make the streets safe for respectable women, defined as the wives and daughters of the citizens. The Nuremberg regulations stated that the reason for establishing the municipal brothel was "for the avoiding of greater evil," that in Munich to prevent "evil to wives and virgins." The rhetoric of the governors lauded prostitution not merely as a necessary evil but as a buttress of the moral order.[2] The necessity of official brothels, however, did not confer respect or privilege on those who worked in them. The benefits for society were purchased at the cost of stigmatizing some of its most powerless members. A necessary evil was an evil nonetheless, and official recognition did not imply respectability.[3]

The towns' financial interests as well as their concern for public order motivated their inspection and regulation of the brothels. Whether the municipality owned the brothel or granted a municipal concession to a private house made little difference in its administration. The officials who ran the houses—in some areas customarily women, in others required to be men—generally paid the town for the privilege, but the job was lucrative enough to be well worth it. In addition to the money they collected from the prostitutes (which in some cases could amount to the entire fee from the customer, the prostitutes themselves keeping only tips), they could also sell food and drink at exorbitant prices, or in some instances require the prostitutes to purchase necessities from or through them. In some towns the brothel also brought in revenue to the municipality itself, and conflict could arise between the brothelkeeper and the town if the latter found the former keeping too much of the income.[4]

The official brothels catered especially to young unmarried men who, established burghers feared, might otherwise seduce or rape the burghers' wives or daughters. Many towns forbade married men access to the brothels, although, like many of the other regulations, this one was often honored in the breach. Priests, although they too could be seducers and disruptive forces in society, were also often banned. One of the functions of the brothel may have been to provide for men who were in the city temporarily without a wife or established mistress. In Florence the customers seem to have been mostly outsiders: fewer than half were even from Tuscany. For young unmarried men, their main clientele in purpose if not in practice, brothels did more than just fill the need for physical release; they also gave young men power over women and thus bonded them into the male community.[5]

Even in towns that had no municipally operated or concessionary brothels, prostitution was often formally condoned within recognized geographical limits. In Paris, for example, brothels were permitted in designated streets, where they were inspected and regulated by the provosts, although the municipal administration found it impossible to restrict prostitutes to those neighborhoods.[6] Similarly, Cologne, which unlike other German towns had no official brothel until the 1520s, recognized privately run brothels in the fifteenth century and restricted them to particular areas of town.[7] In addition to geographical restrictions, sumptuary legislation also played an important part in the regulation of prostitution, even in towns that tolerated the practice without institutionalizing it. In some towns whores were required to wear identifying garments of a particular color or style (which varied from place to place), or were forbidden to wear particular types of clothing or ornaments (which could then be confiscated by the arresting officer). In others the dress of "respectable" women was regulated and whores were exempt.[8] The rationale seems to have been to protect nonprostitutes from harassment by visually marking women who were available for sexual purposes. That men should have felt this necessary for the protection of their wives and daughters implies that they expected men to treat as a whore any woman they did not know to be otherwise.

Most of the towns that recognized and condoned prostitution paid some sort of lip service to the prostitutes' immortal souls and the prospect of their conversion, whether by closing the brothels on Sunday or during Holy Week (which could also serve to keep them from competing with churches for their parishioners), by requiring the prostitutes to listen to sermons, or by establishing Magdalen houses for those who chose to leave the profession. These provisions protected to a certain extent the prostitutes' right to make choices by keeping open the possibility of conversion, but they also reflected a deep ambivalence. If the authorities were really concerned with the souls of the prostitutes, they could have attempted to prevent prostitution in the first place. Because prostitution served what they saw as a vital social function, they used the example of the converted prostitute saints (see chapter 6) as a convenient fiction to justify condoning and sponsoring the whores' continuation in a life which they believed to be endangering the women's salvation.[9]

Municipal or publicly regulated brothels provided some protection for prostitutes. Regulations tried to protect them from falling too deeply into debt to the brothelkeeper, from being beaten, or from being kept in the brothel against their will. Identification as a common woman could also help protect the prostitute from sexual violence, although in some places the rape laws did not apply to whores, since their status implied universal consent.[10] On the negative side, in addition to any psychological stigma it may have caused, public regulation also restricted the prostitutes' freedom of movement and their freedom of association; for example, they were sometimes prohibited from having a special lover. The institution existed for the benefit of the towns, whose interests were identified with their male inhabitants', more than that of the prostitutes, and as the persistence of clandestine prostitution (and forcible enclosure of clandestine prostitutes in official brothels) indicates, the whores were not particularly eager to become part of it.[11]

Despite variations in the operation of legal brothels throughout Continental Europe (which this brief summary has necessarily glossed over), we can discern some overall contrasts with the English situation. The most important difference is that officially operated or regulated brothels were far less common in England, where toleration tended to be unofficial and prostitution seems to have operated on a more casual basis. The brothel was not as thoroughly integrated into the community. For example, prostitutes did not play a formal part in festive observances in England as they did in some places in Europe (although their participation may have been a means of mocking rather than accepting them).[12] The absence of official brothels in most English towns also implies the absence of a strictly delineated class of professional prostitute. The whore against whom English legislation was directed was a much less clearly defined category. Nevertheless, even those English towns without institutionalized brothels shared some fundamental attitudes toward prostitution with towns on the Continent. It was a necessary evil to be deplored but tolerated, and the prostitutes themselves were to a large extent excluded from the community even though their work was considered necessary to it.

Institutionalized Brothels in England

Even though only a few places in England had official or institutionalized brothels, this small number of cases is worth studying in detail because the inferences that can be drawn from them about attitudes toward prostitution may be more generally valid.[13] The legal brothels or stews were well enough known for the women who worked there to appear in literature as exemplars of various kinds of sin. "Janet of the stews" appears, along with Jack the juggler, Daniel the dice player, Denote the bawd, Friar Faker, and Robin the ribald, in *Piers Plowman's* list of practitioners of dishonest trades.[14]

Two of the jurisdictions that had official brothels were port towns, Sandwich in Kent and Southampton in Hampshire, and the third was the London suburb of Southwark. The three sets of regulations do not appear to have been modeled directly on any of the European systems (or vice versa). Local conditions help explain why these three localities had institutionalized brothels while others did not. Southampton and Sandwich had a clientele of sailors to create a demand for prostitutes—and a perceived threat to wives and daughters if that demand were not met. The port town of Hull may have rented dwellings to prostitutes for much the same reason, although there were other port towns that did not do so. In Southwark a tradition of brothels just outside the jurisdiction of the city of London, combined with the desire of the lord both to increase his income and to assert his authority, created the opportunity for institutionalization.

The municipal brothel of Sandwich was a fairly modest enterprise. Whores (not all of them commercial prostitutes) occasionally crop up in the Sandwich records through the second half of the fifteenth century, punished with banishment from the town or with the cucking stool.[15] In 1475 the mayor and commons of the town granted a quitrent in exchange for land "to make a common house of stews called the Galley."[16] That this bathhouse was not simply a place for people to get clean was indicated by a 1494 provision "that a house shall be ordained for common women like as it has been accustomed." The following year the Sandwich council set down the regulations for the keepers of the town brothel. They were to charge "their maids" sixteen pence a week for room and board; to refrain from beating them; and to sell them ale at a fixed price. The keepers at that time were a husband and wife, and there were four women living in the brothel. The

Latin term used for the brothelkeepers, *lenones*, was a loaded and negative one meaning "procurers" or "pimps," but the prostitutes were not called whores or even the more neutral "common women"; they were simply identified as "serving-maids resident in the brothel."[17]

In Southampton sanctioned brothels did not appear before the late fifteenth century. Earlier in that century the authorities were trying to eliminate prostitution from an area of town in which it had become entrenched. The Mayor's Court ordered in 1413 "that all the whores keeping a common inn in East Street shall be entirely removed . . . particularly for the sake of preserving the continence of those walking through the said quarter or going to the churches of St. Mary, the Holy Trinity, and St. Andrew."[18] Apparently the prostitutes continued to create a temptation for churchgoers, for by the 1480s the brothels of East Street were recognized stews. Stews were also built at West Quay.[19] The ordinances governing the official brothels or stews do not survive, but there is enough evidence from court cases involving the prostitutes and their customers that we can infer what the regulations must have been. The stews at Southampton were apparently abolished in 1544, when the council noted that "it hath been in question whether it were better to abolish and put away the name of the stews in East Street and the common women of the same or to suffer them." It was determined that until a decision could be made, "in the meantime the harlots and common women shall be expelled out of the liberty of the town, and that Tristram Harrison, now bawd of the said stews, after this day shall keep no such common woman or harlot in his house. . . ."[20] The stews cease to appear in the court records after this point. The motive for the decision was not stated, but the time coincided roughly with similar proceedings in Southwark and on the Continent, and may be indicative of a generally more repressive attitude toward sexual morality in both Protestant and Catholic countries during the mid-sixteenth century.

So long as they practiced their trade in the stews, Southampton's prostitutes seem to have been fully tolerated. They were not regularly fined as in other towns. The Southampton "Bawd of the Stews" (an official title) could be fined for offenses such as harboring suspicious persons; in 1518 he was fined for hindering the officers in their search of his house.[21] Presumably they were searching for ineligible customers—married men or priests, who could be fined if they were caught at the stews.[22] Occasionally foreigners were fined for being taken at the stews (a Norfolk man, a Dutchman, a "strange man"), but it can hardly have been illegal for foreigners to visit the prostitutes. As in many port towns, foreign sailors must have constituted a large fraction of the prostitutes' clientele.[23] Perhaps as a revenue measure the city routinely arrested and fined foreigners even though they had committed no crime. Men could also be fined for "lying with a quean within the town" rather than at the stews, and the women involved could be fined as well. One woman of the stews was fined forty pence (an unusually large sum) in 1493 "because she was a bawd," presumably acting as procuress for some of her companions, which we may infer was illegal. As elsewhere, the prostitutes had to wear some sort of distinguishing hood when they left the stews; in 1511 "a wench of the stews" was fined "for coming into the town without her token on her head."[24]

The institutionalization of prostitution in Southampton may have been intended in part to make law enforcement easier. Many fines in the Southampton records are for fights or "affrays" at the stews.[25] Concentrating prostitution in one area may have cut down on drinking and violence elsewhere in the town and allowed the constabulary to focus its efforts, but it did not protect the prostitutes. Customers, and even the Bawd of the Stews, were fined heavily for beating the women, an indication that such beatings were illegal but recurrent.[26] Most notably, the institutionalization of prostitution allowed firm official control over the women involved, not only by identifying them but also by monitoring their behavior. An official brothel made it possible to define prostitutes as a formal category, although women of the town who were not commercial prostitutes could still be punished as whores.

The stews of Southwark have left much more detailed information, both about the daily life of the prostitutes and about the nature of regulation, than those of Sandwich and Southampton. Southwark, across the Thames from London, came under the city's jurisdiction in 1327, but certain areas called liberties remained separate and under the control of high-ranking churchmen.[27] It was in the liberty of the bishop of Winchester that the legal stews flourished. The Bankside area in the Winchester liberty was known as "Les Stuwes" by the middle of the fourteenth century; indeed, the London customs that prohibited boatmen from taking any man or woman to "les Estouves" at night may go back to the thirteenth century.[28] It is not clear whether at that time the stewhouses were officially sanctioned brothels.

The surviving code of customs for the stews claims to date from the twelfth century. That claim is clearly fraudulent—the preamble states that it was enacted by the Commons in Parliament in 1162, long before there was anything called a Parliament, let alone a House of Commons—but it is not possible to tell exactly when the customs were established. The earliest manuscript is from the fifteenth century, and includes some additions from that time; the original may have been a good deal older.[29] The attribution to Parliament was an attempt to add the authority of tradition, but it is not likely that sanctioned brothels here predated those on the Continent by centuries. Brothels had probably been common in the Winchester liberty before they were legalized. They were certainly common elsewhere in Southwark, where they were a sore point with the populace. In 1390 the citizens of Southwark petitioned Parliament that "no stews be held in the Borough of Southwark but in the common place ordained for this." They complained again in 1433 and 1436, asking that "none such that have dwelled at the said Stews be suffered to hold any common inn or tavern in any other place within the said Southwark, save only at the said Stews, for the eschewing of murders, robberies and adulteries that otherwise are likely to be had." Court records from those parts of Southwark under the jurisdiction of the city of London in 1539 indicate that brothels were still being kept there.[30] These could have developed as a result of the legal stews and the consequent reputation of the area as a red-light district, but it is more likely that the whole area was notorious for its brothels by the fourteenth century and one landholder, the bishop of Winchester, decided to profit by legalizing and regulating them.

The regulations of the Southwark stews gave the women some protection from abuses by the brothelkeepers, as well as from harassment by the London authorities, but still kept them under tight control. The ordinances claimed to be restoring the old customs "that have been used and accustomed there out of time of mind, which now of late were broken, to the great displeasure of God and great hurt unto the lord, and utter undoing of all his poor tenants there dwelling, and also to the great multiplication of horrible sin upon the single women, who ought to have their free going and coming at their own liberty. . . ."[31] They forbade the prostitutes to live or board in the stewhouses (B1, A2, B10). On holy days from 6 to 11 A.M. and from 1 to 6 P.M. the prostitutes had to leave not only the stews but the entire liberty, and during the sitting of Parliament they were also banned at night (B11, A3, B15, B16). Banning them from the liberty on religious holidays may have been a concession by the bishop to religious propriety; during the sitting of Parliament or a meeting of the king's council, the bishop himself was likely to be in residence in his palace next to the stews and may well have wanted the area kept quiet. As presentments of stewholders show, however, closing on holy days was one of the regulations they constantly infringed; this regulation may simply have served as a pretext for collecting extra money from those who wished to remain open. The same may be true of the prohibition on the prostitutes' boarding at the stews; repeated fines of stewholders show that the regulation was continually violated.[32]

The brothelkeeper had a number of ways of profiting from the prostitutes, some of which the regulations tried to prohibit. Even though the stew was not her residence, the rent the prostitute paid (fourteen pence per week [B2]) was much higher than standard rents at the time.[33] In Sandwich the prostitutes paid sixteen pence, but that was for board and lodging, not just for a place of business. The rules do not indicate whom the customers paid or how much: they probably paid the prostitutes, who then paid the stewholder the high rent rather than a percentage of their fees.

The regulations evinced a great deal of concern that the prostitutes not be exploited financially. In addition to the prohibition on boarding at the brothel (thus preventing the stewholder from overcharging the women for food, as the Sandwich regulations prohibited overcharging for beer), the customs also prohibited the holder from lending money to the prostitutes (A6). If he did so, he was not entitled to bring suit for its recovery. This regulation, apparently intended to keep the women from falling into debt and having to remain in the brothel longer than they wished, was breached in practice. In at least one case, that of Ellen Butler (see p. 57), a stewholder did succeed in having a woman imprisoned because she would not work for him to pay off a debt. Butler claimed not that the stewholder, Thomas Bowde, had breached the regulations by suing her for debt, but rather that she had never contracted any debt in the first place.[34] This indicates either that the regulation against the stewholders' suing for debts was not enforced or that Butler simply did not know about it (if she had known of the provision, she would surely have argued that Bowde's suit was procedurally illegal as well as false).

The regulations also aimed at protecting prostitutes from other forms of exploitation besides debt. Prostitutes could not spin or card wool with the stewholder (B13). This provision could be seen as an attempt to limit the work options of prostitutes (spinning was the most common occupation for women in the later Middle Ages, particularly for single women), but it also limited the brothelkeeper's ability to force the prostitutes to work for his profit. The only comparable provision in any set of Continental regulations is found in some German towns, which took the opposite position: there prostitutes were required to spin for the stewholder when they were not busy with a customer.[35] As at Sandwich, the Southwark stewholders were forbidden to beat the prostitutes.[36] In addition to preventing the stewholder from keeping women in the brothel because of debts, the regulations also required the bishop's officials to search regularly for women being kept against their will, a provision that casts doubt on the free movement of prostitutes which appeared as an ideal in the preamble to the customs. A woman also could not be prevented from leaving a brothel because of a pending legal action (A5).

While appearing to guarantee prostitutes certain rights, the regulations did not respond to the practical realities that must have kept many of the women in the brothels. There was no provision for persuading them to convert and give up prostitution, no provision for Magdalen houses for them to live in as there were elsewhere in Europe, no dowry made available, no alternative means of support if they chose to leave. Still, protecting a woman's ability to leave if she wished to do so was an important step, if a not fully enforced one. The abuses this regulation attempted to prevent were very real.

The rights of the prostitutes vis-à-vis the stewholders may not have been upheld in practice because, at least according to fifteenth-century claims, the stewholders controlled the court system. Henry Saunder complained to the chancellor sometime between 1475 and 1485 that Thomas Dickinson, "a keeper of one of the uncleanly house on the other side of the Thames," after trying unsuccessfully to sue him in the city of London, had had him arrested in Southwark and placed in the bishop of Winchester's prison, "and they that are impaneled in the inquest are occupiers and keepers of such unclean and infamous places as the said Thomas is." Convinced that he would not get a fair trial, Saunder offered to answer Dickinson's case in any court in England except in the bishop of Winchester's Southwark liberty. Alice Skelling, involved in a debt case between 1504 and 1515, complained that the jurors were "only bawds and watermen, who regard neither God nor their conscience but their own appetite and the pleasure of the great officers of that court."[37] The denizens of Southwark outside the liberty who had petitioned Parliament were concerned not only with the brothels in their neighborhood but also with the brothelkeepers from the legal stews, who they feared were taking over not just the courts of the Winchester liberty but inquests and assizes in the county of Surrey as well.[38]

In addition to nominally protecting the prostitute, the customs of the stews also regulated her behavior. There were no restrictions on her dress other than that she not wear an "apron" (B28).[39] The prostitute who had a lover, especially if she maintained him financially, encountered harsh punishments: three weeks in prison, a fine, the cucking stool, and banishment from the lordship (B12, B50). The purpose may appear to have been to protect her from a pimp who would attempt to take her income, though a measure to protect the prostitute would hardly have punished her so severely. Its true function was rather to control her choices about her own sexuality. To work in a public brothel, a prostitute could not have a special relationship with any one man. Similarly, wives or nuns, who belonged to a husband or to God, were not to be received in the stewhouses (B4). In effect, once she had become public, a woman could have no private life, no say in who her sex partner was to be; she was common property to be shared according to men's wishes, not her own.

The regulations also attempted to protect the customer. He was not supposed to be harassed in the street (B13), pulled into the brothel by his clothing (B7, B8), or have his person or belongings detained in the house because of debts (B3, B6).[40] The stewholder could not sell food or other goods in his house (B29) or keep a boat (B21), probably in order to protect the customer from being forced to purchase food or transportation at inflated prices. The banishment from the stews of any woman with "burning sickness" (B25) protected the customer from disease. The nature of this disease is unclear, but whether it was syphilis, some other venereal disease, or leprosy, the fear that prostitutes spread disease was common. One English treatise of the fourteenth century notes that prostitutes are dangerous because "meseles" (lepers) may have had sex with them; other writers thought that prostitutes could be uninfected carriers of leprosy.[41]

Protection of the prostitute and the customer, although concerns of the regulations, were subsidiary to the preservation of public order. A provision requiring a prostitute to spend the whole night with a customer may have been meant to discourage people from wandering around the area at night (B20).[42] The provisions taken as a whole show an attempt to control both the stewholder and the prostitute, to prevent them from harassing people and creating disturbances. Women's sexuality, a disruptive force, was to be kept within bounds: prostitutes were to disappear on holy days, to be unobtrusive, to stay indoors and not walk the streets. The regulation that no one keep bitches in heat within the liberty (B27) may be related to this effort to control feminine sexuality. The prohibition is logical enough; in an urban area where animals run free, a female in estrus can create quite a disturbance. Nonetheless, there are hundreds of equally logical potential sanitary and nuisance regulations that did not find their way into the customary of the stews as this one did. Its inclusion works to stress symbolically the dangers of unbridled feminine sexuality.[43]

The thrust of the Southwark regulations, despite the preamble urging protection of the prostitutes, was to make women sexually available to men while keeping them under tight control. If a woman was not the property of a particular man—a husband—her sexual behavior had to be strictly regulated by the (male) civil authorities. The regulations emphasized this by referring to prostitutes as "single women."[44] If not the property of one man, they were common women and had forfeited the right to choose their own lovers; while remaining available to all, they had to avoid disturbing any.

The city of London and the central government, as well as the bishop of Winchester and his administration, were concerned about disturbances caused by the Southwark stews. The city prohibited boatmen from taking people across at night "lest misdoers from one side or the other be able to come and go."[45] A commission issued by Henry VI noted in 1460 that "owing to the number of prostitutes in Southwark and other places adjacent many homicides, plunderings and improprieties have occurred." The king appointed commissioners to "remove all such prostitutes and others dwelling within the said borough and places," including anyone the bishop of Winchester's officers certified as refusing to accept the church's penalties. As a means of enforcement, this was setting the fox to guard the henhouse. The church had "cited such [prostitutes] and others reporting their sins to the correction of their souls," and the king was ostensibly trying to help with enforcement "because the church cannot compel them to appear for their crimes by ecclesiastical censure only."[46] For the bishop of Winchester to mark out the guilty ones, however, placed him in a hypocritical position, although the subordinates who handled this matter would not be the same ones who handled the accounts of his secular landholding, including the stews. Indeed, this proclamation may have applied only to Southwark outside the liberty, in which case the king would have been helping the bishop enforce his monopoly on legal prostitution.

The bishops of Winchester seem to have been successful in separating their secular landholdings and administration, including that of the Bankside brothels, from their spiritual duties. Although the bishops spent time in their London palace and would have been fully aware of what was going on, they themselves were not personally involved; bailiffs and other officials enforced the regulations. The bishop of Winchester was not the only ecclesiastic in Europe to own and legalize brothels; the bishop of Mainz did the same. By the fifteenth century the bishop of Winchester himself retained actual ownership of only two of the stewhouses, though he maintained jurisdiction over them all, and thus the substantial profits of justice from the repeated fines stewholders paid for violation of the ordinances. The new owners of the houses, who collected steep rents, were mostly ecclesiastical institutions.[47] The customs of the brothels explicitly reinforced the bishop's power as a temporal lord: all residents of the liberty (not just prostitutes) had to sue one another in the bishop's court rather than the king's (A7). The condoning of the brothels, in addition to producing revenue for the bishop, may also have been a means of tacitly asserting his control over the area and his power to institute customs quite different from those in force elsewhere in England. The fact that a churchman owned the most notorious brothels of the late Middle Ages is a sign not of the corruption of the medieval church but rather of the separation of the bishop's function as secular landlord from his religious persona.

Ultimately the central government did take action against the legal brothels of Southwark. The eighteen stews were briefly closed in 1506, and only twelve reopened. The chronicler who recorded this information was not sure of the reason.[48] In 1546 Henry VIII made his ostensible intentions more explicit:

> Considering how by toleration of such dissolute and miserable persons as . . . there without punishment or correction exercise their abominable and detestable sin, there hath of late increased and grown such enormities as not only provoke instantly the anger and wrath of Almighty God, but also engender such corruption among the people as tendeth to the intolerable annoyance of the commonwealth, and where not only the youth is provoked, enticed, and allowed to execute the fleshly lusts, but also, by such assemblies of evil-disposed persons haunted and accustomed, is daily devised and conspired how to spoil and rob the true laboring and well-disposed men. . . .[49]

The concern with public order, with prostitution's connection to other crimes, was cited frequently throughout the Middle Ages (and other eras as well) to justify the regulation or suppression of prostitution. Its invocation at this particular moment might have occurred because crime rates in an increasingly crowded London had become much worse, or were at least perceived as worse. By the mid-sixteenth century the question of morality may also have begun to loom larger in motivating the regulation and suppression of prostitution. Some scholars have attributed this change to religious development, citing the suppression of brothels in Germany at this time, which has been persuasively linked to the Reformation.[50] But the same pattern seems to have been repeated in countries where Protestantism did not take hold: Florence and the towns of Languedoc all closed down their municipal brothels in the sixteenth century.[51] A fear of syphilis has been suggested as the reason for this chronological coincidence, but none of the proclamations cite it, and one can imagine that the officials would have been only too eager to do so had it occurred to them as a serious problem.[52]

The most important reason for the withdrawal of official sanction seems to have been a change in morality—a stricter view of male sexuality in particular. Whereas in an earlier period men, especially unmarried men, had essentially been guaranteed the opportunity to behave sexually as they pleased, the church now took more seriously its own preaching about fornication, and the secular authorities began to adopt it too. The Protestant and Catholic Reformations played a role, but the encouragement of marriage and the criticism of male fornication reflect a change in popular beliefs as well as church teaching. Brothels did persist, as did the sexual double standard, but they became less widely acceptable. The closure of the Southwark brothels in England was part of this movement. But this process seems not to have begun yet in the fifteenth century: there were few objections then to men visiting prostitutes.

Brothel Ownership and Management

If legalized brothels were so profitable or so beneficial to public order, why did more English jurisdictions not establish them? Since those places that did not have them have left no record of whether they ever considered establishing them, we can only speculate. The Continental model may have been influential but obviously was not followed everywhere. The question of who owned and profited from the brothels affected the laws and their enforcement. The bishop of Winchester was obviously an important figure, not just by virtue of his ecclesiastical position and his substantial temporal landholdings, but also because of his high position in the royal administration. Several bishops of Winchester in the period served as chancellors. They could operate with impunity in their own lands. Other lords could have done the same; but any other lord might have incurred ecclesiastical censure, as the bishops of Winchester did not.

Those places that did have official stews seem to have taken an "if you can't beat 'em, join 'em" attitude toward existing concentrations of brothels: if they were going to be there anyway, they might as well be closely supervised and financially exploited. Other towns may well have wished to do the same but were prevented because the existing brothels were owned by powerful citizens who did not want to give up control of the trade.

Although in most towns the leading citizens and major landlords did not have the same jurisdictional rights as the bishops of Winchester and thus could not make prostitution legal, they could often ignore the law with impunity. William Walworth, Lord Mayor of London, owned a brothel in Southwark that was attacked during the Peasants' Rebellion of 1381.[53] Apparently he was not the only leading London citizen to rent to prostitutes or brothelkeepers, for in 1417 the council decreed that "no Alderman, substantial Commoner, or other person whatsoever, shall receive as a tenant . . . any man or woman who has been indicted or charged as of, or known to be of, evil and vicious life."[54] A landlord charging high rents to a profitable business might be able to do very well out of the trade; there are examples of men who owned strings of brothels all over the London metropolitan area.[55] This perhaps explains why some powerful citizens may not have looked kindly on a municipal takeover of the trade, and would have preferred illegality with ineffective enforcement.[56] But where they did exist, the official brothels were clearly not so wildly successful (either financially or as a form of social engineering) that other towns rushed to imitate them.

The wealthy citizens who owned and profited from illicit brothels did not manage them themselves but either rented them to brothelkeepers or (less typically) hired brothelkeepers to manage them. Both men and women worked as brothelkeepers. In the brothels of Southwark the regulations required that the stewholders be men; their wives could accompany them, but no unmarried woman could keep a stewhouse.[57] Nonetheless, fines assessed on stewholders show repeated violations of this provision. Of twenty-two stewholders presented for various offenses in the Southwark court sessions of 1505–6, nine were women. A list of suspicious persons arrested at the stewhouses in 1519 listed the keeper of each house, and again several were women.[58]

Across England brothelkeeping was an important area for female entrepreneurship. In eight jurisdictions analyzed, the percentage of accusations against women alone (as opposed to men alone and married couples) ranged from 34 to 59.[59] Although it is possible that women appear so prominently in the records because the authorities considered brothelkeeping more typically a female offense and were readier to charge women with it than men, it is more likely that women are in fact underrepresented in the records. Because of the way medieval courts viewed the legal responsibility of women, if a married couple committed an offense, often only the husband was charged. If a married woman committed an offense on her own, her husband still might be the one charged for it, whereas a woman would never be charged with acts carried out by her husband alone. Even if the law considered women more likely to be involved in this particular trade, it still did not accord married women an unusual degree of individual responsibility. Systematic error might be expected to work in the other direction in the case of the ecclesiastical courts, since their accusations of moral offenses were less likely to be directed at those deemed fiscally responsible, and women's moral transgressions may have been presented (especially by their neighbors) more often than men's. Nevertheless, the evidence still points to a high degree of involvement by women. On the one hand, the trade may have been especially open to women because it was not considered respectable; on the other hand, the traditional involvement of women in it may have made it even less respectable.

When women managed brothels, men still owned and profited from them. Male property owners in Great Yarmouth were sometimes fined more than the female brothelkeepers to whom they rented. Perhaps the court accorded them more blame, or perhaps it thought they could better afford to pay, but the fact that the male owners were fined at all indicates that the municipality considered them responsible parties.[60] This pattern of men as owners and women as managers cannot be so clearly documented elsewhere, but it fits with general trends in women's occupations in the Middle Ages. The work women tended to do, such as brewing and spinning, required neither capital investment (beyond equipment most households already had) nor year-round activity. Prostitution was a natural outlet for casual unskilled labor, and brothelkeeping worked the same way when it could be engaged in without capital investment, that is, when a male entrepreneur provided the property. The man could be blamed if he knew of the activity; according to one handbook for confessors, such a man was a brothelkeeper even though he did not operate the house himself.[61]

Ecclesiastical institutions and individuals owned brothels, though the bishop of Winchester's Southwark brothels were the only ones that were legally tolerated. In Winchester itself several ecclesiastics were accused as owners of brothels, perhaps because the town authorities, who would certainly have known about the Southwark brothels and the bishop of Winchester's part in them, were hostile to ecclesiastical landholders generally. It is hard to imagine that the landlords would not have known the nature of the business being operated from their premises, even if they did not actively approve or promote it; priests, monks, and friars were certainly among the clients.[62] In York the vicars choral rented property to prostitutes, although this seems not to have been especially lucrative; individual women rather than brothelkeepers were the tenants, and rents were low, reflecting the poverty of many of the women in the business.[63] Many of the customers of York's prostitutes were vicars choral, and as a collective body they cannot have been unaware of what was going on in their tenements. Several individual clerics also managed brothels in London and Westminster.[64] The absence of moral considerations that militated against renting to prostitutes is perhaps not too surprising to a modern sensibility but worth noting with respect to the Middle Ages.

Whereas some brothelkeepers were professionals, others operated on a more casual basis or kept brothels as a sideline. The Nottingham records reveal a wide range of occupations for men accused of brothelkeeping, including cobbler, baker, barber, tailor, dyer, glover, net maker, and simply "laborer" (the women were more often listed by marital status: widow, housewife, spinster, or "wife of").[65] In Exeter all seventeen women listed as brothelkeepers during the period 1373–93 also had other occupations.[66] Although as individuals the brothelkeepers may have had a legitimate identity in the community, this did not mean that they were among the leading citizens. They may have turned to brothelkeeping when their other business was not going well; brothels were not always permanent institutions. The line between brothels and houses of assignation is not always clear. Making rooms available for couples must have been a fairly easy way of picking up tidy sums of money on the side, although one did face the risk of prosecution in the church courts.[67] In Southwark, where the brothels were more formalized and one might expect brothelkeeping to have been a less casual occupation, there was very high turnover of the management, which would seem to argue against stability. Records of stewholders fined in 1506 show that six of twelve brothels had more than one keeper during the year.[68]

Brothelkeepers did not always remain established in the same house.

Especially if convicted and banished from the city, they might move around while still continuing in their occupation. For example, in 1425 Peter Bednot and his wife, Petronella, were keeping a stew (bathhouse) in London, in Grub Street; they gave sureties that it would be an honest one (although there had previously been a brothel-type stew in Grub Street). Ten years later Peter was fined in East Smithfield for "keeping a common brothel and receiving divers night-walking men," and in 1438 it was charged that Petronella "has a stew within her house . . . and in this house she keeps divers malefactors, both thieves and common whores who turn away no one."[69] We do not know the circumstances under which they left London proper, but we may guess that their stewkeeping prompted their expulsion.

Some brothels were very small indeed. The landlord renting a room to a single prostitute could be considered a small-scale brothelkeeper if he or she were involved in making arrangements with customers. Amy Semmestere of York was charged as "a common bawd to whoever wished to lie together, and especially between Joan Clerk, whom she keeps and kept privately in her room . . . and divers men." Amy failed to clear herself of this charge but managed to do so when she was accused again two years later. Medard Leonard, a York goldsmith, and his wife also were charged with operating a small brothel combined with a house of assignation: "[T]hey keep common bawdry in their house between whoever want to commit adultery or fornication. And also they keep a common whore in their house for the desire of whoever wants to take her." Joan Boys of London was similarly charged with being "a common bawd [who] keeps bawdry between Margaret Davy, whom she keeps in her house as a common whore, and Henry commonly called Little Henry of the Steelyard and his other companions."[70] Priests were involved on this level too. In one instance from the bishop of Lincoln's visitation of Thornton in 1518, a woman was accused of having set up shop as a prostitute in the parish rectory: "Joan Thakham is a common whore, and lives in the rectory, and there keeps a common tavern. And the same Joan is also a common scold. And the rector lives incontinently with her."[71] The phrasing here is different from the more usual case of a priest's housekeeper who also sleeps with him; a "common whore" was more public than that. The accusation clearly implies promiscuity and possibly commerciality. Although resentment of a priest's partner could have led to an unfounded accusation, it is also possible that the priest was profiting from her activity.

Some prostitutes who worked in brothels lived elsewhere. Isabella Betisham was charged as "a whore spending the night at a brothel for three nights." Anne Warren was accused of "keeping whores daily in her house," a charge implying that they did not live there. Another woman was accused of "being in a brothel all Monday night," although she resided elsewhere.[72] It may have been the custom with brothels generally merely to rent prostitutes their working premises, as was the case with the Southwark stews. Even when the prostitutes only lived there and did not work on the premises, their presence in a house was undesirable because they gave the neighborhood a bad name. Those labeled as whores needed to be controlled even during their nonworking hours. Landlords could be fined for renting to prostitutes, as with Robert of Stratford, cordwainer, who "presumed to lodge or maintain whores in his rents,"[73] even if the premises were not being used as a brothel or the landlord had nothing to do with the operation. These fines might be based on ability to pay rather than moral responsibility—the municipality had an interest in prosecuting those with deep pockets—but in this situation placing a share of blame on the landlord may not have been too unreasonable. Landlords probably knew what went on in their tenements and who lived there, and raised their rents accordingly. The fines for harboring or maintaining were possibly also an attempt to turn landlords into guardians of the morals of their tenants, and were thus directed not entirely against commercial prostitution but rather against feminine sexual misconduct generally.

Some brothelkeepers were practicing prostitutes themselves, perhaps only for a few favored clients, and we may infer that more were former prostitutes. Elizabeth Saxby of Ipswich, one charge reads, "uses her body as a whore and keeps her house as a bawd, and Thomas Brey several times knew her carnally in her brothel." Elizabeth Moryng, who took apprentice embroidresses, was convicted of whoredom as well as bawdry.[74] In chapter 4 I will discuss further the varieties of work within the sex trade and the movement of prostitutes into brothelkeeping and procuring.

3

; a Prostitute

Why did women become prostitutes? Was the medieval prostitute a victim of economic circumstances, a pawn of unscrupulous individuals, or an agent making her own choices? What were the societal and individual factors that led her into the trade? The medieval authorities considered prostitutes both subject and object, agent and victim. In general, prostitutes were blamed for their actions, which they were believed to commit out of lust (even if they were financially needy as well); but when a brothelkeeper or procurer was prosecuted, the prostitutes could be treated as innocent pawns. These two views might be called the "happy hooker" model (the prostitute who chooses to be so and who enjoys her work) and the "white slave" model (the prostitute who is exploited and bears no responsibility for her actions).

Medieval prostitutes experienced a reality that lay between these two extremes. To say that prostitution is so degrading that no one who had other options would enter the trade is to impose a modern viewpoint.[1] Most medieval prostitutes did have choices to make, except in cases of force and deception. But to treat them as free agents risks losing sight of the extremely constraining circumstances within which they had to operate and the unpleasant conditions under which they had to work, as well as the gendered system of power relations that made them much more vulnerable than their customers. This was no free market: medieval prostitutes were exploited, whether or not they perceived themselves to be. Most prostitutes, though—the ones whose reasons do not appear in the records—probably entered the trade more or less voluntarily. They were coerced by economic necessity and lack of alternatives (owing to both individual situations and general economic and demographic conditions) but not by direct threats.

Demographic Patterns and Economic Opportunities

Prostitution was a choice women made under severe constraints. Those constraints were created in part by the structure of the economy, which excluded women from many occupations, but also by the demographic situation and opportunities for marriage. Whereas for men prostitution sometimes substituted for marriage as a sexual outlet, for women it substituted for marriage as a means of financial support. It was difficult for a woman to support herself outside the conjugal unit, since marriage was the norm in the medieval society and economy. (This is not to say that the overwhelming majority of women and men were married at any given time; but marriage was still a basic expectation, particularly for women.) A woman's marital status determined her role in life. For those who did not marry— whether by choice or by circumstance—options might be limited even under favorable economic conditions.

The at times extraordinarily high numbers of women accused of whoredom are difficult to attribute to the state of the economy at any particular moment. For example, forty women were accused in Exeter in 1324, over 1 percent of the total population.[2] This figure is not typical: numbers of accused prostitutes in London ecclesiastical court records average just over fifty per annum in the late fifteenth century, probably between 0.1 and 0.2 percent of the population of the diocese.[3] Furthermore, although we can derive numbers of accused prostitutes at different times, changes in the numbers of accusations in various sources may be largely due to changes in the nature of the sources or in the enforcement of the laws.[4] The surviving York church court act books leave off approximately when the London ones begin; the Exeter court rolls dwindle in size and number just when one would expect numbers of prostitutes to rise because of demographic change. Thus, it is difficult to compare figures across different cities or across time.

In spite of the difficulty of addressing fluctuations in numbers of prostitutes, however, it is possible to discuss prostitution in the context of economic and demographic patterns during the period from about 1350 to about 1550. The marriage market and the labor market presented women with a range of options, and changes in those options may have led them to prostitution. Scholars such as Richard M. Smith, P. J. P. Goldberg, and L. R. Poos have applied a great deal of ingenuity to the problem of finding sources of demographic data for the late Middle Ages. Their conclusions have all tended to indicate that there was no sharp break in demographic patterns between the Middle Ages and the early modern period—about which we know much more because of the establishment of parish record keeping in the 1530s.[5] In particular, the northwestern European marriage pattern seems to have held in the fourteenth and fifteenth centuries as it did later.

This European marriage pattern includes a relatively late age at first marriage (early to mid-twenties) and a relatively large fraction of people who never marry at all (although marriage may still remain the social norm). It contrasts with the pattern thought typical of peasant society, in which marriage occurs early, as well as with the pattern found in medieval Italy, in which marriage is early for women but late for men.[6] There is general agreement that the European pattern characterized early modern England, and the evidence seems to support it for late medieval England as well.[7] The most detailed work on the relation between women's work and demographic patterns has been done for York and the North. Women found greater opportunities in the labor force after the Black Death than they had had before, owing to the labor shortage, and therefore were less dependent on marriage for their support. It was common for women to spend years in domestic service before marrying.[8] They could afford to be more selective in marrying, and the evidence Goldberg presents for York suggests that they married by personal choice.

In a society in which women married late and a period of domestic service constituted a normal stage in a woman's life cycle, for some prostitution may have been largely a passing phase in the cycle as well.[9] The experience of other societies suggests that women may have practiced prostitution as a contribution to their family's economy rather than in response to their own shortage of marital prospects.[10] But even if some women became prostitutes at the instigation of family members, in late medieval English towns many women and men were relatively independent from their families once they entered the work force. They may have sent some money home, but their decisions seem to have been individual ones rather than part of a family strategy.[11]

Demographic historians generally consider the pattern of late marriage which prevailed in England a sign that various opportunities were available for women. Richard Smith, for example, argues that, unlike in Florence, where the women who ended up in the labor market were those who were unable to marry, in England women entered the labor market by choice. In hard times more women married early because they were unable to find work. When employment opportunities were favorable, many women chose not to marry.[12] This does not mean that women abandoned the prospect of marriage for lucrative employment; they merely postponed marriage and became more selective in their choice of a husband.

Even if the marriage pattern prevalent in late medieval England indicates that there were more opportunities for women there than in other parts of Europe, and fewer pressures on them to find a husband, we should still keep in mind that a period of relatively greater opportunities in the labor market does not necessarily imply that all women found good jobs and that all could marry when they chose to do so. A woman who rejected a prospective marriage in the hopes of employment that did not materialize may well have found herself limited in her choices, and so prostitution may have become an alternative. Those women who never married may not all have preferred independence over marriage; rather, by postponing marriage, some may have found that they had missed out on it completely. The openings in the labor market for women with no capital and no skills were not sufficient to offer all such women a range of appealing possibilities.

Although the work opportunities available to women in England after the Black Death may have been good compared to those in other times and other places in medieval Europe, we should not exaggerate the case. The late medieval "golden age" of women's work is a myth. Women could enter most guilds only as widows of members or as second-class members. Most of the occupations in which women could participate independently (as opposed to family enterprises, in which their contribution was always significant) brought them low pay and low status. Women worked as domestic servants, hucksters (retail traders in food and other small items in the streets rather than in shops), or brewsters (on a small scale). In the textile trades there were a few possibilities for training in a skilled occupation.[13] Opportunities did vary over time, depending on the supply of male labor; when available, men were preferred in the more lucrative and skilled trades. There are many examples of women who did engage in skilled crafts, but most of these were wives or widows of craftsmen.[14] To say this does not denigrate the importance of these women and their work in the economy; women's contribution to the household-based workshop was no less significant because it was made in cooperation with men. This option, however, would have been much less available to unmarried women, unless they remained in their father's household and contributed to his production.

By the second half of the fifteenth century, opportunities for women began to contract; this emerges most clearly from Goldberg's work on York but seems to be supported elsewhere. Women's labor was no longer in such demand, whether because of economic recession or population growth.[15] Women found themselves excluded from many of the crafts and more lucrative occupations and even from domestic service. They became more dependent on marriage for their support, and as the age of marriage dropped, the birthrate rose and the supply of labor increased. Just as the expansion of opportunities for women after the Black Death had occurred all over England, so did their subsequent exclusion from occupations, though perhaps somewhat later in London than in the North. In London after 1480, guilds and livery companies started to exclude from their crafts single women and married women trading as *femmes soles*.[16]

As an example of the limited opportunities for single women in the economy, let us consider brewing. Brewing was a good trade for women in the fourteenth and fifteenth centuries—not as good as some of the trades open mainly to men, but profitable compared to other options open to women. Within the brewing trade, however, it was mainly married women who were able to become professionals, brewing continually and regularly for the market. Single women lacked the social, economic, and domestic resources to do so, and brewed on a much more casual basis. After 1350 the trade began to be more professionalized, and more closed to single women. Thus, even in this traditionally feminine occupation, the chances for a single women to make a good living were slim. The situation was perhaps even worse in crafts not traditionally associated with women.[17]

The availability of economic opportunities for women was not the only factor in late marriage, and the decision may not have been entirely the woman's to make. The period of opportunity in the labor market was fairly transitory, whereas the pattern of women marrying late or not at all, despite some fluctuation, continued throughout the late Middle Ages and into the early modern period.[18] Marriage in one's mid-twenties appears to have become the cultural norm. It is possible that men were not willing to marry women who had not yet saved up some money with which to start a household. No matter what the economic conditions or work opportunities for women, if there is a surplus of marriageable women over marriageable men (as there seems to have been in the towns), many women will not be able to find husbands.

Not every woman who was unable to marry became a prostitute. Brewing, spinning, and other casual occupations could provide sources of income for single women, if not lucrative ones. But "singlewoman" did become a euphemism for prostitute by the early sixteenth century, in connection with the Southwark stews in particular, even if it did not denote this in every instance. For example, one woman presented as a "common woman of her body" was "Katherine Glover otherwise called Singlewoman." Jacob Barber is accused of committing adultery "with a certain singlewoman at the sign of the Rose at the Stews side," one of the Southwark brothels. Alice Clerk and Katherine Marsh were dunked in the Thames (the standard early sixteenth-century punishment for "common harlots") for being "singlewomen," and John Stow's Tudor chronicle of London refers to the prostitutes of the Stews as "single women" and describes the "single womans churchyard" where they were buried. A sixteenth-century ordinance about prostitutes was recorded in the Repertory Book of the London Court of Aldermen with the marginal notation "Singlewomen."[19] That the term could be used to denote a prostitute indicates, first, that marriage was the norm (even though a sizeable group of people remained outside it); second, that prostitutes were expected to be unmarried, an assumption that was not always true but was probably a fair assessment of the general pattern; third, that it was far from unusual for unmarried women to turn to prostitution on occasion; and fourth, that men were made uncomfortable by the existence of unmarried women and saw a need to stigmatize them.

One might wonder, if some or many women became prostitutes because they could not find husbands, where these prostitutes got their customers. If there was a surplus of women, couldn't any man who wanted to marry do so and consequently not need to visit prostitutes (to the extent that the trade existed to fill the need for a sexual outlet)? Just because women were available for marriage, however, did not mean that any man could marry: he also needed a means of supporting a wife and family. Men who worked as servants in others' households or businesses and lived with their employers would not be in a position to marry until they could set up their own households. In any case, the existence of a large number of prostitutes does not necessarily mean that there was enough demand to support them all; this was one reason why prostitutes made such an exiguous living.

In addition to the economic and demographic patterns that drove women into prostitution in the late Middle Ages, cultural factors were at work as well (these will be discussed at length in chapters 5 and 6). The interplay between demographic and attitudinal forces emerges forcefully in later developments. Marriage patterns do not appear to have changed much over the course of the sixteenth century, but the population grew a great deal.[20] This may have had some effect on women's work opportunities, thus forcing more women into prostitution. The sixteenth century, however, also saw a backlash against prostitution as moral standards changed. A higher value was put on marriage and fidelity for men, and this tended to make the official repression of prostitution (along with the repression of gaming, drinking, the failure to attend church, and so on) harsher.[21] This proved to be the case across Europe, and has been attributed to Protestantism's valorization of the family. But since the repression of brothels in the mid-sixteenth century also happened in countries that remained Catholic, any religious interpretation must focus on the moral reform connected with Catholic as well as Protestant reform. But the general change in the mood of Europe toward a morally repressive outlook is not a full explanation either, for it begs the question why; it is here that demographic change may have played a role. Perhaps as population rose, and with it unemployment and the fear of disorder, which became an increasing problem during the sixteenth century, the elites felt sufficiently threatened to suppress prostitution, at least at the level that catered to the lower classes.[22]

Moral fervor for the eradication of prostitution was not as vehement in the fourteenth and fifteenth centuries. The church's teaching against prostitution (which I discuss in chapter 6) was directed at individual prostitutes and customers rather than at the authorities who tolerated prostitution. Nevertheless, as we have seen, those who regulated the trade were very concerned with maintaining social order. The existence of a relatively large number of single women in a society in which marriage was the norm was a threat to that order; and the lack of suitable alternatives for these women contributed to the magnitude of the threat, since prostitution was one of the more prominent possibilities.

Origins and Occupations

Women impelled to prostitution by their unfavorable economic circumstances did not necessarily move full-time into the trade or become what we, or they, would consider professionals. Prostitution was one of many occupations in which a woman could participate on a casual or occasional basis. Work opportunities for single women, while not exactly "golden," may still have been better in England than elsewhere. Goldberg has suggested that prostitution was more casual and less institutionalized in England than in other European countries because in southern Europe there operated a more powerful sexual double standard and a higher premium on female honor, so prostitutes were seen as necessary but were more strictly segregated from the rest of society.[23] Yet we have seen that some English towns did have official brothels, and the European towns with institutionalized brothels had more casual, clandestine prostitution as well. To the extent that prostitution in England was a more informal occupation, it may have been so in part because more opportunities in the labor market meant that women who did practice prostitution did not rely on it exclusively.

Many women turned temporarily to prostitution when they were not earning enough at their primary occupation, often in the highly cyclical textile trades.[24] The evidence for their primary occupation is derived from surnames like Kempster or Sempster (comber or seamstress), which were not family names at this time but rather by-names given to individuals. Spinsters—that is, women who span—came to be associated with theft as well as prostitution, a possible indication of their precarious economic status.[25] Indeed, the term "spinster" occasionally denoted "prostitute," as in the 1543 ordinance from a Southwark Leet Court that "no spinster inhabiting the stews come within the liberty aforesaid, except to the market."[26] Whether this usage reflects an association of prostitutes primarily with women who span or with unmarried women (the term "spinster" had this latter meaning in law by the seventeenth century), it is clear that all three meanings were connected. Women who performed this low-status, low-paying work were likely to be unmarried (though there were exceptions), and both unmarried women and poor women were likely to be suspected of engaging in sexual irregularity for money.

Another occupation that was especially closely connected with prostitution was that of laundress or washerwoman. Whether or not laundresses in fact engaged disproportionately in prostitution, they certainly had an unsavory reputation. London citizens who gave sureties that they would keep an "honest stew" or bathhouse, as opposed to one that amounted to a brothel, had to promise that they would "not permit any laundress or any other but good and honest men" to enter, implying that such women could be expected to frequent men's bathhouses. Courtesy books warned against the dangers to a noble house's honor of having too many women servants in the household, especially laundresses. Regulations from the brothels of Southwark limited the number of laundresses a stewholder could employ. An early sixteenth-century poem on the "Ship of Fools" theme has a boatman address a female passenger: "Thou shalt be my lavender [laundress] / To wash and keep clean all my gear, / Our two beds together shall be set / Without any let." The chronicler Walter of Hemingburgh recounts an apocryphal story of King John's desire for a particular woman. Her husband instructed her to send instead "a whore or laundress, dressed in your clothes," and was later able to tell the gloating king, "You did not have my wife; but in her place a horrid whore and laundress."[27] The equation of laundress and whore was clearly made. Both the prostitute and the laundress had some connection with filth, but laundresses most likely acquired a reputation for prostitution because they were among the few women who frequently came and went from all-male households. Medieval preachers told the tale of the woman who pushed her daughter into a life of sin by sending her, seductively dressed, to the dwelling of a university rector to deliver his laundry.[28] This may have been a common pretext for celibate men to bring women onto the premises. There is evidence of accused whores and laundresses lodging together, an indication that they came from the same social milieu.[29] It is quite likely that women in this trade engaged not infrequently in casual prostitution.

Domestic service could also lead to prostitution. Such employment relieved the immediate economic pressure that drove some women into prostitution but did not protect them against being coerced into the sex trade, for example, when an employer forced his servant to work as a prostitute or to have sex with him. When an employer was accused of acting as a bawd for his or her servant, it is likely that coercion—physical, psychological, or economic—was involved, although it is possible that some cases involved an employer's condoning or facilitating a servant's personal and voluntary relations. When a servant was labeled a "common whore," this often meant that the employer was involved in finding her customers, as with a servant named Alice, whose mistress, Marion Ingleby, acted as bawd, or Nicholas de Presse, cordwainer of Southampton, and his wife, who acted as bawds between their maid and the captain of a Venetian galley.[30] Employers may also have pressured a servant into sexual relations with their friends or relatives on a noncommercial basis. Since children could become apprentices or domestic servants at twelve or younger, they would have been in a very vulnerable position with regard to an unscrupulous employer, as in the 1537 case of an apprentice silkwoman, age eleven, seduced by her employer's brother.[31] This sort of pressure may eventually have led these women into prostitution, as pregnancy or childbearing would have resulted in the loss of employment and a lack of alternatives.

Some prostitutes were in the trade on a long-term basis and could be considered professionals. These are the ones about whom we know the most, and in chapter 4 I tell some of their stories. Prostitutes who worked in stable situations such as institutionalized brothels fall into this group. We might surmise that for women who made a career out of it, prostitution was a more attractive occupation than the others open to them, and they chose accordingly. Yet these women did not necessarily lead easier lives than casual prostitutes, nor was their initial entry into the trade necessarily voluntary, as we shall see. But for some women who catered to wealthy customers under reasonably attractive working conditions, prostitution could be seen as a choice that allowed them to retain their independence. For others, the fact that they were professionals in the sex trade did not give them either status or personal autonomy.

As I have noted, most prostitutes were probably single. (It is not always possible to determine marital status from accusations of whoredom; some women are listed as married, but we cannot assume that those for whom no husband is listed were single. Some may have been widows, though this is difficult to determine since records indicate marital status only for married women.) The use of the term "singlewoman" certainly implies that prostitutes were assumed to be unmarried, and the general suspicion of unmarried women's sexuality encouraged that expectation.

There were, of course, exceptions. Of fifty-five Exeter prostitutes from

1373 to 1393, 15 percent were married.[32] The Southwark stew regulations (B4)[33] had forbidden married women to work as prostitutes in the stews, but this did not affect those prostitutes outside the stews, who were illicit anyway. When married women were prostitutes, their husbands sometimes procured or pimped for them. Husbands who were charged as bawds for their wives may have been encouraging or permitting them to have sex with other men, not necessarily for pay. Some husbands may have pressured their wives into prostitution; other couples may have had a voluntary working partnership.[34] In still other instances the husband had nothing to do with his wife's engaging in commercial sex, as when Margery Smith, charged as a whore, left her husband, "taking with her all his goods."[35] Not all these married women necessarily lived with or under the control of their husbands; in an age without legal divorce, a couple would still be considered married even if they had lived apart for years.

Many prostitutes in English towns were foreigners, not necessarily from overseas (those were called "strangers") but simply outsiders to the towns they lived in. Already marginal because of the absence of kin, they may have felt the force of economic circumstances more harshly than citizens, and for such women domestic service or prostitution was likely to be the only choice open to them. A few may have adopted foreign by-names for the sake of exoticism: "Spanish Nell" may have come from Spain, but more likely she was a native Londoner who wanted to set herself apart from the crowd. Certainly there were prostitutes who had taken for themselves or had given to them erotically suggestive names, such as "Clarice Clatterballock,"[36] and labeling oneself Spanish or French may have had the same effect. But Scotswomen charged in York and the Cornishwomen in Exeter brought with them no exotic eroticism; they had simply migrated to the towns and had difficulty establishing themselves in licit occupations. Not all newcomers, of course, became prostitutes. London's population at all levels, from aldermanic families on down, turned over very rapidly, as did that of other towns, and it is not surprising that prostitutes exhibited this pattern as well. Some migrants arrived with their relatives, and of course not all prostitutes were migrants; in Exeter only 20 percent of prostitutes had no family in that town.[37] Still, kinless and friendless young women were a population ripe for recruitment.

Flemish, Dutch, and Low German women are particularly prominent in the records as prostitutes and bawds. Some did well as brothelkeepers, who were likely to make much more profit than the prostitutes themselves. In these cases the sex trade may not always have been a last resort for lack of other opportunities. "Dutch" brothelkeepers appear to have been particularly common, for example, in Great Yarmouth, where a sizable Dutch community was settled. (The word "Dutch" could also include Germans or Flemings, although in London at least most of them seem actually to have come from Holland or Brabant.)[38] Court rolls from the London suburbs of Southwark (outside the Winchester liberty), Lambeth, and East Smithfield name several Dutch women as brothelkeepers.[39] A Southwark stewhouse attacked by rebellious peasants and Londoners in 1381 was managed by Flemish women. An editor's marginal heading in John Stow's account of this event reads, "English people disdained to be bawds. Froes [women] of Flanders were women for that purpose,"[40] indicating a certain satisfaction in thinking of immoral women as being mainly foreigners. Perhaps not coincidentally, Flemish women were prominent as prostitutes in Florence as well.[41] Crises in the cloth industry in Flanders occasionally did send Flemings, both male and female, elsewhere in search of work, but it could also be that in the late Middle Ages Flemish women were in particular demand as prostitutes, as are members of other ethnic groups today.

The sources mention the age and place of origin of prostitutes only in special cases. Although the majority of prostitutes were not foreigners, foreigners may have been disproportionately represented. Nor were the majority young girls corrupted by wicked procurers, although that problem was real enough, as I will show later on. The sorts of factors that drove women into prostitution—unemployment or underemployment, lack of family support, unwed motherhood—affected women of all ages and origins, if some more than others, and must account for most of the prostitutes whose background the records do not reveal.

Recruitment

Court cases often accused bawds of fraud and force in recruiting women into prostitution. Except in cases of procuring, however, they do not tell us how prostitutes came to enter the trade, so we do not know whether most prostitutes would have cited coercion. Nonetheless, to acknowledge that the sources are systematically biased toward forced recruitment is not to deny that such coercive tactics victimized young, vulnerable women, particularly domestic servants with no families of their own in the towns where they worked. In some cases we must follow the medieval courts in seeing the prostitute as victim. Seduction and abandonment or pressure from an employer were among the most common reasons for initial entry into prostitution, at least for those who entered the trade full-time.

Where prostitution was illegal, clandestine, and relatively informally organized, women entered and left the trade casually, repeatedly, and voluntarily. The more organized the brothel, however, the greater the need for regular means of recruiting and retaining workers. The stews of Southwark faced a demand for prostitutes that outran the supply, and the stewkeepers were willing to go to considerable lengths to procure women. Ellen Butler (see p. 38) had been looking for a position as a servant in London when she met a man named Thomas Bowde, who asked if she wanted a good job. He took her to his house on the Stews side of the river and "would have compelled her to do such service as his other servants do there." When she refused, he brought an action against her in the court of the bishop of Winchester in Southwark for a sum she would never be able to pay, so that she would have to remain in prison unless she agreed to work for him as a prostitute.[42] Henry Whitehere took "a certain Margaret to the Stews side brothel and there sold her to a certain bawd." Anna Chester allegedly sold her maidservant to a man who took her to the stews. The stewmonger Nicholas Crook was accused of "deceiving many virgins and servants of divers upright men within the city, enticing them by allurements to wicked intercourse," and of taking Christina Swynowe "to Southwark to a certain stew and by force and money compelling and enticing her to fornication and cohabitation."[43] Elizabeth Troubled (alias Vaughan) "procured a young maiden to go to the Stews and thereupon conveyed her thither." In 1495 Thomas Togood, a "bawd of the Stews," was put on the pillory in London for having enticed two women "to become his servants and to have been common within his house at the Stews."[44] One distressing story was told to the Court of Aldermen in London in 1517:

> John Barton, tailor, confessed that on Thursday last, in the highway coming from Our Lady of Willesden, he faithfully promised to one Joan Rawlyns, a young woman born at Aldenham in Hertfordshire, to bring her to a good and honest service in this city. Whereupon she, putting her trust and confidence in him, went with him throughout all the city until he, unknown to her, had brought her to the Stews side and there left her in a waterman's house, and then went immediately to a bawd there and made covenant with her to set the said maiden with the said bawd. In the meantime, the said maiden perceiving by the said waterman's wife that she was in such an evil-named place, knelt down on her knees and besought her for Our Lady's sake to help convey her to this city; which accordingly she did honestly in this city, where she now remains in honest service.[45]

Barton was convicted, imprisoned, and punished with a procession through town, the pillory, and banishment.

These stories all entail the kidnapping and what modern society would consider the rape of unsuspecting young women. Those whose voices emerge from the records—Ellen Butler and Joan Rawlyns—claimed coercion; in other cases we do not know how the woman felt. But the fact that the bawd was the subject of the prosecution implies that the prostitute was considered a victim. Notwithstanding the humanitarianism of the anonymous waterman's wife who saved Joan Rawlyns, many other young women who were looking for work in a city where they knew no one must have been forced or tricked by procurers as well as by circumstance into prostitution. Once they realized what had happened, violence forced them to remain.

Violence was part of the routine of brothelkeeping, even when discouraged, and it helped coerce women into remaining under the control of the keepers. The brothelkeepers of Sandwich and Southwark had to be prohibited from beating their prostitutes, and those in Southampton were fined for doing so.[46] It was not only prostitutes who were subject to physical abuse by their employers; male as well as female apprentices and servants in medieval London were often powerless.[47] Thomas Bunny, an apprentice sheather whose contract was sold to Joan Hunt, a stewkeeper in Southwark (but apparently not in the Winchester liberty), won a case against her for not teaching him a trade; part of his testimony was that Hunt had had her lover beat Bunny, and when he fell ill as a result, she turned him out of the house.[48] This endemic violence, though not unique to brothelkeepers, could keep prostitutes from leaving the trade—or a particular brothel—when they chose.

Joan Rawlyns managed to escape through her appeal to feminine solidarity: it was not the waterman but his wife who responded to Joan's entreaties. Joan's invocation of the Virgin Mary may also have been an appeal to feminine sympathy, although devotion to the Virgin was by no means restricted to women; indeed, Barton himself had been coming from his devotions to the Virgin when he first met Rawlyns. But the sympathy of one individual woman for another does not mean that women were opposed to prostitution in general. Women were apparently involved in the recruitment of girls into prostitution as much as men were (although often as men's agents). Indeed, Ellen Butler was persuaded to go with the stewholder by the woman in whose house she was staying.

Sisterhood was also conspicuously absent in cases such as that of Elizabeth Moryng in 1385. Moryng took in a young woman named Joan as an apprentice embroidress (or so Joan thought) "and retained the said Joan and divers other women . . . and bound them to serve her in that art, whereas in truth she did not practice that art, but after she retained them she exhorted the said Joan and all the other women living with her and serving her to live in lechery and go with friars, chaplains, and all others wishing to have them." Joan does not seem to have understood what was expected of her:

> [Moryng] ordered the said Joan at night that she would go with the said chaplain to his chamber to carry a lantern for him . . . with the intention that the said Joan would spend the night there with the said chaplain, the said Joan knowing nothing of their agreement, as she says. But she remained there with the said chaplain the whole night and the next day came back to her mistress's home. . . . Elizabeth asked her if she brought something with her for her work that night, to which she answered "no." For this the said Elizabeth reproached her and ordered her to go back to the said chaplain the following night and take whatever she could get for her work.

Joan went back and spent another night with the man, and stole a breviary which Moryng subsequently sold for eightpence. Moryng was convicted of bawdry on Joan's testimony and eventually was banished from London.[49] Evidently her business, run under the cover of an embroidery workshop, operated fairly informally: Moryng and the chaplain did not set a fixed price, nor did Joan even seem to understand the essentials of the trade.

Elizabeth Morying represents a different segment of the sex trade from that of the bawds who kidnapped or deceived women into working at the stews. She was running a prostitution business on the side, not a permanent full-time brothel. But an apprentice, once initiated into prostitution by her employer in this way, might well remain in it; it might be more lucrative than embroidery, especially if she was not in fact being trained in embroidery skills as she had expected. With other employers, too, the sexual use of servants or apprentices may have been occasional, but it did represent an initiation into the sex trade, if only on an informal basis.

Moryng was not the only woman accused of forcibly prostituting her apprentices or servants. Alison Boston was sentenced to the thew (a pillory for women) in 1424 because of the thirteen-year-old Joan Hammond, "a young damsel innocent of sin, that was put to her by way of apprentice here to learn her craft, [whom] she let to hire to divers persons for divers sums of money to execute and exercise with them the horrible vice of lechery," in particular a barber living at Charing Cross, from whom she received eight shillings fourpence. The council did not mince words about Boston, "a woman not dreading God nor ashamed before the world, but continually using the abominable custom, maintenance, and counseling of sin, lechery, and bawdry." Robert Cliff and his wife were charged as common bawds, "especially between Elizabeth Mountain their maid and divers merchants; and four or five years ago they sold a certain Agnes Smith, a young girl and that time servant to the said Robert, to Lombards for forty pounds."[50]

People exploited not only their own servants but other people's as well. Any young woman in a domestic job who found the work arduous or tedious was ripe for temptation or deception by someone offering a new position. In Great Yarmouth John Saddler was fined forty pence for receiving "his neighbors' women servants in his house, and men to have intercourse with them; and he is a common lodger of whores." Richard Peryn of London and his wife, Margaret, were imprisoned not only for receiving whores and for condoning immorality in their house but also because of their behavior toward "a certain Isabella Putnam, a pure virgin, servant of Thomas Harlow and living in his service." The charge continues: "[S]hrewdly, with enticing words, they removed and took her from his service and led her to their house . . . and there shut and sealed her, against her will and crying out, in a room, and conveyed and sold her to a certain George Galliman [presumably Galleyman or Italian merchant] and others to deflower and to use shamefully."[51] Two features of this account typify the way the legal system depicted women's entry into prostitution. First, the woman was young, completely innocent, and enticed; second, the customer was often a foreign merchant. Although the courts generally blamed the bawd and not the customer, the customers were still part of the story, and foreigners made the best villains. The charge against Hendrik van Hove, doubly suspect as a foreigner and a bawd, was that he "persuades young girls and virgins to whore and especially he keeps a certain young girl of twelve or thereabouts in his room; she was sold to him by a bawd at the sign of the Bull in Thames street."[52]

Several of the cases just cited indicate that the traffic in women in fifteenth-century London included the outright sale of young women for sexual services. Many women charged as bawds were accused of procuring girls for what we would call rape rather than prostitution, although a life of prostitution may well have followed. Agnes Turner, nine-year-old daughter of the lace weaver Margaret Turner (probably a widow), brought a case against Agnes Smith, who

> with enticing words fraudulently drew her into her house . . . secretly concealing a certain young man named Robert, a clerk of the royal chapel of St. Stephen of Westminster, the said Agnes Turner knowing nothing about it, and then, the door of the said house being falsely and damnably closed, the said Agnes Turner would have been damnably deflowered by the said youth except for the people who came running at the cries of the said Agnes Turner, and she was easily rescued.

Agnes Smith was sentenced to the thew for three market days. Margaret Hathewyk and Margery Bradley in 1439 took Isabella Lane and another girl "to the houses of divers Lombards," who paid "certain sums of money received by the said Margaret from them for her own use" and "deflowered [Isabella] against her will." Hathewyk then arranged with "a certain gentleman" to have Isabella Lane kept in the Southwark stews for three days "to be used in lustful acts." In 1440 a "young girl" named Margaret testified that "she went to a gentleman of my lord of Gloucester called Caxton to bring a bag there, and the said Caxton kissed her and lay on top of her on the bed and repeatedly violated her . . . and this was done with the procuring of Christina Moorpath." Moorpath was convicted, while Caxton was not prosecuted. Elizabeth Knight was convicted of being "a bawd to a certain person who committed the foul and detestable sin of lechery in her house with a young girl of the age of thirteen years." The girl testified that

> the wife of one Everard Carpenter . . . came to her five times at the time of St. Bartholemew's Fair and provoked her to go to Elizabeth Knight . . . saying to her that she should have a good service and a good wage of the said Elizabeth, and thereupon she went with a man to the said Knight's house, and when she was come there she was sent up to the chamber and the said Elizabeth Knight shut fast the lower door and there she found the said man ready, who took her in his arms, and she cried, and he stopped her mouth and against her will he had to do with her.

Although most of these young women sold for rape were servants enticed or deceived with promises of employment, some were actually kidnapped. Peter Manyfeld, according to the accusation, "violently and secretly ravished a certain Alice Burley against her will from the home of her father and mother, and kept her in his chamber for a long time, committing the crime of fornication with her, and, after he was satiated with her, sold her to a certain Easterling [German merchant] at the Steelyard."[53]

The fact that these cases found their way into court indicates the concern of both ecclesiastical and secular authorities to prevent this sort of abuse of young girls. Nine-year-olds did not bring cases and successfully prosecute their kidnappers without help, nor most likely did their widowed mothers. It must have been very difficult for a young woman who had been through this experience to testify publicly about it. The scanty records of the courts do not reveal who initiated the prosecutions of these procurers. Friends or family may have helped the victims bring their complaints before the appropriate body, but more likely neighbors reported the cases. One does not need to have a naively trusting view of the medieval legal system to surmise that the authorities simply found the sexual abuse of children to be wrong. But the circumstances under which the records depict its having happened are revealing of medieval assumptions about sexual transgressions.

Even where there were no claims of force, coercion, or deception, the bawd is the villain of the piece. Those accused of procuring young women in this manner are disproportionately female. Although Richard Wunderli argues that "from surviving information about the few who were convicted, we cannot make a composite picture of a typical pimp,"[54] it may be more relevant to the way medieval English culture understood bawdry to consider those who were accused. Of accusations against procurers (pronubae) in London church courts, 324 were against men, 1,593 were against women, and 810 were against couples.[55] Of those accused of corrupting young girls (iuvenculae or puellae), 14 were women, 11 were couples, and none were men alone. Persuading women into sin seems to have been blamed particularly on women, especially when the victim was young, a servant, or in some other way dependent.

Accusations against female procurers confirm the powerful literary motif of the old woman who corrupts young girls, found in tales such as that of the weeping bitch.[56] This story appears in England in a number of exemplum collections and as "Dame Sirith," a freestanding fabliau. A young man (sometimes a cleric) asks an old woman to persuade a young married woman to have sex with him; the old woman feeds her puppy mustard to make it cry and then tells the young woman that this was her daughter, transformed into a dog because she would not yield to a lover's advances. The blame for corrupting the young woman is placed squarely on the bawd, not on the man involved.[57] The elderly bawd who corrupts a young woman is a topos found in all types of literature; it reflects the same unease about old women living alone as did later witchcraft accusations.[58] Although the image may have roots in an older literary tradition rather than in contemporary reality, it corresponds with the stereotype found in the court records of the old woman who corrupts the young. Even when the responsibility is taken off the prostitute or the woman who engages in illicit sex and she is presented as a passive victim, some other woman is made to bear the blame. Literary representations and court prosecutions worked together to construct an image of the bawd that reflected a deep distrust of the sexual nature of older women.

The strategy of placing the blame on female bawds rather than on the young women themselves was not based on an understanding of adolescence as a period of immaturity, a part of childhood.[59] Although the law in many jurisdictions today does not consider a girl under sixteen capable of giving consent and terms any sexual intercourse with her rape, in medieval England the age of consent for marriage and vows was set at twelve for girls, and society deemed them capable of making their own decisions. So the girls in these cases do not appear passive because of a notion of childish innocence and purity. Rather, the legal discourse underscored the sin of the corrupter, localizing blame on the female go-between rather than the prostitute or her male customer. Even though it was the man who provided the money and committed the sex act, it was not he but the woman who had facilitated it who was held responsible for deflowering the girl. In the church courts both parties to the sex act as well as the procurer might be accused, but in the secular courts it was usually only the procurer. The debauching of the chaste was a heinous crime, and one that the courts usually pinned on women, including mothers and those in the position of mothers.

Some families in fact forced or at least pressured their daughters into prostitution. The widow Juliana Colson was accused of being a bawd for her daughter, "and she permits her to go at night to the Stews side and return the next day"; Katherine the Dutchwoman was "especially a bawd to her daughter and beat her because she did not want to go to the home of a certain Lombard, by whom she afterwards had a child." Elizabeth Brouderer (possibly the same woman as Elizabeth Moryng) allegedly took her daughter Alice to spend the night with various men. In 1523 Agnes Catstrey was charged "because it is supposed she hath sold her daughter divers times and hath taken money for the same."[60] In Lichfield Joan Cooke acted as a bawd for her daughters. Another Joan, widow of John Chapman of Sandown in Kent, was charged with whoredom and also with being "a bawd between a certain Alice, her daughter aged fifteen years, and the Easterlings and Flemings in the Downs." She was banished from Sandwich for thirteen years after being paraded through town and placed on the cucking stool.[61] Far more rarely were fathers blamed. The mother who corrupted her daughter was the extreme case of the mistress who corrupted her servant or apprentice.

The legal system ignored any evidence of free will or cooperation between mother and daughter. In cases such as that of Katherine the Dutchwoman, the allegations of beating make it clear that the daughter's eventual cooperation was not voluntary, but in other instances we might interpret the parents' promoting the daughters' prostitution as part of a family economic strategy. In some societies the prostitution of one or more daughters for the benefit of the family is a common pattern. Viewing prostitution this way, however, obscures the question of who in the family makes the decision, and whether the prostitute herself has a choice.[62]

Not all of those recruited into prostitution were necessarily as vulnerable or as passive as the court records would indicate. The courts, in repeatedly referring to "young girls" without specifying ages, may simply have been infantilizing the prostitutes. The way the legal system prosecuted bawds may have shielded an element of volition on the part of some of these young women. Rightly or not, a young girl might believe that being a prostitute was more glamorous or profitable than being an embroidress.

The case of Katherine Flood, "an honest damsel being in service with an honest citizen of this town," illustrates the limited extent to which women who were "sold" may actually have cooperated. Joan Moody, the record alleges, persuaded her "to depart and go out of her said master's service and to commit the filthy and detestable crime and sin of lechery" (this strong language is typical of the rhetoric used in the presentation of a case). Moody "did afterward sell and deliver the same Katherine unto a Lombard of this city who kept and used her a long season as his concubine and harlot."[63] That Flood entered into a long-term relationship with the Lombard suggests that she went along with the scheme, but Moody is still portrayed as a debaucher. Flood's behavior can be considered voluntary, within the constraints imposed by her society. She made a choice, whether for economic reasons (better food and clothing, easier work) or for affective ones, so we need not regard her as merely a victim. Still, we must always remember that for poor women the choice was between greater and lesser evils, and the fear of violence, although not cited in this particular case, may have influenced the decisions they made.

The bawds were accused of obtaining young girls for what might be considered the high end of the sex trade: for the institutionalized brothels and for particular customers who were in a position to place an order. Prostitutes who entered the trade on a more occasional or casual basis probably did so more of their own volition. Although a bawd might make a connection for such a woman or point out to her the advantages to be gained from prostitution, most women could probably figure it out for themselves, and would have known which streets or taverns were good places for picking up customers. Middlemen or -women were more likely to be found in that segment of the trade in which there were high profits to be made, which was not the case with most prostitutes.

Blaming the go-between, bawd, or procurer took some of the onus off the prostitute herself, but at the cost of denying her capacity for independent action. The courts did attempt to protect women from abuses such as deceptive employment and physical force. But the protection of women by the prosecution of procurers was a two-sided coin. To accuse only the prostitute would be to blame the victim, since the procurer and customer were both responsible. Yet to blame only the procurer was to view the prostitute as passive and easily manipulated. The customer, for whose benefit the whole system operated, was the least often blamed.

The Sex Trade in Practice

In many ways prostitution resembled other urban trades. The term covered a wide array of workplaces and a variety of ways of organizing that work. A prostitute's working situation could range from the level of the streetwalker to that of the courtesan, and determined her freedom of choice in entering and leaving the trade, her prosperity, and her relation to the community.[1] Some prostitutes operated out of their homes; others had their place of business separate from their residence. Some worked in brothels, whether officially sanctioned or a good deal more casual. Some catered especially to wealthy foreign merchants, others to servants and apprentices. Some prostitutes had to share their remuneration with pimps, procurers, brothelkeepers, and go-betweens; others remained more independent, while yet others procured for one another or, if they remained in the trade long enough, became brothelkeepers themselves.

The great diversity within the trade makes it difficult to generalize about prostitutes' social standing. The more institutionalized prostitutes were not necessarily better off; rather than indicating social acceptance and integration, institutionalization or other types of formal recognition contributed to prostitutes' being set apart from other people. Illicit prostitutes had to find a place to live, in many cases a trade other than the prostitution they practiced on the side, and a network of acquaintances who could support them in legal difficulties, connections through which some may have been better integrated into the community than those in the licit brothels. Yet all prostitutes interacted to a certain extent with the society around them. As a group they helped set the boundaries of sexual behavior by serving as the extreme case against which the norm could be defined.

The structure of the sex trade in medieval England does not lend itself to the clear-cut hierarchies historians have identified elsewhere.[2] The records do not reveal anyone we can identify as a courtesan, that is, an educated, refined prostitute. Courtesans may have existed, especially around the court, but the sources simply do not discuss them as the Italian ones do. The women whose customers were primarily foreign merchants and who remained with the same man for a period of time and were paid more than the normal fee might be considered to verge on the courtesan. Certainly there was a distinction between the professional who worked in an established brothel and the barmaid who occasionally engaged in sex for pay, but we should beware of casting it in strictly hierarchical terms: casual prostitutes were not necessarily poorer than professionals, and they had a wider choice of customers and occasions. The situation seems to have been fairly fluid, as women moved from one form of the sex trade to another.

Indeed, the overall picture of prostitution as it was practiced in medieval England is one of transience, variation, and adaptability. Women entered and left the trade as their economic situation dictated; they moved from place to place as harassment by the authorities became onerous. They cooperated with other prostitutes or with brothelkeepers when it was to their advantage to do so. We cannot identify a "typical" prostitute among the wide range of practices, but the efforts of authorities to demarcate and stigmatize prostitutes gave them a collective identity, one that was on the fringes of the socially acceptable but that was nonetheless integral to society's functioning.

The Careers of Prostitutes

The careers of those prostitutes whose lives can be reconstructed from court records reveal a long-term participation in the trade. This is largely a function of the sources. For only a few prostitutes or other women in the commercial sex trade—indeed, for few urban women generally—is it possible to piece together a life story. The longer a woman stayed in the sex trade, the more likely she was to turn up in court, so it is easiest to trace those who remained involved the longest and much more difficult to find out what became of those who appear in the records only once or twice. Several of the women discussed here continued to earn a living in sexual commerce, as bawds or brothelkeepers, even after they were no longer working as prostitutes themselves. These women might be considered the most degraded or marginalized in that they were not able to move out of the sex trade as others presumably were. But in other ways they are less marginal than women who left the trade once they were too old to work as prostitutes, in that they managed to establish themselves in a permanent career and station in life. Those who were able to achieve some stability and long-term income from the trade were very much the exception to the general rule of transience and the makeshift nature of the profession.

Isabella Wakefield began a career as a prostitute and keeper of a brothel in York at the beginning of the fifteenth century: in 1403 she was accused of fornication with a priest and of being a common bawd, and in 1404 of being a "common bawd, keeping immorality in her house" between a woman named Isabella Scot and two priests. Before entering the sex trade, she had apparently been an apprentice seamstress and had become involved in a sexual relationship with Thomas Fox of Snaith, whom she unsuccessfully sued in 1402 to enforce a marriage contract.[3] She may have turned to prostitution after being seduced and abandoned by Fox; alternatively, Fox may have been a customer she hoped would marry her and enable her to give up prostitution. Wakefield continued to be charged with fornication and adultery, as well as bawdry and brothelkeeping, especially catering to priests.[4]

She also provided rooms for couples to commit adultery in her house. The priest first cited in her case, Peter Bird or Bryde, continued to live with her, and the two were repeatedly charged with fornication. In 1405 she did penance and abjured him on pain of a twenty shilling fine; she later returned to him, and also continued to receive a variety of other men as customers. In 1412 she cleared herself (by compurgation, bringing other women to swear on her behalf) of fornication with Bird and fornication and adultery with two other men. In 1417 she was still being presented for being "a common bawd promoting sin in her house between many people coming there," for fornicating with Bird, and for being a common defamer of her neighbors, and in 1418 and 1420 for practicing bawdry. In 1427 she was once again accused of fornication with a different man, in 1428 of being a common bawd, and again in 1431 of fornication.[5]

If we assume that Wakefield began her career at fifteen (a low estimate given that it would mean she was involved in marriage litigation at fourteen, whereas women often did not marry until their mid-twenties), then she was still operating as a prostitute at forty-three.[6] No doubt by that time her income derived mainly from brothelkeeping, but the stability of her career is still remarkable. That she carried on a long-term relationship with a priest indicates that she had an established place in this ecclesiastical town (albeit one censured by the authorities). More tellingly, in several of the cases in which she was charged, she was able to find the requisite number of compurgators (oath helpers, something like character witnesses)—"honest women" of the town—to purge herself. Thus, she was not without friends respectable enough to testify, even when the court increased her required number of compurgators from three to twelve (six was usual). Marginal is not the term that comes to mind to describe Isabella Wakefield.

Margaret Clay of Goodramsgate, also in York, followed a similar career in the sex trade. In 1449 she was charged with fornication with four different men (by one of whom she claimed to have had a child) and adultery with one, as well as bawdry in her house. She was charged again in 1455 with bawdry, and in 1456 she purged herself of the charge that she "was a bawd in her home to whoever came there wanting to have intercourse with each other." She also was charged as a bawd to her fellow brothelkeeper Medard the goldsmith and a woman who was apparently a prostitute, and was accused of committing fornication with a servant to Baron Graystoke. In 1459 she confessed to providing rooms to couples and did penance. In 1460 she was accused of receiving in her home a pregnant woman (Joan, servant to William Smith) and acting as bawd to her. In 1461 she did penance for being a bawd to three other couples, and she also purged herself of a charge of fornication. The charge in 1462 was that she was "a public and common bawd." In 1466 one of Margaret's servants was accused of fornication with a vicar choral (a priest serving at the cathedral); the record does not even identify the woman by name but only as a servant of Margaret Clay, who by that time was apparently notorious (and required more than the usual six compurgators). Margaret herself was accused again of bawdry on several occasions in 1466 between three vicars choral and other ecclesiastics and a certain Margaret Bugtrot living with her.[7] Her career in commercial sex extended over decades. In the beginning she was a prostitute as well as a brothelkeeper and provider of rooms. The repeated charges, her successful purgation, and the fact that she does not seem to have moved her residence indicate that she too was more or less established and accepted in the community.

Alice Dymmok of Great Yarmouth also operated as a bawd and brothelkeeper and possibly as a prostitute as well.[8] In 1487 "the wife of Thomas Dymmok" was fined for quarreling and for selling ale against the assize, and her husband for keeping a "suspicious house." Thomas Dymmok was apparently quite a substantial man, for in 1489 he was cited for occupying as a citizen (behaving as though he had been admitted to the freedom of the city) and ordered to take up the citizenship or else be fined, whereas a number of others were simply fined and not offered the choice. In 1491 Alice Dymmok was presented as a bawd and fined twenty pence (by comparison two other women were fined sixpence for the same offense), and was also fined twenty pence for lodging suspicious persons in her house (compared with fines ranging from sixpence to six shillings eightpence for six others fined at the same time for the same offense). In 1493 the wife of Thomas Dymmok was fined for promoting immorality in her house. It is not only the similarity in the offenses that points to the identification of Alice as the wife of Thomas. In 1493 John Robbins was fined six shillings eightpence for assaulting Thomas Dymmok so that his life was endangered. This same John Robbins was evidently Alice Dymmok's lover, for the next year the two were fined, forty pence and six shillings eightpence respectively, for committing adultery with each other.[9] Alice was fined again for harboring suspicious persons in 1494 (six shillings, whereas those charged with her were fined sixpence). Two years later she was fined for "promoting immorality" and scolding (ten shillings, compared to twelve to twenty pence for her fellow offenders), and six shillings eightpence for "suspiciously and illicitly associating with John Robbins." At the same time, Robert Peacock was fined sixpence for maintaining John Robbins and Alice Dymmok "suspiciously in his house several times," and John Robbins forty pence for "suspiciously associating with Alice Dymmok and knowing her carnally." In 1497 her fine for "keeping and promoting debauchery and a brothel in her house" was only twelvepence, though this was more than the fines of the people charged with her; she was also fined threepence for selling ale against the assize.

By 1498 Alice had moved. She was fined forty pence as a common whore (another woman charged at the same time was fined threepence) and was fined three shillings fourpence for being a "quarreler" (compared with fines of threepence to sixpence for others). The next year the fine was three shillings fourpence for "keeping a suspicious house, and bawdry, and cursing her neighbors," the same amount for abetting her son in beating two women, and twelvepence as a common quarreler. In 1500 the fine was sixpence for cursing her neighbors. In the same year she was also banished from the city as a "leper" on pain of ten pounds (the term could be used of anyone with an unexplained skin rash, possibly including those caused by venereal disease). She evidently did not comply, for in 1501 she was fined six shillings eightpence as a "common quarreler and sower of discord among her neighbors," three shillings fourpence for "keeping a house of ill-governed and suspicious persons," six shillings eightpence for assaulting people in her house, and twelvepence for milking other people's cows.

The wide variety of phrasing in the immorality charges against Alice Dymmok indicates that the specific offenses were not very clearly defined. She must have been considered a particularly egregious offender, since her fines were higher than others'; she was generally unpopular, as evidenced by her quarreling and creating quarrels, which may have contributed to her frequent prosecutions; and she was fairly independent, not restricting herself to one particular lover or having a landlord who was considered responsible for her activity. That she could afford to pay such high fines means that she must have been doing reasonably well financially. Unlike Isabella Wakefield and Margaret Clay, she moved about a good deal. Combined with her prosecutions for creating disorder, this transience indicates that she was not accepted within her community but could be called a marginal figure. The repeated fines and prosecutions may have stigmatized her, but they did not stop her. She herself may not have been a prostitute: she was fined only once as a whore, and, given the wide range of charges against her and her general unpopularity with the authorities, it is easy to imagine her having been convicted on this count simply on the basis of a bad reputation.

The biography of Margaret Morgan (alias Smith) of London further illustrates the transient side of the prostitute's life. Whether this description of her life is true or not (it was given in order to disqualify her testimony), it indicates what the witness considered a plausible career for a London whore. Morgan testified in the London Consistory Court in a marriage case in 1491. In an attempt to impeach her testimony, a hostile witness testified that three years before, when Morgan was living with John Hay and his wife in Langbourne ward and selling their ale, she had been "of ill fame and in the said parish commonly said, held and reputed an adulteress and a whore." The alderman had expelled her from the ward. She then went to another parish, where, the witness said, she married, kept an immoral house for three years, and committed adultery. Expelled again, she went to Farringdon ward, where she sold ale and harbored suspicious people; expelled, she went to the home of Margery Hor (possibly a nickname, "Whore"), a "bawd and infamous woman," and committed adultery with a number of men. Again expelled, she went back to Langbourne ward, then to Billingsgate, where she was again expelled. According to the witness, when she lived in Langbourne ward, she used to sing "like a whore," "foul and scurrilous songs," and called passers-by to "lechery and immodesty."[10] If the description is true, Morgan may have become a prostitute at the instigation of her employers. Despite this activity she was able to marry, although she does not seem to have remained with her husband long, and the marriage may never even have been solemnized. Her interval as a brewster or ale seller is typical of women who took up prostitution as one of several casual occupations, though her transient mode of life is characteristic of the lower end of the social scale among prostitutes.

The prostitute about whose actual practice in the trade we have the most detail is, ironically, a man, John Rykener. Since at least before, and possibly even after, the act his partners took him for a woman, the circumstances under which he operated were probably not atypical of female prostitution. Rykener, calling himself Eleanor, was arrested with another man in London in 1394, having been accosted in the street and taken his customer to a market stall to commit "that detestable, vile, and ignominious vice." He testified that he had recently spent five weeks in Oxford as an embroidress, fornicating with several students, and six weeks in Burford as a tapster at an inn, having sex for various sums of money with foreign merchants and friars. Female prostitutes undoubtedly traveled about in much the same way. He originally got his start in the trade with a certain Elizabeth Brouderer, probably the same as Elizabeth Moryng, the embroidress who put her apprentices out as prostitutes.[11]

These stories illustrate several of the themes to be developed in the rest of this chapter and the following one: the adaptability of prostitutes as they moved about and changed the way they operated according to circumstance; the persistence of their ties with the sex trade; their connection with other sorts of offenses besides the sexual; and their ambivalent relations with the community. Isabella Wakefield and Margaret Clay made real careers for themselves in the sex trade and became substantial and established businesswomen, though we do not know how prosperous they were. Alice Dymmok and Margaret Morgan, while not as well established or accepted in their communities, were also able to eke out a living—in Dymmok's case apparently quite a good one—by practicing prostitution and/or bawdry. The courts that recorded the alleged activities of these women saw them not as innocent victims but as sinners and criminals. Nor should we see them solely as victims: they were women doing the best they could in difficult circumstances, and occasionally making quite a success of it, although at the same time they were repeatedly harassed by the authorities and deprived of respectability because of the sexual nature of their offense.

Varieties of Prostitution

The most independent sort of prostitute was a fairly transient one who found her customers on her own. A woman who practiced this sort of prostitution did not have to make arrangements with bawds or brothelkeepers; she could just seek a customer whenever the financial need arose. It would not have been difficult for a woman who wanted to have sex for money to find customers if she was not too particular. Any woman walking the streets at night was presumed to be available for sex. John Britby accosted "Eleanor"

Rykener on the street, "asking him as he would a woman if he could commit lechery with her." "Eleanor's" clothing did not mark her out as a prostitute: it is noted only that he was "dressed as a woman," not "dressed as a whore."[12]

Picking up customers in the street was thus a form of prostitution easily accessible to those who entered the trade temporarily, part-time, or in cases of necessity. The courts noted notorious places where streetwalkers gathered or passed: in 1421 in one London ward "the men of the inquest have indicted the postern in Langhorn Alley for the entry of whores there by night," and another ward inquest found that "behind the Pye [a tavern] at Queenhithe there is a privy place which is a good hiding place for thieves, and many evil agreements are made there, and many whores and bawds have there their shelter and leisure to make their false covenants."[13] Prostitutes and their customers may sometimes have had sex in back alleys rather than indoors.

Women who were labeled "vagabonds," harbored in people's homes where they "slept during the day and stayed up at night, playing illicit games and promoting immorality," had a similar transient status.[14] Unlike those who worked in an established brothel, they did not have the potential to build ties within the community and establish a client base. They remained more independent; yet because of their lack of a steady clientele, their income would have been low and the threat of violence by strangers would always be present.

Even casual prostitutes had to live somewhere, and some operated out of their dwellings. Prostitutes sometimes rented houses or rooms in groups without necessarily organizing as a brothel. The London Eyre of 1276 noted several violent crimes that took place at such houses. For example, Henry Peticors and Roger le Stedeman were killed in a quarrel with some foreign merchants at a house occupied by six whores. The woman who rented to them appeared in court but was acquitted; since she was not referred to as a bawd or brothelkeeper, the prostitutes were evidently considered independent operators.[15] Many prostitutes took rooms in someone else's house, an arrangement under which it would have been difficult to conceal their profession from the landlord. Landlords of this sort were often fined less than brothelkeepers. Women who operated in this way were likely to be transient, seeking new dwellings as they were fined and expelled from successive wards.

A tavern was both a good place for a casual prostitute to meet potential customers and, since most taverns would have had private rooms available, a convenient spot to carry out the bargain if she could not take the man to her home. Men knew that they could find sex partners, whether for pay or not, at a tavern. John Derby, a vicar choral of York Cathedral, was presented in 1472 for frequenting "the tavern of John Betson every night and there having colloquies and conversation with various whores and especially with Matilda Crossey, to the great danger of his soul."[16] John Somer, a barber, was accused of adultery "with Joan Wilson and with another whore in a house at the sign of the Bell."[17] In the sixteenth century the London Wardmotes were ordered not to allow anyone "keeping any tavern, alehouse, cellar, or any other victualling house or place of common resort to eat and drink in . . . [to] permit or suffer at any time hereafter any common women of their bodies, or harlots, to resort and come into their said house or other places aforesaid either to eat or drink, or otherwise there to be conversant or abide, or thither to haunt or frequent."[18]

Taverns were places where casual prostitutes might drop in, but there were also prostitutes who were regulars. Prostitutes sometimes had special arrangements with tavern employees to steer customers their way for a share of the profits (or, if landlords, for the benefit of the additional business the prostitutes might bring in). The innkeeper at the Bell in Warwick Lane in London was accused in 1485 of "keeping whoredom in his house" by "harboring suspected women"; the ostler was accused of fornication with Joan Singlewoman. In 1498 Joan Blond, the tapster there, was also charged as a whore and Agnes Thurston, who apparently worked there, as a bawd.[19] The landlord of the Three Cranes in London was charged as a bawd for German merchants, and a brewer and his wife at the Elephant in Smithfield were similarly accused. Roger and Margery, landlord of the Windmill in London and his wife, were alleged bawds to Joan Goldsmith and a retainer of the Duke of Gloucester.[20] A case from 1519 shows how prostitutes operated with the help of tavern employees. Elizabeth Tomlins went to an alehouse beside the Bell inn, sent for the ostler of the Bell, and asked whether a priest, Gregory Kyton, was there. The ostler told Kyton that the woman had asked for him, "and he answered that he would have her into his chamber, and then the ostler said that if he would go to the George in Lombard Street she should come to him, and then the ostler conveyed her to the George into a chamber there and after came the priest. . . . [T]hey went to supper all three and the priest paid for all."[21] In this particular instance the ostler may have gotten nothing for his efforts besides a good meal, but this must have been an everyday occurrence and an income supplement for him and other tavern staff.

Not only did many towns see taverns as a haunt of prostitutes, but some also connected tapsters with prostitutes. In Coventry, for example, no one was to "receive nor favor any tapster or woman of evil name." Presentments of whores or bawds with the surname or byname Tapster, or accusations of fornication against those working as tapsters, were not uncommon.[22] Any woman frequenting a tavern could be suspect. Respectable women were not often associated with taverns, although the reasoning here could be circular, as any woman who frequented or worked in a tavern was ipso facto not respectable. Prostitutes who frequented a particular tavern may have been part of a group or community of regulars, but it was still a transient mode of operation and dependent on the cooperation of others.

Women who picked up customers on the street or in a tavern could bring them to houses of assignation, which made premises available to couples who needed a private place to meet. Adulterous couples might also need such facilities, and some of the couples who used them were involved in long-term relationships that were not (as far as we can tell) commercial. Such houses of assignation were distinct from brothels in that the customers did not come to them seeking prostitutes; the couples met elsewhere and then came to use the space, the equivalent of today's hotels that charge by the hour. The line between such houses and brothels is not always clear, however. The Southwark stews, like other brothels, made rooms available for couples as well as for the prostitutes permanently working there, and it could be the man's initiative to take a prostitute there, as with Robert Hosteler, who "fornicated with Helena and with Denise whom he took with him to the stews."[23] A stew in Grub Street was indicted in 1422 as a "common house of whoredom and bawdry, and in which thieves and also priests and their concubines are received."[24] In a case in 1292 in which a man refused to solemnize his marriage on the grounds that he had previously had sex with a relative of his betrothed, witnesses testified that they had peeked into a private room in the bathhouse of Fulk the barber near the Tower of London and seen the couple lying naked together in bed, the man on top of the woman, the coverlet up to their shoulders, having "carnal connection."[25] Bathhouses and other houses of assignation were places where people in whatever sort of illicit relationship could meet conveniently.

Some prostitutes would go to their customers' homes or lodgings. These women were the medieval equivalent of an escort service, operating via go-betweens. The customer had to be wealthy enough to command privacy: no apprentice or servant would be able to bring a woman to his room. He also presumably had to be unmarried, or at least living apart from his wife, which may explain the large number of priests who employed prostitutes in this way, as well as foreign merchants such as the "Galyman" in whose home Katherine Clerk and Margery Goodwin were arrested.[26] Richard Wyer was convicted in 1529 of being "a common bringer and conveyer of certain single women to merchant strangers' places . . . there to use and occupy the foul and detestable sin of lechery and bawdry."[27]

The involvement of foreigners may be formulaic, as is the condemnatory language, but the repeated occurrence of similar accusations indicates that foreigners were at least thought of as among the main clientele. One woman defamed a man by saying that "he took a certain Colette to the chamber of Lombards." Agnes Hutton was accused as a common bawd on the grounds that she "procures and solicits young girls and the servants of divers men to commit the crime of fornication with divers men, and also leads them to the chambers of Lombards, Spaniards, and Easterlings."[28] She was apparently seeking out women to serve an established customer base. The most successful bawds would have had networks of both prostitutes and customers and would have been able to match them up according to the customers' wishes. A man might have heard of a particular prostitute and would ask the bawd for her; the bawd would comply, taking a large cut of the fee. This procuring was not limited to providing a woman for one night; it could involve recruiting a mistress. The prostitutes who operated in this manner may have been at the high end of the trade, as such customers were relatively wealthy. Yet, as we have seen, not all the women procured for wealthy merchants came voluntarily, and a high wage (if the woman even got to keep it herself) would not have been much consolation for rape.

Making the arrangements between prostitutes and wealthy merchants was only one of the activities that fell under the title "bawd." The term could imply any sort of matchmaking other than that leading to marriage; the transaction did not have to be commercial, although it often was. This sort of activity was extremely easy to practice on a casual basis—it required no capital, unlike brothelkeeping, and only a minimum of skill—and it was usually connected with women. Like "whore," "bawd" was a common term of insult for a woman and sometimes carried a general imputation of shady sexual dealings rather than a specific denotation.

A bawd could be the equivalent of a pimp, finding customers for a prostitute and living off her earnings. Some people, for example Edward Newton and his wife, Margaret, apparently pimped for prostitutes of the stews, procuring "both priests and laymen" for them.[29] Many women were accused of being both whores and bawds. These were probably cases of a prostitute finding a woman for her customer's friend. In this way two prostitutes might act as bawds for each other, as in the case of Joan Wakelyn and her friend Margery:

> A certain Margery came to the house of a certain Joan Wakelyn . . . and made an agreement with her that she would take her to the house of a powerful Lombard, to satisfy him with wicked and illicit sexual intercourse, if she would give her part of her payment; to which the said Joan agreed, and fulfilled, for which the said Joan received twelvepence as the wage for her sin from the said Lombard, and gave fourpence of this filthy lucre to the said Margery. . . . [Three days later Joan came to Margery's house] . . . wishing to repay the said Margery and do in return what she had done for her, the said Joan procuring the said Margery to sin for a very large fee in the home of a certain very free-spending Venetian; to whose house the said Joan brought the said Margery in the evening of that same day, so that the said Venetian could eagerly carry out with the said Margery his venereal acts, for which for the wage of twelvepence for the space of one night she remained in fornication.[30]

Margery and Joan had made a habit of this practice, and cooperation proved profitable for both: as the text stresses, the shilling they received was a very high wage.

There are many other examples of prostitutes helping one another link up with customers. In York in 1422 Elizabeth Frowe (possibly a Dutch or Flemish woman) allegedly fornicated with several Augustinian friars, with another woman acting as bawd; Elizabeth also acted as bawd between friars and other women. Again, this amounted simply to finding partners for her customers' friends. Although the court records do not label Elizabeth Frowe a whore, that term is rarely used in the York records; it is likely that she was a prostitute, as Joan Plummer of Goodramgate was charged in 1409 with "receiving in brothel Joan Montague and Elizabeth Frowe with ecclesiastical and other men."[31] Such cases indicate an element of cooperation, even solidarity, among prostitutes, although, since the aid was mutual, the cooperation was self-interested.

Bawds also served as go-betweens for couples of long standing. Especially if one or both parties were married, it could be difficult to arrange to meet without an intermediary, and some of the bawds who appear in the court records acted in this sort of situation. When the courts charged that someone "keeps whoredom [lenocinium] in her house" or even "keeps a brothel [for] anyone who wants to fornicate," we cannot always assume that she provided prostitutes; she may have been providing a meeting place for couples.[32] "Bawd" could even mean a woman who had facilitated the rape of another woman. An unnamed widow was accused of being a bawd between a woman sharing her bed (people of the same sex staying in the same lodging often shared beds) and a certain man: "[A]nd when the man came to them, then the widow got out of bed and went out of the tavern, leaving the man closed up with the woman."[33]

The fact that the woman who arranged this encounter was called a bawd indicates that the term was not restricted to the context of prostitution. A man might ask a bawd to procure for him a particular woman in whom he was interested, not as a prostitute but as a mistress. This may have been the case with Alice Shelton, "bawd to priests, by the token that she wished to take a certain woman who lives with Margery Crompe to a priest, and because the said woman did not want to go with her, became angry with her."[34] Such cases imply that men, even priests, assumed that any woman would be available for a price, and typically sent a female procurer to handle the negotiation.

The brothel, discussed in chapter 2, was the most formal and organized workplace for prostitutes. Although brothels were the rule in Southwark and existed elsewhere, too, they seem to have been relatively uncommon in London proper, compared with houses of assignation. There were certainly illicit stews and other brothels, but in the Wardmote records that survive for one ward (Portsoken) between 1465 and 1481, there were numerous presentments for whoredom and bawdry but none for brothelkeeping, unless that was subsumed under the category of bawdry.[35] Working in a brothel does not seem to have been especially attractive to prostitutes. Perhaps the formal regulation of the official brothels restricted their economic activity or their personal freedom too much, inclining them to seek work elsewhere. In Southampton a bucket maker's wife was fined "because she was bawd to the queans of the stews in her house," and an Italian was fined for taking a woman from the stews to the town.[36]

Prostitutes—or at least women accused of prostitution—were scattered throughout London, although concentrations could be found in particular areas such as the ward of Farringdon Without, beyond the city walls to the west. There were concentrations in the suburbs as well. There was a good deal of geographical as well as social mobility among prostitutes. The words with which Joan, wife of Richard Barrey, defamed Margaret Ward, whether or not there was any truth to them, show that a prostitute was expected to move about: "Thou art a common whore, my husband did keep thee a twelvemonth, and thou wast at the Stews six weeks, and a Lombard did keep thee at Galleys."[37] Women could drift in and out of long-term relationships and work as prostitutes when they did not have lovers to support them. They may also, like Margaret Morgan, have had to move about a good deal when the authorities in a particular ward took measures against them.

Customers and Fees

Where prostitution was licit, it was intended as an outlet for those men who did not have legitimate access to women through marriage, and these were in fact the main groups prostitutes served. Apprentices, servants, foreigners unaccompanied by their wives, and clergy were all excluded from conjugal relations, at least temporarily, but their sexual desire was nonetheless privileged because society presumed it was unavoidable that men would seek (and find) sexual outlets somewhere. The authorities judged it better to abandon a small group of women to sin and corruption in order to serve these men than to subject the whole society to the disorder that would otherwise ensue.[38] Married men visited prostitutes as well, but according to statements in legislation about the avoidance of greater sin, the function of prostitution was to channel the lusts of men who had no other outlet.[39]

Keeping apprentices and male servants in order was one of the reasons given in Continental European towns for the licensing of brothels. In England, whatever the benefits to the social order, individual employers were not particularly happy to have their male domestics visit prostitutes. They feared that servants or apprentices might steal their property to pay the prostitutes' fees (as in the case of Isabel Martin, "a common harlot who of late hath provoked many honest men's servants and apprentices to waste and spend their masters' goods upon her and to commit fornication with her"); a similar concern was expressed about servants' spending their masters' money on drink. The charge against Alice Staneyge of Nottingham, presented in 1515 for "bawdry and keeping other men's apprentices at cards and other games for money," was not unusual.[40] The women here are depicted as voracious for both money and sex; they are the temptresses, the ones to blame for the misbehavior of male servants. Some companies explicitly prohibited their apprentices from visiting prostitutes: the Fullers' Company of London in 1488 ordered their apprentices "not to use or haunt the stews side, nor the skittles, nor any other riotous games"; in 1371 a York apprenticeship indenture for a bowyer stipulated, "[L]et him not play at dice; let him not habitually frequent taverns, checkers, or brothels, let him not commit adultery or fornication with the wife or daughter of his master. . . . ."[41] Yet servants did visit prostitutes, and some prostitutes seem to have catered to them in particular, such as Joan, the wife of James Brewer, who was accused as "a whore by the token that she brought men's servants into her house where she kept them for a long time."[42]

Clergy were slightly higher than apprentices and servants on the social scale of customers, and probably hired better-established prostitutes. The authorities tended to see clerics as one of the main client groups; the relatively large number of prosecutions of clergy for visiting prostitutes may reflect a harsher attitude toward this activity on their part than on that of laymen.[43] Gloucester's regulations of the early sixteenth century, in addition to legislating against prostitutes in general, went on to ordain punishment "if any such priests or religious daily haunt queans within any Ward of the town, or walk by night suspiciously, or practice unlawful demeanor with whores, strumpets, or with men's wives."[44] Yet, from the point of view of the temporal authorities, who were busy prosecuting the clergy for adultery and fornication with the wives and daughters of the burghers, prostitutes were by far the better alternative.[45] Priests feared being prosecuted for adultery: John "Eleanor" Rykener, the transvestite, managed to extort two gowns from a priest he had had sex with, saying that if the priest tried to get the gowns back, "Eleanor"'s husband would prosecute him.[46]

Some prostitutes were perceived as catering especially to priests, as in the stewhouse in the London ward of Cripplegate Without condemned as "a common house of whoredom and bawdry, in which both thieves and priests and their whores are greatly received."[47] In Canterbury one Reginald Schakston, according to witnesses, "kept bawdry in his house . . . between various men, both religious and others, and especially between certain friars of Sandwich and also a certain chaplain, and the wife of the said Reginald." Another witness alleged that Schakston "kept a dishonest house for a long time between his wife and a certain Matilda Goldsmith, his relation, and various friars of whom some were from Sandwich and some from Canterbury."[48] Here was a brothelkeeper who specialized, at least to the extent that friars were his best-known customers. The transvestite John Rykener testified that he would rather have priests than other customers because they would pay more, and female prostitutes may have felt the same way.[49]

Even though some prostitutes specialized in priests as customers, they seem to have mocked them. Elizabeth Chekyn was convicted in 1516 of being "a common harlot and strumpet, and also was now lately taken strolling and walking by the streets of this city in a priest's array and clothing, in rebuke and reproach of the order of priesthood." When she performed her ritual of punishment, parading through the streets of London with a striped hood and white rod, she had "on her breast a letter of H of yellow woolen cloth in sign and token of a harlot, and on her left shoulder a picture of a woman in a priest's gown." Of course anyone could have mocked the priesthood in this way, especially in the early sixteenth century. But a prostitute was more likely to be outspoken than other women—and more likely to be prosecuted for it. Elizabeth may have had a better reason than most to be anticlerical, knowing clerical unchastity at firsthand: at the time of her arrest she was in bed with two priests.[50]

The rule of clerical celibacy was often breached in this period, and many clergy had partners who were for all practical purposes their wives. The term "priest's whore" for these women was used even when the speaker meant a woman in an ongoing relationship with a particular priest, not a prostitute. When John Ward called Alice Pepinell a "priest's quean" and said that the priest John of Ronchcliff came to her "commonly whenever he pleased,"[51] he implied a permanent liaison. Still, not all women who were involved in ongoing relationships with priests were the equivalent of wives: Katherine Brady or Braby was "a common whore and also adulteress with master Robert Grene, rector of St. Olave in Southwark, who thus kept her for the space of ten years here and elsewhere . . . and also the said Katherine is named with divers others. . . ."[52] It is hard to draw the line between the prostitute who may have had a particular priest as a regular customer and the woman who acted as a more permanent partner, because the courts that punished them did not make the distinction.

Foreign merchants, another main source of clients, made up 2 to 4 percent of the population of London, and probably a similar percentage in other port towns.[53] They were not likely to have their wives with them, and their household servants were even less likely. From the London court records it would seem that these merchants tended to prefer young women, whom they purchased as concubines, rather than paying for the one-time services of a prostitute. It may also have been foreign merchants who created the demand for foreign prostitutes in places like London and Great Yarmouth. Perhaps, besides being interested in "young girls," they wanted women who spoke their own language.

Not all foreigners in London were wealthy, and not all who sought the company of women could afford to purchase concubines or invite high-class prostitutes to their lodgings. There were brothels that catered especially to foreigners, like the one in East Smithfield where a married couple was said to "keep and sustain in their house common prostitutes, and serve refreshments to Lombards and Galleymen living lustfully with the said prostitutes, and keep common gaming." Many foreigners probably lived in quarters such as those of Zenobius Martin, who "kept a lodging-house for aliens" and was indicted as a common bawd for admitting prostitutes to his house.[54] The prostitutes may simply have been lodging in the same house as the foreigners; but more likely Martin was arranging for them to service his tenants sexually. The prostitutes who served a transient clientele of foreigners were likely to be transients themselves.

Foreign merchants were not the only ones with largely male households. A lord traveled with his male retinue, and even at his main residence would have had very few female servants.[55] Whether or not this was intended to preserve the order and honor of the household, his retainers would have had to turn elsewhere for sex. The retainer of the duke of Gloucester for whom a young girl was procured (see p. 61) was not atypical. In Lichfield one prostitute boasted that when the duke of Clarence was in town, she had had sex fourteen times with members of his retinue.[56] Members of the royal household dealt with prostitutes too. Joan Burdon was charged as a whore with "Easterlings and gentlemen of the court"; and a woman called Alice was accused as "a common bawd especially between gentlemen of the court and whores living within the precincts of St. Katherine," a liberty near the Tower.[57] Various kings issued ordinances against prostitutes' being kept at the court; in 1318 it was decreed that a woman caught a third time would be imprisoned for forty days. This law apparently had little effect, for in 1370 a marshal of the court prostitutes was appointed. He was to take fourpence a week from each whore who followed the court.[58] Whether they were more or less formal mistresses who restricted themselves to one man or ordinary prostitutes who had sex with many, camp followers were certainly not unknown.

The fee a woman received for sex depended on her customers and her working conditions. References to fees are usual enough in the sources to indicate that anyone called a whore was commonly expected to take money, although this was not necessary in order to be categorized as one. The fees cited range from less than a penny's worth of food to several pounds. This latter amount, however, was not for a single act but for the purchase of a woman, and the large amounts received by some bawds were probably also payments for brokering long-term relationships rather than portions of a prostitute's earnings. Robert Flowerdew and his wife sold a girl to Benedict Spenell for four pounds. William Redwood and his wife, Isabella, were "bawds for divers women and received from divers men sums for these women, from some twenty pence, from some thirty pence, from some forty pence, and from some four shillings at the most." Alexander Elwold kept two whores in his house, "one called mistress Helena for whom he received weekly two shillings from a certain priest"; it is not clear how much Helena herself was paid or by whom. Eden Johnson, accused of being a bawd, had demanded payment from John Parnesse and his lover, saying, "I have been bawd between you two a dozen times and thou owest me sixteen shillings," to which he responded, "I paid thee at the stews side, thou whore."[59] Johnson was clearly a go-between for an established couple, not a procurer of prostitutes, but the case gives some idea of the scale of fees involved, when compared, for example, with a daily wage of one and a half pence to twopence daily plus board for women agricultural workers or an annual wage of fourteen to eighteen shillings plus board (somewhat less than a penny a day) for laundresses.[60]

In some cases a large payment could be in the nature of a bribe. Richard Dodd, a tailor, received forty pence from a priest named William Langford for acting as bawd for his wife, Margaret.[61] We could analyze this as an instance of the exploitation of women within the family—the husband selling his wife like property—or as an example of husband and wife cooperating in the household economy, with the wife earning and the husband negotiating her wage. Margaret was accused as an adulteress, not a whore, so the court did not imply that she had transgressed with more than one man or that any of the payment had gone to her. This was perhaps not so much a case of payment for sexual intercourse as one of payment for Dodd's relinquishing his rights over his wife.[62]

The amount that the prostitute herself received may have been minimal. In the case of Elizabeth Moryng, who sold for eightpence the prayer book her apprentice stole from her clerical lover, the court found that "the said Elizabeth retained for her own use this sort of filthy lucre received from the said Joan and her other servants."[63] In this case the prostitute is clearly presented as having been victimized by the rapacious bawd. John Tanner, who "used to lead women living in the parish of St. Dunstan in the East and sell them to various men," apparently did not share his fees, although the women presumably could have negotiated an additional payment themselves.[64] Joan Wakelyn and her friend Margery, who took only a threepenny cut of each other's twelvepence, were unusual both in the low percentage to the procurer and in that the customer paid the prostitute directly, not the bawd; but they were peers and apparently trusted each other.

When prostitutes operated on their own, without a bawd, they do not seem to have made very much either. The penny that Margaret Weston received from a man for having sex with him was probably typical of the lower end of the trade, though a woman could also defame another by saying that she would take any "man that would meddle with her for half a penny." Another woman was charged with saying that whoever wanted to might sin with her servant for a halfpennyworth of ale. Margaret Bird got twopence from a priest known as "holy Sir John." Sometimes the prostitute would take goods instead of money. The priest Clement Munyell paid "Prone Joan who lives with Spanish Nell" fourpence for their first night together and "a farthing cake and a farthing worth of single beer" for the second.[65] A penny, of course, was not a negligible sum. But given the irregularity and uncertainty of payment, prostitution can hardly be seen as a lucrative trade for its practitioners. There is no evidence as to how many men a prostitute might have sex with over a given period of time; but many of the records refer to spending the night with customers, so it seems likely that the women did not turn a large number of tricks in one night. Prostitution, except at the highest levels, was not a route to riches.

Sometimes a prostitute took it upon herself to improve her pay scale by theft. The courts were no doubt quite ready to believe that whores were also thieves, but it is likely that the accusations were based on actual occurrence as well as on a general connection of prostitution with criminality. The sanctioned stews were supposed to protect the customer from theft, but it undoubtedly still took place there as elsewhere. Sometimes prostitutes participated in violent robbery, victimizing not only their own customers but also passers-by. A country vicar from Bedfordshire was accosted by Alice atte Hethe, who took hold of him and pulled him into her inn to drink with her, whereupon the ostler and another man appeared and took his cloak, ring, and purse at dagger point. In the records for 1262--63 we find one such situation that led to murder: "Richard Valet came up to the door of a house . . . where lived Beatrice de Wynton', Isabel de Staunford, and Margery de Karl', prostitutes; they immediately came out of the house, dragged Richard inside, and took from him a buckle . . . worth 6d., whereupon Richard drew his knife and, intending to strike Beatrice with the handle, instead struck her beneath the breast with the blade, so that she died."[66] Theft could also be less violent. A prostitute of Southampton was fined for taking money from a Frenchman's purse at the stews, and another stole ten pounds in gold from a Spaniard (who paid the town a third of it upon recovery). Agnes Sampson of Sandwich, a serving woman, was punished with the cucking stool and banishment not only for whoredom but also for stealing silver spoons from the kitchen of Richard Howet, presumably when she was in his home for sexual purposes, and one London priest who had two rings stolen from his purse by a whore found himself charged with fornication when he complained.[67]

Marriage and Children

Prostitution was for many young women a practice in which they could engage for a while before they married, though it often hampered a woman's ability to find a husband. There is some direct evidence of prostitutes marrying and leaving the trade, from defamation cases in which a witness accuses a married woman of having been a whore or makes other references to her past, and from cases such as that of Margery Smith, of whom the record states, "[A] certain man took her from a brothel at Hull and married her so that she would leave her ill governance." The church considered it a good work to marry a prostitute in order to reform her, but this was apparently ineffectual in Margery's case, since she left her husband, taking all his goods.[68]

Such an altruistic motive for marrying a former prostitute was probably rare in practice. If a woman had been a prostitute—or was suspected of still being one—this could seriously compromise her husband's rights over her. In 1382 Henry de Wilton sued a priest, Thomas Norwich, for trespass, claiming that he "took, eloigned, and carried away Joan, the wife of the said Henry, and divers of his goods and chattels, viz. woollen and linen cloths, silver plate, dishes, pewter saltcellars, and iron and brass pots and pans." The jury found in favor of the plaintiff as far as the goods were concerned, but "as to the eloigning of the wife, they say that she is and was a common whore, so it is not eloigning."[69] In effect, if the wife's reputation as a whore was strong in the neighborhood, the husband was unable to collect the damages to which he would otherwise have been entitled. Such cases must have been cautionary to anyone contemplating marriage to a former prostitute, even if he hoped that she would continue to work and support him.

Although in some parts of Europe efforts were made to redeem prostitutes by providing communal houses for them if they left the trade, or dowries to make them attractive marriage prospects, these practices were less common in England. In London, less than 1 percent of all charitable gifts were marriage subsidies to provide dowries for poor girls. Although these were not intended specifically for prostitutes, they may have relieved the pressure on some women to engage in prostitution. Similar charity was practiced in York and other towns.[70] Earlier English pastoral manuals gave a good deal of attention to the redemption of former prostitutes, but this did not necessarily translate into practice, especially in the late Middle Ages. The fact that England, unlike other countries, had no foundations expressly for repentant prostitutes may indicate either that prostitution was perceived as a lesser social problem there, or perhaps that English people did not approach with the same zeal the religious goal of eliminating prostitution by conversion.[71]

Whether or not they married, prostitutes did have children, although we do not know how common this was. Medieval physicians believed that prostitutes were sterile because their wombs became clogged with dirt, because the great quantities of semen they received made their wombs slippery, or because they commonly got no pleasure from sex and therefore did not emit seed.[72] If prostitutes were in fact less fertile than other women, perhaps it was because they practiced some form of contraception or abortion, or because of venereal infections.[73]

Contraceptive information would not have been handily available in textual form even for those few prostitutes who were able to read, as it was suppressed in translations of gynecological treatises intended for women. Information may have circulated by word of mouth, however. A reference in one medical manuscript to "whore midwives" suggests that prostitutes were thought of as knowledgeable about reproductive matters, although this may have been a disparagement of midwives rather than a statement about prostitutes.[74] Those who wrote the texts assumed that prostitutes would practice contraception if it were available: one Middle English translation explains that contraceptive information had been omitted "because whores would use it."[75] They may also have practiced nonprocreative sex. The testimony of the transvestite prostitute John Rykener gives us a clue to the actual sexual practices of prostitutes. If his testimony is to be believed, and many of his partners never found out that he was a man, this would seem to indicate that prostitutes were not expected to take their clothes off (obvious enough in the case of streetwalkers having sex in stalls and alleys, less so in the case of liaisons indoors and in private, as were many of Rykener's). It also suggests that customers did not necessarily expect to penetrate a prostitute vaginally. Rykener did not indicate that his performance "as a woman" was in any way unusual. If the practice of other than vaginal sex by prostitutes was common enough that Rykener could pass as a woman without occasioning any questions, the most likely reason is fear of conception.[76]

Nevertheless, some did become pregnant. Wet nurses accused of whoredom presumably had to have borne children of their own.[77] It is not clear how many prostitutes abandoned their children and how many reared them. There were no foundling hospitals in London until the mid-sixteenth century.[78] Richard Whittington, mayor of London in the late fourteenth and early fifteenth centuries, gave a charitable donation to establish a special room in St. Thomas's Hospital in Southwark "with eight beds for young women that had done amiss, in trust of a good amendment. And he commanded that all the things that were done in that chamber should be kept secret . . . for he would not shame any young woman in any way, for it might be the cause of hindering her marriage."[79] Some prostitutes may have been among the unwed mothers so cared for, but Whittington's grant did not specifically provide for their children. In 1552, when three common harlots were to be punished, only two were dunked in the Thames; the other "being with child [was] spared."[80]

One case survives in which a child was abandoned: Agnes Tyler, a "maintainer of the foul sin of lechery and the offenders committing the same," took a female child born in fornication (presumably to one of the women to whom she was a bawd) and abandoned her "suddenly and quietly in the night time at a substantial merchant's gate . . . leaving it there crying without any manner of comfort, in no little peril of its utter destruction."[81] That she abandoned her at the doorstep of someone who could afford to care for her implies that infanticide was not the intention; nevertheless, the entry in the court book is far more condemnatory in tone than most of the references to whores and bawds, stressing that she must be punished or her crime would set a bad example. This may have been one of the services bawds provided for the women who worked for them. The infant's mother was not punished. Defamation cases occasionally involve women accused of killing their children, but not necessarily in connection with prostitution.[82]

The paucity of references to prostitutes' children may indicate a high rate of nonprocreative sex, contraception, abortion, infanticide, or abandonment. Yet an argument from silence is dangerous. Surely prostitutes bore children. There is no evidence to indicate whether such children grew up alongside other children and were treated normally, but there is no reason why there would be: since the sources for information on prostitutes are mainly court records, much everyday behavior does not appear there. Children born to prostitutes would have shared their mothers' lives of poverty, and if they were girls, they might have had few alternatives but to follow in their footsteps.

The degree to which prostitutes were able to marry, and the degree to which their children were accepted, would have depended a great deal on popular attitudes. Where prostitutes were accepted members of the community, an individual prostitute's marriage prospects are likely to have been a good deal better than if they were marginalized. In the next chapter I turn to the question of the prostitute's status in the community, especially in the context of marriage.

Marriage, Sexuality, and Marginality

Popular attitudes toward the practice of prostitution and other variations on feminine sexuality were not necessarily the same as the attitudes inscribed in the law. Those who made and enforced the law enshrined their views in the records, where they are much easier to discover than the views of prostitutes themselves and those among whom they lived. Even though the law of church and state treated their profession as a crime and a sin, individual prostitutes may not have felt degraded but may simply have felt that they were earning a living as best they could. Still, it would not be fair to assume that to the prostitutes and those around them, prostitution was just another trade. A prostitute was encumbered with moral and ideological baggage as a baker or an embroideress was not.

Some historians consider the medieval and early modern prostitute a figure on the margins of society, along with those who lived by other shady means such as gambling, begging, or theft.[1] Others argue that brothels, especially legalized ones, were central to town life, and that prostitutes only became marginal later, as they lost official sanction.[2] Official recognition and some degree of protection under law, however, need not imply inclusion in the community.[3] To the extent that prostitutes did play a formal role in civic life, as in Germany, it was not a respected one. Prostitutes were often physically located on the margins of cities—outside the town walls, in the suburbs—and were labeled and stigmatized through court proceedings and through the requirement of wearing distinctive clothing.

The voices we hear that constitute the prostitute as marginal, however, are those of the civic and ecclesiastical authorities. We lack the voices of women who may have had their own interpretations of their lives. Becoming a prostitute, especially on a temporary basis in time of need, did not always cut a woman off from her community; and, as we have seen, some prostitutes as well as others involved in commercial sex—brothelkeepers, procurers, landlords—aimed for and attained respectability.

One factor promoting the prostitute's integration into society was the way she fit into the gender system. Prostitution linked feminine sexuality and financial exchange in a very visible way, but other aspects of medieval culture, such as marriage, linked them too. Although the whore fell on the wrong side of the law, she was perceived as in some ways no different from the married woman whose sexuality was also a commodity.

Class, Marriage, and Sexual Behavior

To determine whether the prostitute was marginal to or accepted in the community in which she lived and worked, we need to ask whether the label "whore" was one applied from above to describe behavior condemned by religious or secular authorities but considered normal by other social groups. In other periods some of the women who have come down to us in the court record as prostitutes were not engaged in commercial sex but merely had a different notion from that of the middle classes about what constituted appropriate sexual behavior.[4] It is worth exploring whether the prevalence of what we identify as prostitution and what medieval England labeled "whoredom" was perhaps due to the failure of some groups within the society to accept the church's model of sexual behavior.[5] In particular, given the changing understanding during the Middle Ages of what constituted marriage, we can see how some women who considered themselves married might have been condemned as whores.

Marriage in the Middle Ages meant the formation of a household. It was also a sacrament; it created a spiritual as well as an economic unit. In the church's view marriage legitimated sexual intercourse and procreation. It took centuries, however, for the church's definition of marriage and sexuality to be accepted throughout Europe.[6] The general public's views on the licitness of sexual behavior related to marriage differed greatly from those of the church. The church held that marriage was indissoluble but relatively easily created. It did not require a church ceremony; although the parties could be punished for entering into a marriage without the blessing of a priest, their marriage was still valid. All that was required was the consent of the parties, phrased either in the present tense or in the future tense, followed by sexual intercourse.[7] From cases of disputed marriages, however, it is clear that regardless of what the canon law held, people tended to regard the exchange of consent as merely a betrothal, which could legitimately be followed by sexual intercourse, but which was not binding. According to R. H. Helmholz, "What the law regarded as a complete and indissoluble marriage, many men regarded as a contract to marry."[8] The licitness of premarital sex among the betrothed was also an issue in the Middle Ages.[9] Although a couple might have to perform public penance if their marriage was followed by the birth of a child in less than nine months, this hardly resulted in their ostracism from the community or from respectability. Only gradually over the course of the Middle Ages did the church manage to impose its model, and even then it was not able to do so completely. The high rates of bridal pregnancy in the sixteenth and seventeenth centuries indicate that couples commonly behaved as though betrothal entailed permission to have sex.[10]

Although there may have been continuing disagreement on this point, recent studies have argued that by the late Middle Ages the church's model of marriage as permanent, indissoluble, and created by publicly expressed consent had been imposed across the entire social scale. It is true that some cases appearing in the church courts as late as the fourteenth and fifteenth centuries still involve clandestine marriage, in which the parties treated marriage as a private contract, but clandestine marriages were much more likely to be in dispute than those publicly celebrated in church. Larry Poos speaks of "a popular culture of marriage that generally recognised the gravity and perdurance of unions formed by mutual vows, even when these were not entered in the canonically optimal manner." People did take marriage seriously and cared about the legitimacy of their children.[11] Thus, it seems unlikely that most of the women categorized as whores by the courts simply belonged to a social group that took a different view of marriage from that of the mainstream. Nonmarital sex may have been deemed more acceptable in some milieux than in others (priests' domestic partners, often called concubines or whores, who might be wives in every respect but legal recognition, are one example), but this does not explain the prevalence of accusations of whoredom.

Regardless of whether all social groups accepted and internalized the church's view of marriage, not all women who transgressed that view and became involved in quasi-marital or nonmarital relationships were considered whores, at least in legal terms. Court records are full of adulteresses, fornicators, and women said to be "ill-governed of their body" or similar circumlocutions, yet not referred to as whores. Probably many of those who appear in church and temporal court records as adulteresses or fornicators were women living in more or less permanent relationships with men whom they could not marry because of a previous marriage that now existed in name only, or to whom they considered themselves married even though the union had never been formalized by the church. By contrast, the whore was usually a woman who was common (indeed, the phrase "common whore" was very often used), that is, who was seen as promiscuous in giving her favors to more than one man, often for money, or whose behavior in some other way scandalized the court officials.

To the extent that those called whores were so labeled because of multiple sex partners, we may wonder to what extent this behavior was considered acceptable by different groups in medieval society, or to what extent sexual mores varied by social class.[12] Did the general public accept the church's teaching on multiple sex partners as it had the teaching on marriage? Could accusations of whoredom have arisen as the church attacked behavior that seemed perfectly normal not only to the individuals involved but to their peer group? It was not "the church" as an institution that brought women into court as whores: the bishops' officials accused them based on information from their neighbors. Standards of morality were being imposed from within the community as well as from without.[13] Women who engaged in sex with more than one partner were censured not just by social elites but also by their peers, although the church's teaching was less widely accepted with regard to men's sexual behavior.[14] The categorizing of some women as whores cannot be interpreted as the imposition of bour-geois morality on the working class, as it may have been in later.periods.

Even if attitudes toward sex with multiple partners were not class-related, attitudes toward sex for money could have been. Perhaps those who recognized women's financial need were more sympathetic toward the sexu-al irregularity it prompted. (Then again, perhaps not: canon lawyers recog-nized financial need as a motive for prostitution, but not a mitigating fac-tor.)[15] The simple fact of being poor may have affected one's attitude toward the exchange of sex for money. And since men of the upper and middle classes often assumed that women of the lower class were there for the taking (domestic servants in particular), these women may have decided that if they were going to be pressured into sex anyway, they might as well get paid.

William Caxton's translation of *The Book of the Knight of the Tower* recognizes that the reasons for engaging in what he considered sexually immoral behavior were different among different social groups:

These sorts of women which take as their paramours and love such folk [married men, priests and monks, and servants and "folk of naught"], I hold them of no esteem or value; they are greater harlots than those who are daily at the brothel. For many women of the world do that sin of lechery only because of need and poverty, or else because they have been deceived into it by the false counsel of bawds. But all gentlewomen who have enough to live on, who make their paramours such manner of folk as before is said, it is by the great ease wherein they are, and by the burning lechery of their bodies.[16]

But even if some medieval authors found sexual license more excusable for the poor than for the rich, this does not mean that lower-class women actually had different norms or morals than the wealthy.

The fact that marriage in the Middle Ages could be entered into without a public ceremony did mean that the nature of the financial arrangements involved could be confusing, and on occasion the line between the pros-titute and the wife was a fine one. In 1470 a woman named Agnes sued William Knollys, claiming that the two had contracted marriage. He testi-fied in the bishop of London's Consistory Court that he had given her a set of knives, fifteen pence, and a pair of gloves, but that "he did not give these gifts to the said Agnes with the intention of having her as his wife, but to please her so she would continue with him in sin."[17] She testified that she had given him gifts in return, and that she had understood both sets of gifts as being in token of matrimony. He may have promised her marriage and deliberately misled her; but it is also possible that the two had completely misunderstood each other, and that he had in fact thought that he was purchasing her sexual favors. It does not matter whether his claim was true in this specific case; the fact that it could have been true indicates that the line between a respectable woman and a whore was a vague one. Exchange was part of matrimony as well as of prostitution. Although by the fourteenth century the monetary economy was no longer a new phenomenon, late medieval Europeans were still grappling with the shift from a society based on lineage and loyalty to one based on cash.[18] Sexuality was not exempt from the dislocation of social and intellectual patterns caused by this change. It affected the way people viewed marriage and its relation to financial exchange.

The exchange of women is a feature of many societies both primitive and complex. Dowries in land had figured prominently in earlier medieval marriage politics.[19] When cash became the measure of the dowry a woman brought to her marriage, the woman became that much more obviously a commodity. The dowry never became the crucial economic issue in England that it was in Italy, where whole urban economies depended on the investment of dowry funds, and where dowry inflation made fathers bewail the birth of daughters. But even in England, marriage could be thought of in terms of a market. Dowries helped daughters of rich merchants marry into the nobility; and cash could dissolve some of the distinctions between estates during the late Middle Ages.[20] Financial arrangements constituted a more important part of marriage the higher one went in society as marriage became less a personal relationship and more a family alliance. But they were not unimportant for workers; indeed, one of the reasons for the late age of marriage was the need to save money until one could afford a family.

Secular Literature and the Commodification of Sexuality

The fine line between financial exchange that led to marriage and financial exchange that constituted prostitution is evident not only in the court records but also in the literature of the late Middle Ages. The pervasiveness of venality in representations of feminine sexuality, within and outside marriage, indicates that it was not merely her acceptance of remuneration that placed the prostitute at the margins of society.

The impact on gender relations of thinking in cash terms went far beyond the area of dowry. Dowry was an exchange not between individuals but between families. What was being purchased was not sexual access to the woman, or even her childbearing capabilities, but rather, since by the late Middle Ages it was the woman's family that paid the dowry, respectability for their daughter. Medieval writing about marriage, however, emphasizes the role of money in another way, depicting it as an exchange of sex for cash. If wives are shown as venal, engaging in sex with their husbands not for love or duty but for money, they are in effect not very different from the commercial prostitute. I do not mean to suggest that contemporary literary representations necessarily reflect the way women in medieval England actually behaved; it is pointless to ask how accurate such depictions are.[21] What I am concerned with here is the mental world of a past culture. Literary texts convey, if not actual events and social relations, at least the concerns and preoccupations of the time.[22] At the same time they are constitutive of their culture because they establish the framework within which people think and write and behave. The language of literary texts can be a "social agent" as well as a "social mirror."[23] In medieval society the literate—the upper classes, the clergy, and the bourgeoisie, especially men rather than women—were the ones with power. Whatever affected the mental world of those in authority would affect the way society was structured, in numerous ways that impinged on everyone's lives. The tremendous interaction between oral and written medieval culture means that works of imaginative literature may be used as an indication of cultural attitudes in general.

The commodification of sexuality in medieval literature reaches its extreme in some of the French fabliaux, tales that may have been known in England as well.[24] In the fabliaux body parts themselves become commodities. For example, in "Du Moigne" a monk dreams of finding himself at a market where the wares displayed are female genitalia; in "Li Sohaiz desvez" a woman has a similar dream about a market where penises arrive by the wagonload. In "Les Quatres Sohais Saint Martin" a wife wishes for her husband's body to be "covered with pricks." When her wish comes true, she describes herself as rich: she wanted them not for sexual purposes but as symbols of wealth.[25] Greed for sexual organs (which serve as characters in their own right in 13 percent of the extant fabliaux) is connected to economic greed. Male organs become currency more often than female, and women's desire for the disembodied member implies both feminine covetousness and a wish for the power symbolized by the phallus.[26]

The fabliaux also contain several portraits of prostitutes. Once again, we cannot assume that the social relations depicted there correspond to reality;[27] they do serve, however, as evidence of how medieval society imagined the prostitute. Fabliaux, like other literary genres, reveal not sociological detail but an author's version of the values or ethos of the culture.[28] And the fabliaux adopt a moderate rather than a condemnatory tone toward prostitutes. There is no difference in the description of the actions of a prostitute and those of a countess, or between the lovemaking of a married couple and that of a prostitute and her client. The prostitute is part of the community. The fabliaux, according to Marie-Thérèse Lorcin, make the same point the city fathers made whenever they established official brothels or bathhouses: that clerics and other unmarried men should go to the brothel and not seduce respectable girls and women. The prostitute thus serves as a protector of the family. One example of this is the fabliau "Du prestre et d'Alison," in which a priest who wants to seduce a twelve-year-old girl (and offers her mother money for this) is tricked into having sex with a prostitute instead.[29]

Nevertheless, the prostitute is still not a completely accepted member of the community of the fabliaux, but she threatens that community through her greed rather than her sexuality.[30] In seeking to extort more than her legitimate wage from her clients, she becomes the quintessence of feminine sin and threatens to ruin men. In one fabliau the prostitute Richeut deliberately becomes pregnant in order to extort money from three of her clients, making each believe the child is his.[31] In the story of Boivin de Provins, the tables are turned and the greed of a madam "who knew more about trickery and guile than any woman that ever was" allows a customer to trick her.[32] The prostitute Alison, who helps foil the priest's attempt to buy a young girl's virginity, does so not to help the girl and her mother, nor for the love of sex or of trickery, but rather for the large sum of money he promises. The priest is thoroughly tricked: "God! how he will be deceived, / Because, for one penny, / he would have been able to have his pleasure / With the one who slept with him."[33] There is not much sympathy in this poem for the priest, who gets his just deserts. Nevertheless, the poem incorporates the theme of the prostitute's greed and her attempt to milk every last sou from her customer, along with the notion that all women are for sale. This notion is put more bluntly in the fabliau "Des trois boçus," where it has little to do with the plot: "[N]ever yet has God created / A girl whom money couldn't get."[34] Prostitutes are not the only greedy women (or men) in the fabliaux. The butt of the satire is often not the avaricious prostitute but the priest who wants to sleep with her, as in the story "Des Putains et des lecheors," which describes how God entrusted the clergy with the protection of whores: they took care of them so well that they spent all the church's goods on them.[35] Here the women's greed is only a backdrop to the lustfulness of the clergy. But those features of the story that are the backdrop rather than the main focus often indicate clearly the assumptions the society makes; and here the venality of the prostitute is central.

The venality of the prostitute comes to the fore in English literature also. In *Piers Plowman* the financial aspect of prostitution is clearly understood:

> Lechery loves not a poor man // for he hath but little silver
> Nor does he dine delicately // nor drink wine often.
> A straw for the stews! // They wouldn't stand for long
> If they had no other custom // But of poor people.[36]

Women of the brothels are used repeatedly as an example of people who are good-for-nothing: the plowman grows food for everyone no matter how worthless, "a waster or a wench of the stews."[37] Such a wench is unproductive yet venal, taking money for that which should not be bought. Yet the commerciality of sex in English medieval literature extends well beyond the prostitute.

The thirteenth-century French *Roman de la Rose,* which Chaucer knew and translated, made the connection between sex and exchange a close one.[38] In that work the Jealous Husband complains about the cost of his wife's clothing, which he finds only an encumbrance: "[T]rumpery that bothers me all day / And adds not to my pleasure in the night. / How profit I from it unpawned, unsold?" (ll. 8848–50). He asserts that her body "belongs / Alone to him who should your seignor be, / Who keeps you, feeds you, clothes you, buys you shoes" (ll. 9181–83), and complains of the expense of the clothing and jewelry he has provided for her. His stress on expense emphasizes her venality, as does his suspicion when she wears a dress he has not given her (ll. 9146–47). As a good bourgeois husband, he fears not so much his wife's lust as her greed, which puts him to such expense and may cause her to cuckold him. The Jealous Husband is so suspicious as to make himself ridiculous. But his words do not simply satirize the speaker; they condemn all women in terms familiar from a long misogynist tradition.

La Vieille ("Old Woman" or "Duenna"), whom Jean de Meun presents later in the *Roman*, also emphasizes the economic motive for women's sexual activity. A modern audience may sympathize with much of her discussion of feminine behavior—for example, she claims that wicked women in classical literature were made so by the men who deceived them—but even if she struck similar sympathetic chords in some medieval minds, La Vieille was not meant to be an admirable character.[39] In a masterpiece of misogynist speech put in the mouth of a woman, she describes how women tempt and deceive men. Her purpose in attracting lovers is strictly financial:

> . . . her care
> Should be to leave to none of them the means
> Of living well, and bring them one and all
> To such great poverty that each will die
> Most wretchedly in debt and leave her rich . . .
> (ll. 13440–44)

A woman should not love any man unless she gets gems or money in advance. The woman's accomplices, maids, relatives, and so on should also help fleece the lover by demanding gifts for themselves or by criticizing his insufficient generosity to his lady. The reason La Vieille presents is not simple greed but the fact that men often deceive women; you cannot trust promises, she says, you can only trust cash. The other reason, of course, is that, as Chaucer's Wife of Bath echoes, men value most what they pay most for: "The thing that's dearest bought is dearest held; / But what men get for nothing they despise" (ll. 13515–56).

La Vieille, the reader discovers, has not practiced what she preaches. In her youth she loved a man who mistreated and beat her; she nevertheless stayed with him and supported him until he had spent all her money. No wonder, after such bitter experience, that she counsels her protégées to place their faith in material things. But whatever her motivation, La Vieille's advice places sexuality firmly in the marketplace: "Just so a woman, mistress of all marts, / Who makes her bargains in pursuit of gain, / Should take her toll from all . . . " (ll. 13121–23). Women trade with what they have—their sexuality. This allows them to compete with men in the marketplace, but it also turns them into commodities. Men trade in objects; the objects in which women trade are themselves, even when they are trading with their own husbands.

Chaucer's Wife of Bath, who echoes La Vieille in many ways, is the most obvious and frequently cited example of the intersection of sex and money in fourteenth-century England. For her the two intersect in marriage, not in prostitution, yet she uses a vocabulary of sale and purchase, and connects greed with lust as motives for her marriages.[40] In wedding her five husbands, she has "picked out the best, / Both from their lower purse and from their chest" (ll. 44a–44b). The wife despoils her husband's money box as she drains him sexually.[41]

The concept of the "marriage debt" (that each spouse owed the other sexual access and had to engage in intercourse on demand) was not a result of the new monetary consciousness, for it was part of Christian doctrine all through the Middle Ages,[42] but the Wife endows it with a more pecuniary connotation through her desire to have her husband "both my debtor and my thrall" (l. 155) and her description of how she made her husbands work hard and give her land and money (ll. 201–6). "For winning [earning] would I all his lust endure" (l. 416): the Wife acknowledges that, like a prostitute, she exchanges sexual for financial favors. She even refers to the possibility of selling those favors outside of marriage when, in response to her husband's jealousy, she replies, "[I]f I would sell my *bele chose*, / I could walk as fresh as is a rose; / But I will keep it for your own tooth" (ll. 447–49). Her implication that she would be able to get more for sex on the open market than from her husband puts the gifts and clothes he buys her on the level of the profits of prostitution. She also makes this equation through the use of market metaphors: "With disdain we set out all our merchandise: / Great press at market makes dear wares, / And too great a bargain is but little prized. / This knoweth every woman that is wise" (ll. 521–24). When a woman is in great demand, she raises her metaphorical price. Men and women are adversaries in the market, each trying to fulfill his or her desire at the smallest expense. Women sell their merchandise, if not by exacting a price for specific sex acts, then in general by becoming men's possessions in the hope of receiving other possessions. The Wife of Bath's use of market metaphors for relations between the sexes may be Chaucer's way of satirizing the bourgeoisie or artisan class of his time for their acquisitive attitudes.[43] It also shows a thorough integration of economic thinking with sexual thinking.

In "The Shipman's Tale" Chaucer commodifies feminine sexuality both through the venal wife's adultery for money and through repeated puns on the word "taille," meaning both a tally or account and female genitalia. The merchant is very concerned with money, as one might expect from his calling, and as punishment he becomes the butt of the story. The tale's use of technical legal and financial terminology (found in none of the analogues on which Chaucer may have drawn) emphasizes its concern with money. The tale commodifies not just feminine sexuality but all interpersonal relations.[44] The merchant's close friend, a monk, is enamored of the merchant's wife, who complains to him about her husband's miserliness. She asks the monk to lend her one hundred francs to buy clothing appropriate to her station. The monk then goes to the merchant, who is about to leave on a journey, and asks him for a loan in the same amount. In the merchant's absence, "this fair wife accorded with sir John [the monk] / That for these hundred francs he should all night / Have her in his arms bolt upright [flat on her back] / And this accord performed was in deed" (ll. 314–17). The husband comes home, in need of ready cash. When he mentions this to the monk, the latter tells him that he gave the money back to the wife. When the husband asks his wife for the money, she says that she thought the monk had given it to her not for her husband but to do her honor. If the husband wants the money repaid, she says,

> You have slacker debtors than I!
> For I will pay you well and readily
> From day to day, and if so be I fail,
> I am your wife; score it upon my taille [tail or tally]. . . .
> You shall my joly body have as pledge;
> By God, I will not pay you but abed.
>
> (ll. 413–16, 423–24)

Chaucer concludes the tale with another pun: "God us send / Tailling enough until our lives' end" (ll. 433–34).

Chaucer both implicitly and explicitly equates all unfaithful wives (and even faithful ones) with prostitutes. The Wife of Bath and the merchant's wife in "The Shipman's Tale" are willing to exchange sexual favors for gifts or cash, whether with their husbands or other men, and in "The Miller's Tale" Absalon at least expects that Alisoun will do the same, though in fact she chooses a different lover, one who does not pay.[45] Chaucer also presents, in the fragmentary "Cook's Tale," a commercial prostitute: her husband is connected with a criminal underworld of gambling and riotous living. She "kept for appearance / a shop, and swived for her sustenance" (ll. 4421–22). The difference between this woman and the other three respectable wives, who nonetheless can be bought, may be seen in class terms: one sells herself for her support, the others for luxuries. Yet none are called whores, and no sharp distinction is drawn between them in moral terms. Chaucer, in fact, has another of his pilgrims explain, in "The Manciple's Tale," that

> There is no difference, truly,
> Between a wife of high degree,
> If of her body dishonest she be,
> And a poor wench, other than this—
> If so be they both do amiss—
> But that the gentlewoman, in estate above,
> Shall be called his lady, as in love;
> And, since that other is a poor woman,
> She shall be called his wench or his leman.
> And, God knows, my own dear brother,
> Men lay the one as low as lies the other.
>
> (ll. 212–22)

Chaucer's main audience—the lower gentry, as well as to some extent both the court and the upper bourgeoisie—are here being told by the cynical and embittered Manciple that class distinction makes no difference, that all women can be whores.[46] This message is conveyed in a way that emphasizes the bonds between men—"my own dear brother"—against women. Indeed, the lady who is the object of noble love or the woman who marries a yeoman may be as involved in a system of exchange as a lord's concubine or a common prostitute, just at a different price.

The monetary world is similarly pervasive in *The Book of Margery Kempe*, an autobiography from the early fifteenth century. It consists of Margery's own words (dictated to and probably edited by an amanuensis). Monetary language permeates it, as it does the language of Chaucer's fictional Wife of Bath. Margery herself, the daughter of a mayor of King's Lynn, came from the world of the bourgeoisie. She was a failed entrepreneur several times over. Thinking in cash terms crops up throughout Margery's autobiography, as she records her expenses on pilgrimage, expresses her fear of being robbed of her money, accounts for the alms she is given.[47] The most direct relation between money and sexuality appears in Margery's attempt to free herself from her husband's demands for sex in payment of the "marriage debt." He agrees on three conditions, one of which is that she will pay all his debts.[48] This text by a woman presents her not selling but buying back the right to sexual access to her person, something that only a woman of the bourgeoisie with access to money of her own could do. Whether buying or selling, feminine sexuality, even the wife's sexual relations with her husband, is still subject to the market.[49]

More popular literature such as ballads also emphasized the importance of money to women's sexual behavior. A fifteenth-century ballad of Sir Penny is explicit about what money can do: "With Penny men may entice women, / Be they never so strong of will, / So oft may it be seen."[50] Even popular lyrics on the common theme of the young girl seduced by the cleric could make the assumption of monetary exchange:

> Sir John to me is proffering
> For his pleasure right well to pay,
> And in my box he puts his offering—
> I have no power to say him nay.
> . . . .
> Sir John gives me glittering rings,
> With pretty pleasure to assay—
> Furs of the finest, with other thing:
> I have no power to say him nay.[51]

This poem operates on the assumption that a young woman may be had for a few gifts, especially by a priest wise in the ways of the world. Another lyric, also in the first person, describes how a serving maid's lover buys her ale on Sunday to quench her thirst, then has sex with her and gets her pregnant.[52] The woman is depicted as desiring at least the man's company if not the sex. She is not given a commercial or avaricious motive, but exchange is nonetheless part of the process.

In sum, the connection of sexuality, greed, and commerce permeates the view of gender relations presented in late medieval English as well as Continental literature. If prostitutes in real life were marginalized by their treatment under the law, the institution of prostitution was integral to medieval English culture's concept of what it was to be a woman, for all women threatened to introduce sex into the world of commerce. The prostitute presented that threat most forcefully, but she was not so different from the married woman.

The Prostitute and the Community

If whoredom was not just an elite name for typical working-class sexual behavior, and if commerciality was just the extreme case of a characteristic attributed to all women, what was the effect of these beliefs on the actual relations of prostitutes with the other members of the community in which they lived? This is perhaps the most difficult to answer of all the questions posed in this volume. The evidence points in several directions, but the overall picture seems to be one of day-to-day pragmatic acceptance of individual prostitutes coupled with a generalized resentment of prostitutes as a group for the disorder they caused. The legal regulation of prostitutes and the attendant stigmatization cannot help but have had an effect on their relations with others. The use of sexual insults in defamation cases shows that "whore" had serious negative connotations. But prostitutes, especially those who practiced prostitution on a casual basis, were not a separate subculture, nor were they limited to one particular geographic area; they inevitably formed part of the life of the entire community.

Nonetheless, the presence of prostitutes in a community could cause significant disruption. The phrase "to the nuisance of her neighbors" found in presentments is conventional and formulaic, but the juries of presentment would have included some of those neighbors (chosen from the higher ranks of local society), and it was they who decided what behavior fell within the formula. Some references to disruption caused by whores go beyond the formulaic; the details are specific enough to indicate that neighbors found brothels offensive as focuses of disorder. Angelo Taylor's stewhouse was accused of causing "many quarrels, beatings, and hues and cries at night." Several "malefactors and disturbers of the peace" harbored at Petronilla Bednot's stew "about midnight, on several nights, when the neighbors living thereabouts were in their beds, came with sticks to their windows and beat on them maliciously and said to the neighbors, 'You who are in there, come out and be beaten!'" In King's Lynn, Henry Cook and Nicholas Wick quarreled when the former interrupted the latter with three prostitutes; the incident led to Henry's death from a stab wound in his cheek.[53]

Some people reacted to houses of prostitution in their neighborhoods by taking direct action. In 1305 the prior of Holy Trinity in Aldgate ward was accused of trespassing in the house of his neighbor; he responded that because it had been presented at the Wardmote that prostitutes lived in the house, and the owner had not evicted them, "the Beadle gathered the neighbours, including the Prior &c., and removed the doors and windows." After the prior won his case, the inquest jury was ordered to eject the prostitutes, who apparently had remained there doorless. Thomas, vicar of St. Sepulchre, claimed that the doors of the butcher William Cock in Cock's Lane had been torn down for identical reasons.[54] In each instance the neighbors did not take action spontaneously but rather acted at the instigation of an ecclesiastical institution; nevertheless, they were ready enough to join in. Such hostility toward prostitutes in the neighborhood could also be used as an excuse for crimes against them. In 1366 some men charged with breaking into the house of Joan Upholdstere pleaded that she was a "woman of evil condition [who] received men of ill fame" and they were members of the watch and were simply trying to catch her with men in her house. They were acquitted.[55]

As this example of members of the watch exploiting their position to rob a woman indicates, the prostitutes' relations with the local law enforcement officers were often ambiguous. The duty to arrest them must have caused some animosity—in 1298, for example, Christina of Gravesend had her lover beat the sergeant who came to summon her—but it is likely that the pattern of bribes noted in 1344, when the beadle of the ward of Farringdon Without "maintained the whores living in his ward and took payment from them so that the said whores could practice their immorality there," was repeated elsewhere.[56]

Prostitutes who operated independently or on a more casual basis were perhaps less offensive to and more integrated into their community than those who worked in brothels. They interacted with other women, even giving them information about the sexual prowess of potential marriage partners. In 1515 Robert Harding of London testified that Katherine Worsley, who had been accused of whoredom, "reported to divers women of the said parish that certain young men which were in contemplation of marriage with them had not what men should have to please them and that she knew it for a truth, by reason whereof the said men were refused by the said women, to their great hurt." Harding was afraid that Worsley "should have made like report of him to the said rich widow whom he wooed, by reason whereof the said widow should have in like manner refused him." It is not clear in this case whether Worsley was actually taking money for sex, but she clearly had such an unsavory reputation that people labeled her a whore.[57] The incident shows Harding's fear of a feminine conspiracy against him. He is concerned that the widow will turn against him not because he has been having sex with someone else but because of his inadequate performance, an indication that women demanded some degree of sexual satisfaction from their husbands (as the church indeed recognized with the doctrine of the marriage debt). Even if the circulation of such gossip among women was a figment of Harding's imagination, there was evidently a realistic possibility that Worsley might fall into conversation with the rich widow he was planning to marry. In other words, her reputation did not result in her being ostracized by respectable women of the community.

Occasional though rare testaments indicate that at least the wealthier prostitutes and brothelkeepers also thought of themselves as respectable citizens. In her 1494 will Alice Stapleton, a convicted brothelkeeper in Suffolk, left money to the local church for a canopy over the altar, gowns to some of her women friends, and to a boy (who may have been the son of one of her friends) six shillings eightpence for his school fees.[58] A pious bequest to the church, money to send a boy to school: Stapleton can hardly be considered a member of a counterculture or an underclass. The fact that a brothelkeeper was willing to offer such donations indicates that she shared many of the values of the dominant culture. Canonists and theologians had been debating since the twelfth century the extent to which charitable donations from whores were acceptable.[59] Unfortunately, hardly any identifiable prostitutes left wills that have survived. Either they did not own significant property to bequeath, or they were too alienated from the ecclesiastical court system to make a last testament.[60]

Prostitutes were on rare occasions respected enough to serve in an official capacity in the church courts, although not ostensibly by virtue of the fact that they were prostitutes. When one party to a marriage sought an annulment on grounds of impotence or frigidity, the truth of the matter had to be investigated, and prostitutes were called into service to do this (see fig. 1). In one case a witness testified that she had "exposed her naked breasts, and with her hands warmed at the said fire, she held and rubbed the penis and testicles of the said John. And she embraced and frequently kissed the same John . . . the whole time aforesaid the said penis was scarcely three inches long, . . . remaining without any increase or decrease." The witness and her companions cursed the man "for presuming to marry a young woman, defrauding her if he could not serve and please her better than that." In another case, however, witnesses testified that the man's penis was "large enough for any woman living in this world."[61] Although the women who undertook this examination have been identified by P. J. P. Goldberg as prostitutes on the basis of their appearing elsewhere in the church court records, their depositions did not identify them as such. In fact, they had to affirm that they were respectable women and of good character, and their oaths to this effect were not challenged.[62] Canon law required "women of good opinion, worthy of faith, and expert in the works of marriage" to inspect the woman in impotence cases; it made no mention of the inspection of the man.[63] But these oaths of good character were necessary to fulfill a formal requirement and do not reflect how prostitutes were viewed in general. The fact that they could be regarded as expert witnesses at all, however, accords them some

Fig. 1. In a case of annulment of marriage on grounds of impotence, two women examine a man's genitals. In England prostitutes at least sometimes performed this task. From a late thirteenth-century manuscript of Gratian's *Decretum*, probably northern French or Flemish. Walters Art Gallery, Baltimore, MS W.133, fol. 277r. *(Reproduced by permission of the Walters Art Gallery, Baltimore.)*

degree of respect. Still, we must note that this was limited to sexual cases, in which their presumed lack of shame as well as their experience made them the best choice.

Being a prostitute, or having been one, could in other cases detract from the validity of one's testimony. In order to impeach witnesses in church courts, one could bring testimony that, for example, they were "poor, low, common, and wretched persons, of evil fame, dishonest conversation, and guilty life and untrustworthy opinions, infamous in law and deed, and suspicious persons." One woman was criticized as an untrustworthy witness because she had lived with a man out of wedlock for many years and had had children by him; another because she had had sex with a priest "and has carnally known many other married and unmarried men in adulterous and fornicating embraces"; another because she had had children by three different men; others simply as common fornicators and adulteresses. The London, Canterbury, and York church courts all heard evidence impeaching witnesses on these sorts of grounds.[64]

Although male witnesses were not often impugned on the basis of their own sexual activities, they could be discredited by accusations of bawdry. In one London matrimonial case witnesses on either side disparaged one another: William Green testified that John Waldrey was a common bawd who "kept an inn of whores and bawds at the Stews side at the sign of the Rose and the Fleur de Lys and the Tower, and in these houses kept public immorality, living by wicked deeds and whoredom," and that he lived with a whore who was not his wife; another man then testified that William Green "had spent time at a brothel at the Stews side promoting immorality between many men and women and does not care of what sort they are as long as they pay him," and that he had been the keeper of the Hart's Horn, had married a whore who worked there, had kept a public brothel and then moved to another inn where he employed whores as servants. (Green's own testimony identified him as "the king's constable at the Stews side.") Another witness was said to have "two tenements at the Stews side in which common bawds and receivers of whores live," and to have provided them with bed furniture and linens. In another case a couple were accused of testifying for money and impeached as unreliable since they had moved from parish to parish and ward to ward eight years before "because of the bawdry or whoredom had and used in their homes."[65] Bawds were the sort of people suspected of being available to give suborned testimony. Yet Thomas Togood, a stewholder, was able to testify in another matrimonial case without mentioning his occupation, and the opposing party did not mention it either.[66]

The fact that the testimony of a prostitute or other sexually deviant woman was not considered acceptable would seem to point to her degraded status; but some women who clearly were practicing prostitutes were able to find enough respected women to act as compurgators in the church courts that they were able repeatedly to escape conviction. This was the case with both Isabella Wakefield and Margaret Clay of York (see pp. 66–68). Margaret Valentine, accused in the London church courts of adultery with a beadle, allegedly claimed that satisfied customers would serve as her compurgators: "I will please a beadle, a sergeant, a yeoman, and a summoner, for they will bear me out against all courts." She did in fact purge herself, both of adultery and of making the statement.[67] Of course, it is impossible from our distance to pronounce on the guilt or innocence of parties in medieval court cases. People may have been charged on the basis of gossip and then rightly succeeded in purging themselves.[68] Nonetheless, when we find the same person presented year after year for offenses involving commercial sex, we may assume that she was a practitioner and that her successful purgation reflects local networks of influence rather than any lack of culpability.[69]

Although prostitutes were accepted to some degree within the dominant culture, to the extent that their activity was criminalized they became part of a criminal class or subculture. But they were criminals because their activity was against the law, not because commercial sex has an inherent affinity with theft and violence. It is true, however, that the legal status of their work threw them into unsavory company. This was true of broth-elkeepers as well. In borough and manorial courts leet, presentments for whoredom were juxtaposed not only with commercial offenses but also with offenses involving disturbing the peace, like assault. Indeed, disturbing the peace was part of the formula for presenting people for keeping brothels or harboring prostitutes and, though less frequently, for practicing prostitution itself: for example, "keeps a brothel and supports brawlers and vagabonds in her house, to the nuisance of her neighbors," or "keeps and promotes immorality and a brothel in her own house between divers men and women, against the peace."[70] The formulaic nature of these statements reveals nothing about the nature of the particular disturbance; they tell us only that any brothel was considered to be a disturbance against the neighbors and the common peace, and that this was in fact what people found threatening about it.

Those who kept brothels or received prostitutes in their homes or rented to them were often also accused of receiving thieves or vagrants, or of promoting gambling or other illicit activities.[71] The city of London's clerk in 1281 could lump together a group of men arrested "for divers trespasses, as for homicides, robberies, beatings, assaults, and for being vagrants by night after curfew in the [c]ity with swords and bucklers, and for instituting games near the [c]ity and keeping brothels."[72] Not only was receiving and harboring prostitutes connected with the harboring of thieves, but prostitutes were also connected with other crimes—in Exeter, for example, with receiving stolen goods. In King's Lynn a number of people were convicted of whoredom or bawdry in the context of multiple offenses: regrating (reselling), night-walking, eavesdropping, dice playing, harboring thieves and whores, and failing to appear at the leet.[73] The connection of whores with scolds—the courts often grouped them together—further indicates that they formed part of a subculture of disorderly women. The same women, in fact, were often accused of both whoredom or procuring and scolding (see pp. 138–40). What was seen as promiscuity, whether sexual or verbal, threatened the order of society, and their activity placed these women on its fringes.

The degraded status of the prostitute in the eyes of the community meant that accusations of whoredom might be used against women who were resented for other reasons. This may have been the case in the 1423 accusation of Maud Sheppster of London, that "[she] holds open shop and retails, and is not a freewoman [admitted to citizenship and free trade in the city]; also she is a strumpet to more than one and a bawd also."[74] Perhaps she was a prostitute, or at least had multiple sex partners; perhaps not. Whatever the truth of the accusation, it probably would not have been brought had there been no concern over her commercial activities. The case of Joan Grubbe in 1311 in the town of Ramsey may be similar: she was charged with "being a thief of geese and hens and stealing her neighbors' geese, hens and dregs, to the value of 10d., and for being nothing more than a common whore."[75]

The prostitute may not necessarily have been readily identifiable by the community, whether because her activity was not public or because people were not quite sure whether that activity constituted whoredom or not. The vagueness of the line between whore and non-whore appears in a pair of cases from Ipswich. Hugh Moon was accused of raping Alice Hill, and in the same court session Alice Hill was accused of being a common whore with Hugh Moon and others.[76] Several other cases also follow this pattern. Probably Alice complained of rape and Hugh responded that she had been willing, which involved accusing her of being a whore. The jury of presentment did not know which offense to present. The continuum good woman–whore–prostitute was difficult to divide clearly into segments, and it was not immediately apparent to the community, from which the jury was drawn, where any particular woman fell. This would, of course, have been especially true in the case of casual prostitutes.

The extent to which prostitutes, or women who had been accused of whoredom, were able to marry, or the extent to which their children were accepted in the community would be good indications of their degree of marginalization, but we have no strong evidence on these matters. Certainly a number did marry and were not seen as tainted for life; others remained in the trade but did well out of it and were respected by their neighbors. Those women in particular who did not spend their whole lives as prostitutes were not excluded from society, although they may have remained marginal in the sense that they were among the poorest and most vulnerable, the nearest to the margin of subsistence.

Saints and Sinners

Like law, like secular literature, the teachings of the medieval church did not promote a unitary understanding of what it meant to be a whore. The whore's fundamental distinguishing characteristic was sexual immorality, yet the connection with financial exchange was pervasive enough to give all references to whoredom, indeed all considerations of female sexuality, the taint of venality.

All of the late medieval church's teachings about prostitution and about whoredom must be seen against the background of a general hostility to sexuality and a widespread misogyny. This chapter first presents this background, then focuses on medieval analyses of the sin of lust in particular. I then move on to the specific discussions and representations of commercial sex in medieval pastoral texts and saints' lives and analyze how these texts constructed the image of the whore. The focus is especially on negative attitudes toward women based on their sexuality. I do not argue that the church's view of women was univocally negative, nor that women internalized this negative view. Medieval culture was not monolithically hostile to women; queens, holy women, even ordinary wives and mothers could be respected and revered. And women developed their own spirituality which affirmed and valorized their connection with the flesh.[1] The antifeminist tradition discussed here was only one part of a complex mix of attitudes that composed medieval constructions of gender. But it was an important part, certainly the most important part for understanding the place of the whore in medieval culture, and it was expressed in ways that affected women's lives.

Some of the material discussed in this chapter is *about* prostitutes, but very little is directed specifically *at* prostitutes. There are no examples of English clergy who took it upon themselves to preach to and convert prostitutes, as there are for other countries.[2] In part this is because late medieval England gave rise to no popular urban preachers like Bernardino of Siena—at least none whose sermons survive. The pastoral works that circulated were far more concerned with the danger prostitutes posed to others and the risk of women's falling into prostitution than they were with the condition of the prostitutes themselves. Overall, the tendency of the culture's images of the prostitute was not sympathetic.

The Church, Gender, and Sin

The church's teachings during the Middle Ages conveyed consistently negative attitudes toward sexuality generally, which tended to spill over into attitudes about women. The origins of these attitudes, whether in Jewish or Hellenic asceticism or elsewhere, need not concern us here; we need only recognize that by the late Middle Ages sexual desire was almost universally condemned within orthodox teaching as a force destructive of social order and threatening to individual salvation.[3] Sexual activity outside of marriage was wrong, and even within marriage most authorities held it proper for reproductive purposes only; some considered it sinful to take any pleasure even in licit, potentially reproductive sex.[4] This aspect of the church's teaching was not on the face of it gender-biased; both men and women sinned in sexual desire and behavior. But since for most of the male writers women were the objects of desire, women came to take the blame for arousing that desire.

Medieval writers added weight to their arguments by drawing on earlier authorities, especially the church fathers, many of whom had directed their attacks against marriage. They wanted to persuade men to the celibate life, and hostility toward women was a by-product of that goal. Even though condemnation of women was not their main purpose, however, the arguments they used to dissuade men from marriage were certainly misogynous.[5] The most important patristic text in the medieval church's attack on women was the tract "Against Jovinian" by Saint Jerome, the fourth-century theologian, ascetic, and translator of the Bible into Latin. Part of this text was a diatribe against marriage, including condemnatory language about women. In the context in which he wrote, Jerome's attack on women had its logic.[6] It was part of a general criticism of the flesh, and did not deny women a spiritual worth so long as they repudiated the flesh. Jerome's particular reasons for attacking women in this tract, however, were irrelevant to the transmission of his writings, which in subsequent centuries did women a great deal of harm. The portions that medieval authors excerpted and repeated were understood not in the context of Jerome's purposes but in the new context in which they were presented, with Jerome serving to authorize them.

The medieval repetition of Jerome's attack on marriage and therefore on women was situated largely in the monastery, at least through the twelfth century. To monastic authors, women were both a sexual temptation in themselves and a symbol of all the temptations of the flesh that a monk had to flee. Hostility toward sexuality could easily shift into hostility toward women. In the late Middle Ages a spate of writings outside the monastery, both antifeminist in general and antimatrimonial in particular, drew on Jerome as well. Antimatrimonial literature may have been particularly promoted in the universities. As all-male institutions with a mainly clerical student body, they had an interest in seeing their clerks remain and progress in orders.[7]

The antifeminist tradition found its way into the public consciousness through preaching. A number of the most common exempla, tales told by preachers to make moral points as well as to enliven their sermons, came more or less directly from Jerome's tract. Texts like John of Wales's *Communiloquium* and the *Alphabet of Tales* also repeated Jerome's arguments against marriage, and by extension against women, almost verbatim.[8] Preachers to the medieval laity were not trying to persuade people not to marry. Nevertheless, they made the same points against women and told the same stories about sinful feminine behavior as those told to celibates. If this did not discourage marriage, it certainly affected attitudes toward women both married and unmarried.

Antimatrimonial literature was not, however, the exclusive rule, even within ecclesiastical discourse. A fourteenth-century tract, "On Wedded Men and Wives, and Their Children Also," for example, although it still agreed that virginity was preferable to marriage, praised marriage as an honorable institution and criticized those who gave it up to become priests.[9] Many sermons and other religious texts also presented far more positive images of women. The church venerated women as virgin saints and martyrs, and praised the virtues of both nuns and worthy matrons.[10] The emphasis here on misogynistic aspects of the church's teaching because these are relevant to the development of attitudes toward prostitution should not obscure the existence of other aspects that may have mitigated them. The more favorable representations, however, tended to focus on individual women and not on women as a group. Misogyny was not the sum total of the church's attitude toward women, but it constituted a significant part. Not only did it reside in the tracts of theologians but it was also copiously transmitted to the laity.

By the thirteenth century the church was making a concerted effort to transmit its doctrine to the whole community of the faithful. To remedy the problem of lay people's poor understanding of the faith, the Fourth Lateran Council's decrees (1215) required regular, competent preaching to the laity as well as annual confession by all Christians. In England, from 1281 on, parish priests were required to preach in English, four times a year, the six main points of Christian religion: creed, commandments, works of mercy, virtues, vices, and sacraments. The issuance of this decree did not necessarily mean that parish priests were not preaching actively before this, but it did mean that the archbishop believed that important doctrine was being neglected.[11]

Franciscan and Dominican friars, members of orders founded in part to supplement the activities of parish priests in teaching the laity, also preached in towns and villages.[12] They wrote a variety of sermon aids and model sermons for the use of their brothers in the order and for any priest who wanted to preach.[13] Some preaching aids were compendia of quotations (*florilegia*) not only from the Bible but from all sorts of useful authorities, including the pagan classics.[14] Other compilations grouped together edifying tales or exempla. There were also treatises on the matters required to be preached—the seven deadly sins, the seven sacraments, the ten commandments —which could be used in the construction of sermons.

Sermons, and devotional works which would have been used by preachers in preparing sermons, are worth studying for the ideas to which medieval men and women were regularly exposed. The messages those men and women took with them from sermons and related literature undoubtedly varied widely. The fourteenth-century Dominican John of Bromyard commented on the preferences of different groups for different sorts of sermons: "It pleases men when they preach against women, and the converse. It pleases husbands, when they preach against the pomp of wives, who perhaps spend half of their goods on their ornaments. It pleases wives, when they preach against husbands, who spend their goods in the tavern. . . ."[15] But because of the power men wielded over women, sermons that changed or reinforced their views of women had great potential to touch women's lives. Women, too, may have accepted these teachings to some extent and interpreted their own experiences in that context.

Exempla are particularly useful in analyzing popular mentalities and the ways in which the laity would have received the church's teachings. These tales were inserted in sermons to make points in ways that would catch the audience's attention. They were meaningful to the listeners because they depicted situations from everyday life. The majority of the exempla that late medieval preachers used can be traced to learned sources; compilers got them not from contemporary folk culture but from other texts.[16] When the same tales are told century after century, we may attribute them to the literary tradition and not the tellers' actual experience. Yet the tales would not have been retold nor criticisms repeated if they were not consistent with their tellers' view of the world, and the ideas were not less meaningful to those who read and heard them because they were conventional. To be appreciated, exempla had to be adjusted to fit the social relations of their day; they thus represent the adaptation of theological ideas to popular mentalities.[17] What people respond to—what they find humorous or interesting, poignant or frightening—varies over time and space, and the compilers and preachers must have chosen their exempla accordingly.

Teaching also reached the laity in written form.[18] During the fourteenth and fifteenth centuries, a number of didactic treatises and devotional texts in the vernacular were written and copied for the use of the laity, and many of these also found their way into early printed editions.[19] Handbooks on sin were used by preachers from the thirteenth century on, but could also be read by clerics, monks, or lay people preparing for confession.[20] For example, the *Destructorium Vitiorum*, or "Destroyer of Vice," compiled in 1429 by Alexander Anglicus or Carpenter, circulated not only in England but also on the Continent as a handbook of sin in general and the seven deadly sins in particular.[21] It was original neither in its conception nor in its exempla, but the large number of early printed editions indicate its popularity. Another widely used text, in English rather than Latin, was *The Pricke of Conscience*, a poem that survives in 114 manuscripts, indicating the growing lay use of vernacular devotional works in the fourteenth and fifteenth centuries.[22]

The overall effect of the availability of these model sermons, compendia, and other pastoral works was the development of a common pool of moral teaching, "a truly mass literature which in one form or other reached absolutely everybody."[23] Different preachers who used a given sermon aid would never preach exactly the same sermon, but preachers who used the same or similar aids would be working within the same conceptual vocabulary, illustrating the same themes.[24] The teaching of the church was presented more uniformly than it would have been if every parish priest were drafting his sermons on his own. Thus, although it may be difficult to determine what individual common people were thinking in the Middle Ages, we can get a good idea of the building blocks available to them to construct their mental worlds. We can look at the teachings presented to the laity as a crucial source for the medieval understanding of feminine sexuality. As G. R. Owst noted in 1933, medieval preaching popularized and perpetuated, even if it did not create, a stereotype of women that influenced Chaucer, Shakespeare, and indeed modern thought as well.[25]

Vice, and woman's vices in particular, were not the only subjects for sermons; the primary concern of medieval preachers was belief, not behavior. When preachers used stories involving women as tools to speak about some other issue, however, their assumptions about women peered through. To take one example, in the Gesta Romanorum, a popular book of moralized tales used by preachers and exemplists, women were often allegorized as the human soul, in many cases unfaithful wives as the soul unfaithful to God. The use of allegory does not obscure the fact that the unfaithful wife was a common theme.[26] Constant presentation of women as equivalent to the sinful soul, or to the flesh, would have had its effect on the audience.[27]

One could argue that if preachers presented examples of good women along with examples of bad, they were not misogynists; if they presented examples of both male and female sinners, they did so because they felt that sin was the human condition, not because they were anti-woman. There are three answers to this objection. First, most of the good women are individual examples, whereas the criticisms of women come not only by way of individual example but also in the form of general attacks on the sex. One collection of exempla gives tales under the following rubrics, provided by either the compiler or a copyist: "That one should flee from the countenance of women," "On the enchantments of women," "Against the false tears of women," "Against women," "Against women who always swear the contrary," "On the heat of women," and "Against evil wives." Nicole Bozon titles his chapters, for example, "That the society of women be fled," "Against the wanton," "That younger adorned women are to be avoided," "Of the power of women," "That it is not safe alone with a woman," and "That virgins are corrupted through the counsel of shameless old women."[28] Men are not considered under such categories;[29] they are presented as wicked individuals or wicked because they are human, not because they are men. There are few blanket condemnations of men as snares of the devil. The second answer is that "balance" does not mean lack of bias. Someone who today stated that Jews are grasping but also intelligent, or that blacks are lazy but good athletes, would be considered not "neutral" or "balanced" but anti-Semitic or racist. It is not the question of whether the good or bad qualities attributed to a particular group preponderate that determines whether prejudice against that group exists; it is simply the fact of stereotyping. The third response is that the negative tends to stick in people's minds. Praise of individual pious women is not as vivid or as memorable or as generally applicable as polemics against the group.

The important question here, though, is not whether medieval preaching, and thus the teaching of the church as it reached the general public, was misogynist overall—surely everyone can agree that it included misogynistic elements—but rather what particular negative views of women it presented. In late medieval England those negative views primarily concerned sexuality. Women were lustful and therefore dangerous to men. All the other criticism of women ultimately came down to the sexual threat that they presented, and even good women presented that threat, despite their intentions.

Of all the deadly sins (sloth, avarice, gluttony, envy, wrath, lust, and pride), that of lust was most closely connected with women.[30] A list of twelve abuses of the age included "a wise man without works, an old man without religion, an adolescent without obedience, a rich man without alms, a woman without modesty, a lord without virtue; a contentious Christian, a proud pauper, a wicked king, a negligent bishop, the masses without discipline, a people without law."[31] The abuse to which women were particularly susceptible was specifically sexual. When works of art depicted sinners, lust was exemplified by a woman more frequently than were the other sins (although it also was sometimes represented as a pair of lovers). Often lust appeared as a woman with her breasts gnawed by serpents.[32]

One way to determine the association of particular sins with women is simply by counting examples, and here lust clearly predominates. John of Bromyard's *Summa Praedicantium*, compiled around the middle of the fourteenth century, is a good choice for such a count because it is the most comprehensive encyclopedia of exempla and other sermon material, unoriginal but widely used.[33] Out of the 1,300 exempla, about 14 percent include female characters. Women make up 13 percent of the avaricious characters, about the same as their percentage of total vicious characters; this is also true of the other sins to which Bromyard devotes fewer exempla. In the case of lust, however, women make up fully half the sinners, despite the fact that so few total exempla include them. This overrepresentation may not be surprising, since lust so often involves two people; but even in the exempla that mention only one sinner, women make up half the examples.[34]

Lust, then, was the woman's sin par excellence, not only in Bromyard's work but in other sources as well. Women did not figure as importantly in most texts as did men, but when they did, they were disproportionately lustful. Even when it was men who committed the sin of lust, they were frequently tempted by women or demons in the shape of women; and though these tales may not have explicitly shown women sinning, they reinforced the medieval tendency to blame women for tempting men rather than men for lusting after women.[35] These tales may originally have been intended for the monastery, to make the monks understand that threats to chastity come from the devil, but they were being told to the laity in the late Middle Ages.

The particular attribution of lust to women was in part an effort to displace onto them the responsibility for the sins of men who could not control their own temptations. The placing of blame also indicated a real fear of women—that they would disrupt the established order of things by leading men astray, by causing bastards to inherit, by destroying clerical celibacy, by polluting the nunnery. The arena of sexuality was the only one in which women could compete with men in importance—their degree of control over money, for example, was so much less than men's that it is not surprising they did not appear as disproportionately sinful in regard to the getting and hoarding of wealth—and it was the one in which men most feared they would not be able to control them. The treatment of prostitutes in the Middle Ages must be seen in this context.

Among the various sexual offenses attributed to women, adultery was the most common. Adultery is not necessarily the focal point of the stories, but adulterous wives were taken for granted as backdrops. Even when adultery was presented as a masculine sin, the implication was that wives were generally available for adultery.[36] Some exemplum collections gave very detailed versions, which could be elaborated in sermons to present vivid and horrific images of lustful women. One of the most common tales is that of the priest who has a vision of his dead mother in hell tormented by vermin, particularly snakes or toads hanging from her breasts in token of the adulterine sons she had suckled there (paralleling many earlier artistic depictions of personified lust). One fifteenth-century version of this tale adds that her head was tormented "because of the whorish ornamenting of my hair" and her lips and tongue "because of vain speech and adulterous kisses."[37] The story connects women's adornment and garrulousness with sexual immorality; whereas other versions of this tale stress the harm adultery does to legitimate succession, this version stresses the lustfulness.

Priests' partners were among the women most harshly criticized for their sexual behavior, though sermons rebuked the priests, too: for example, Bromyard, the Franciscan Nicholas Philip, and the monk Robert Rypon all sharply attacked priests who polluted themselves by embracing whores.[38] They failed to distinguish between prostitutes who had sex with priests and women who lived with priests as wives. Even when the exempla blamed women's greed, the fact that their greed led them to sexual irregularity induced writers to assume that their more serious sin was lust: Bromyard placed ten of his fourteen stories about the damnation and punishment of priests' sexual partners in his chapter on lust.

By condemning the women who lived with priests more than they condemned the priests themselves, the stories reinforced the theme of women's lust. A fifteenth-century handbook for parish priests, discussing penances to be enjoined for sexual offenses, states: "If any [priest] commit fornication or adultery with a woman through sudden chance or by the woman's manipulation and not of his own purpose or deliberation, then much less penance should be enjoined to him."[39] From a modern point of view the priest would be the more guilty partner, since the woman has no vows to break; but to late medieval writers she bore at least equal if not greater guilt.

These tales cautioned men (not only priests) that lust was not without its financial price, and that women were only after their money. Bromyard repeated a story about a woman who weeps because she has not been able to despoil her priestly lover of his cloak. In another tale a priest has to choose between his partner and his benefice, and chooses her; she immediately rejects him because she can no longer profit by him.[40] The emphasis on women's greed thus places the sexually irregular woman—even the life companion of a priest—in a class with the professional prostitute. Women may have lived with or been supported by priests because of a real financial need if they could not find husbands, but the tales emphasize sexual immorality.

In Bromyard's view even women who were raped were guilty of sexual sin. In one tale a woman charges her attacker with rape; the judge tells the defendant to take the plaintiff's money from her. She fights for it tooth and nail, and he is unable to seize it. The judge then declares that if she had fought for her chastity as fiercely as she did for her money, she would have been able to keep it. Bromyard classifies the story under lust, implying that the woman's own desires prompted her to invite the rape. The tale also illustrates women's venality: in another version told by the influential French Dominican Étienne de Bourbon, the woman agrees to have sex with the man for money, then later charges him with rape.[41]

Women's lust, in the view of pastoral writers, grew not only from their greed but also from their pride. Discussions of pride in appearance, clothing, and ornaments were closely connected to lust. Bromyard often cross-referenced his sections on lust, ornament, and beauty. He and others accused women of adorning themselves in order to tempt men. This criticism was not leveled exclusively at women. Robert Rypon noted in a sermon: "[M]any men have their clothes so short that they barely hide their shameful parts, and certainly, as it appears, to show women their members so as to provoke lust. Similarly, too, some women artificially decorate themselves by painting their faces to please the eyes of men. Indeed, those who do so have the true likeness of whores."[42] Although both men and women were criticized for their vanity in dress, however, exempla on the subject decidedly overrepresented women.[43]

Moralists also criticized excess in clothing on the grounds that it involved too much attention to the things of this world (hence pride), that it looked ridiculous, and that it wasted money.[44] But these objections were more commonly used against men; in the case of women the criticism was generally connected with lust. One sermon compared display of the body to a tavern-keeper's setting out his sign to attract customers to drink the wine of lust: "And doubtless many people are steered oft, yea! and assent to lust by the wanton array of women. And such assenting is deadly sin, and they that are steerers to these sins are the devil's underlings."[45] John Waldeby, an Augustinian friar from Yorkshire, wrote that not only do women insult their creator by attempting to improve upon his work, but also they "exhibit and offer their bodies as weapons of the Devil, with which the souls of men are killed."[46]

Even if a woman did not intend to kindle lust by means of her clothing, she was still to blame for letting the devil use her as his tool. As an owner was responsible for the deeds of horned beasts, so a soul was responsible for the deeds of a horned body, that is, the ornaments that tempted others to sin (one of the items most criticized was the horned headdress).[47] Bromyard relates two tales of women who pray for disfigurement because men are attracted to their beauty, and another of a young woman who closes herself in a cell for life because she gave a man temptation to sin.[48] The *Fasciculus Morum* is relatively restrained, condemning "those foolish women who on feast days wear luxurious clothes on their heads and bodies in order to excite men to sin," but also claiming that "a woman can dress herself decently according to the custom of her country without committing a sin, nor is there anything reprehensible in this unless it is a matter of superfluous fashion and hence a source for evil." But the *Destructorium Vitiorum* holds women responsible for men's lust even if they excite it inadvertently:

> And if some say that women decorating themselves exquisitely to improve their beauty do not have an evil intention in doing it, I respond, nor does the sword have an evil intention when someone is killed with it, but still he who turns the sword to unjust killing has an evil intention, thus the devil who uses women thus adorned like a sword has an evil intention. . . .
> Who gives the occasion of harm, gives the harm.

If a man falls into sin because of a woman, it would be better for her if she were mutilated or a leper because "in this case the soul of the man who fell will be required at the hands of the woman," that is, she will be held responsible for causing his sin.[49] Preachers recognized other causes of men's lust besides women's beauty, but they still argued that women bore a moral responsibility for the effects of their natural appearance great enough to justify self-mutilation.[50] This line of reasoning directly supported the blame of prostitutes rather than their customers for the social disruption caused by their trade.

Women's pride in appearance was connected not only to their sexual license but also, once again, to venality. The Middle English translation of the *Gesta Romanorum*, in allegorizing the game of chess, describes the queen: "This queen betokens virgins and damsels, who go from chastity to sin, and are taken by the devil, for gloves or such manner of gifts."[51] Several of Étienne de Bourbon's tales claim to prove that "the clothing of a whore is the sign of the behavior of a whore." Women who decorate their hair "show themselves venal: these are the signs of lightness and whoredom."[52] Any superfluously fancy or seductive clothing thus justifies considering the wearer a whore. Women are assumed to be willing to commit adultery in order to get better clothes.[53]

Like vanity and greed, the other criticisms leveled against women in late medieval English preaching were also related to lust. Preachers expanded on the stereotype of women's foolishness. It consisted not in a lack of common sense but in being easily led astray and used by the devil as temptation for men: "[Demons'] snares, decoys, and traps are wicked and foolish women, who in their contrivances and deceptions catch men and deceive them"; "as a foolish woman strives to have a beautiful appearance, to please evil men; thus all good people strive to have a chaste and beautiful soul."[54] Foolishness was opposed not to wisdom but to chastity. Women's garrulousness was also assimilated to lust. This talkativeness could consist in idle chatter, as indicated by the extreme popularity of the exemplum of the demon who records women's idle words,[55] as well as in nagging and quarrelsomeness. Preachers attacked these vices by calling women unchaste of their tongues, relating verbosity to bodily unchastity.[56]

Women who wandered abroad rather than remaining in the home were also suspected of lust. The extremely common fable of the singed cat connects women's gadding about with their love of finery; the implication is that both are intended to arouse men's lust. The Franciscan preacher Nicole Bozon commented, "So I say to you of women, should they be foolish, shorten their tails, or disarray their heads and discolour their clothes, they will not be then so desired of folk."[57] Women who walked out in public were automatically suspect of sexual sin, and as we saw in chapter 4 the practical effect was that any woman walking in the street could be considered a whore.

None of these attacks on women were new; they all formed part of the misogynist tradition that drew on Saint Jerome and other sources, and the same tales and criticisms had appeared in thirteenth-century (and earlier) collections as well as those of the late Middle Ages. New or not, they were among the main preoccupations of fourteenth- and fifteenth-century preaching about women, and they emphatically labeled women's nature not merely as sinful but as sexually sinful.

Religious Images of the Whore

The discussion so far has dealt with women in general, not with prostitutes in particular, but the implications for prostitution of the church's teaching about women and sexuality were manifold. The public was taught to place the blame on woman as temptress. Laymen were hardly ever criticized for their lust; and though clerics who broke their vows were criticized, the women with whom they did so were also blamed and categorized as whores. The widely acknowledged threat of female sexuality made it easy to regard any woman who stepped out of line in any way as a whore.

Nonetheless, writers of the various genres of religious literature—moral treatises, sermons and sermon aids, saints' lives, and other pastoralia—also recognized a specific category of commercial prostitutes. They did not, however, draw a sharp dividing line between them and other sexually sinful women. Rather, prostitutes were considered only the most extreme examples of a general female tendency to lustfulness. We can see this by examining the formal classifications medieval writers constructed for different types of lust, and then looking at the actual representations in religious literature of those labeled as whores.

Treatises and compilations on the seven deadly sins often divided each sin into branches, which in the case of lust corresponded to gradations of increasing seriousness. The relative severity of each type of lust was calculated from a masculine viewpoint: the concern was not with how sinful it was for a virgin, widow, nun, prostitute, and so forth to have sex, but with how sinful it was for a man to have sex with a woman from each of these groups. John of Bromyard in his *Summa Praedicantium* followed one tradition, which did not specifically mention prostitution or whoredom: least sinful was simple fornication, then the deflowering of a virgin, adultery, ravishment, sacrilege (sex with a nun), incest, and "the vice against nature." Many other texts, including one by John Wycliffe, the intellectual father of the Lollard movement, followed this schema, with minor variations (some omitted sacrilege; some added flirting and impudence as levels below fornication).[58]

The clergy used the seven deadly sins to organize their interrogation of their flock in the confessional. Concerning the sin of lust, according to John Mirk's fifteenth-century manual of instruction for parish priests, they were to ask if the parishioner had had sex, with whom, under what circumstances, and, in the case of a woman, "whether it were for covetousness / Of gold or silver, or anything of his / For then the sin would be double / And needs penance much more."[59] Here again we meet the assumption that all women were, if not prostitutes, at least venal in their sexuality.

Other texts discuss prostitution specifically. According to the *Fasciculus Morum*'s discussion of the subdivisions of lust, "[W]hile fornication is any forbidden sexual intercourse, it particularly refers to intercourse with widows, whores, or concubines. But the term 'whore' must be applied only to those women who give themselves to anyone and will refuse none, and that for monetary gain."[60] The author here explicitly equates the "whore" with the prostitute. But he also assumes that any woman would be either a virgin (in which case sex with her is defloration or sacrilege), a wife (in which case it is adultery), or a widow, a whore, or a concubine. There is no category for a single woman who engages in sex other than for money; this suggests that any single woman who was not chaste risked being considered, and treated as, a prostitute. Nonmarital feminine sexuality was assumed to be venal. Another tract, stressing the mortal sin inherent in fornication (even though many lay people felt that simple fornication was only venial),[61] equated the unchaste single woman with the whore: if a man asked a woman to be his lover, it meant that he considered her a whore, for if he thought she were chaste, he would not have asked.[62]

The *Speculum Vitae*, or "Mirror of Life," a fourteenth-century poetic compilation of the sins, explicitly refers to prostitution as the second branch of lust, in terms of seriousness falling between simple fornication (sex between two single people) and sex with a widow:

> The second degree the deed may be
> Between a single man, it seems to me
> And a common women of a brothel
> Who often seeks her body to sell.
> This is a sin that is much graver,
> And with the Devil more in favor,
> For it is held to be more vile,
> And more it may the soul defile,
> Because such women of life unclean
> Perchance are wedded, as oft is seen,
> Or are women of religion
> Who have forsaken their profession,
> . . . .
> And refuse none of the same kin
> Who have the wish with them to sin,
> Father, nor son, nor cousin, nor brother:
> This sin is more grave than the other.

The reasons given for the harm of prostitution—that it amounted to adultery, sacrilege, or incest—would seem to make it one of the worst branches of lust, so it seems odd to find it ranked only as more serious than simple fornication.[63] Indeed, the degree of gravity in all the texts seems discordant until we realize that it is based not on the prostitute's sin but on her customer's; prostitution is ranked low not because the woman's sin was insignificant but because the viewpoint behind the texts was so masculine.

The *Speculum Vitae* also included prostitution under the sin of avarice, the ninth branch of which consisted of sinful trades. Whereas the passage just quoted stresses the indiscriminate nature of sexuality and mentions the selling of sex only in passing, under avarice what is mentioned in passing is the indiscriminateness ("they refuse no man") and what is stressed is the notion of financial gain: "[F]or their livelihood they do nothing else . . . by charging they earn their sustenance, they have no other merchandise."[64] More than most other texts on the sins, this text, and the textual tradition to which it belonged, make the connection between the prostitute's lust and her greed. Although these texts relied heavily on French sources, this connection was more fully developed in the English versions.[65]

Another group of texts classified prostitution not merely as a separate branch of lust but as the most serious. This tradition was based on the thirteenth-century Anglo-French work *Manuel des Pechiez* (Handbook of Sins). This text enjoyed a great deal of popularity in England, probably among both confessors and the laity. The fourteenth-century English translation, Robert Mannyng of Brunne's *Handlyng Synne*, gives a detailed analysis of why this branch of lust was the worst.[66] We read:

> Full foul is that public one
> Who is common to all, indeed;
> Therefore, whatever is in your thought,
> Common women take you not,
>
> . . . .
>
> One [reason] is, she may take your brother,
> Father, or relation, as well as another.
> Another, for quarrels and foul strife,
> You may, through her, lose your life.
> The third is the worst defilement:
> Lepers, people say, use them;
> And he who takes them in that heat
> May soon lose the purity of his body.
> Much woe, then, it is to take such,
> For the sake of these three problems;
> And much may be that woman's moan,
> For she shall answer for every one
> Who has done any sin with her
> On Judgment Day, the day of wrath.[67]

Here, once again, along with the warnings against prostitutes on the grounds of incest and disease is the attribution to them of responsibility for men's souls. In this tradition prostitution was considered separate from, and worse than, fornication; it was not just a subset but the bottom of a slippery slope of lust. In the late fifteenth century Peter Idley's book of advice for his son drew heavily on *Handlyng Synne* in urging him not to visit prostitutes. Idley apparently viewed them as an alternative to marriage, for his additions to Mannyng's text include, "Alas! that man's appetite cannot be satisfied / To be pleased with one woman alone," and "Therefore live according to God's law and take a wife."[68] The *Speculum Sacerdotale*, a fifteenth-century text, also implied that unmarried men were the most likely to visit prostitutes: "There are many that commit fornication with strumpets, because they have no wives."[69]

Treatises and sermons on the ten commandments also sometimes discussed various forms of lust under the sixth commandment, explaining that it forbade any sort of sexual behavior outside marriage and thus included prostitution. As the fourteenth-century preacher Robert Rypon of Durham put it:

> In this commandment are prohibited corporeal adultery, that is all illicit use of the genital members and all carnal desire attacking chastity, such as adultery among the married, fornication among the single, whoredom which is in a common manner without shame, incest which is lust between cognates and affines, the sin against nature which is the worst and most vile, the violation of virgins or nuns.[70]

The late fifteenth-century *Dives and Pauper* lists sex with common women as the second of nine branches of behavior prohibited by the sixth commandment.[71]

Occasionally a text discussed prostitution in a way that placed the blame on men and showed some understanding of and even sympathy for the socioeconomic factors that drove women to it. One such text reads: "Many men sin much, for they defile many women and keep them from matrimony, and ruin them in this world and sometimes are cause of their damnation, for they become common women when they lose their families and have no craft to live by."[72] The *Book of the Knight of the Tower*, a book of advice by a Frenchman to his daughter, distinguishes between the prostitute and the lustful woman, recognizing the compulsion of financial necessity. But most works blamed all sexual misconduct on lust and greed, largely women's.

The depictions of commercial prostitutes—or of women who are not commercial prostitutes but who are still labeled whores—in religious literature further reveal to us the medieval understanding of this term. Once again, the line between commercial prostitution and other forms of sexual behavior is a very fine one. Sometimes this was made explicit, as in a fourteenth-century exemplum manuscript claiming that "the custom of the Romans was that when any married woman was convicted of adultery, so that she could be perpetually humiliated, she should be enclosed in a brothel and offered for sale by the bawds," who were to announce the reason for her punishment.[73] An adulteress is forced to become a prostitute in the flesh as she has already become the equivalent of one in the spirit. Such literary representations cannot be taken as depicting actual social practice, but they reflected and influenced the way people thought about their world.

The story of the nun Beatrice, found in many European languages and several literary genres, indicates the slippage between the categories of unchaste woman and prostitute. This nun, the trusted sacristan of her convent, has been devoted to the Virgin Mary all her life, nevertheless leaves the convent for a life of sin. In some versions she leaves for a lover, who later abandons her so that she has to turn to prostitution to support herself. In others she leaves the convent not for a particular man but out of sheer lust. Years later she returns to the convent as a beggar and finds that the Virgin Mary has been impersonating her the whole time so that no one would

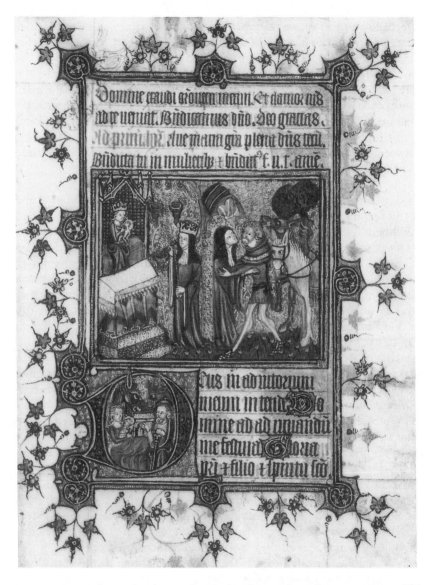

Fig. 2. A nun embraces her lover; the Virgin Mary replaces her as sacristan. This miniature illustrates the story of the sacristan who left her convent and became a prostitute. Bohun Psalter, English, ca. 1370. Oxford, Bodleian Library, MS Auct. D.4.4, fol. 200r. (*Reproduced by permission of the Bodleian Library, Oxford.*)

know of her absence (see fig. 2). Many versions of the story, Continental and English, acknowledge a financial motive for the nun's entry into prostitution. The *Alphabet of Tales* reads: "And when he had deflowered her, within a few days he left her and went away; and she had nothing to live on, and was ashamed to go home again to her cloister, and fell to be a common woman."[74] But recognition of need did not imply sympathy, since it was her own lust that brought her into distress. The story also recognizes a distinction between the prostitute and the nun who lives in sin with a man; the deflowered nun was not ipso facto a common woman. Of two earlier (thirteenth-century) Anglo-Norman texts, one says only that she had been leading an evil life of debauchery, making no reference to money, and the other has her living with her lover for seven years and bearing him children.[75] Yet, just as in real life an abandoned mistress might have nowhere to turn but prostitution, in literature a woman who in one version has sex with one man becomes a whore in another.

The point of this miracle tale and others was the intercessory power of the Virgin. A whore devoted to the Virgin could be saved no matter what her sin.[76] One medieval variant on the "whore with a heart of gold" theme concerns

> a woman who loved not chastity
> Her life she led in great wantonness
> In filth and lust of lechery
> She forbore with no man to sin
> From whom she hoped to earn money.

This prostitute prays on behalf of a holy hermit; the Virgin Mary then intercedes with Christ in favor of the whore and he forgives her, even without her repenting her sin.[77] Again, promiscuity seems to have been her main sin, but it is financial exchange that characterizes her activity.

Other exempla also used the image of the whore to stress the hopeful message of repentance. One popular tale concerns a bishop who could read the state of people's souls in their faces. Seeing two women with radiant faces, he inquires about their virtue. God tells him that "the two women that shine above all others were two common women of full evil life; but when they came into the church they took such repentance in their hearts that they made a vow to God that they would never do amiss after. Wherefore God of his high mercy has forgiven them. . . ."[78] In one "desert fathers" tale, a monk goes to town to try to convert his sister, who is a whore. She agrees to repent her sin. She follows him back to the desert, walking behind him so that if they encounter anyone he will not appear to be traveling with her. Eventually discovering that she has fallen behind, he returns and finds her dead. God then reveals to him that because of her repentance, she has been saved. The woman's life as a whore is not described in detail, but the texts stress the motive of promiscuity rather than cash. Henri D'Arci's Anglo-Norman *Lives of the Fathers* says that "she was common to all those who wanted her, and many souls by her were led into temptation." A fifteenth-century Latin version from England also says that she was the "perdition of many souls," blaming her for the sins of her lovers.[79]

The evil of such women's sin made the message of repentance plainer. In another exemplum a preacher comes to a town full of brothels, chooses the most beautiful whore, and begins to preach to her. Converted, she does penance and persuades her companions to listen to the preacher.[80] Similarly, a preacher converts a whore by asking her to have sex with him in the marketplace; when she answers that she could never do it where so many people are watching, he asks her how she can do it where God is watching.[81] Although the story of Saint Thaïs (discussed later in this chapter), to which these tales are related, emphasizes the whore's relation to money in impoverishing her customers, none of these tales makes any reference at all to financial exchange. The audience probably understood from the term "common woman" and the brothels that the women were professionals, but the financial transaction was not to be considered part of the sin. Any sexually sinful woman could have served the same function as bearer of the message of repentance.

The conception of the whore as promiscuous rather than as professional emerges in a tale from the Middle English *Gesta Romanorum* of a woman brought to whoredom through incest. She becomes pregnant by her father and kills her newborn child. When her mother curses her, the young woman kills both her parents and goes to another country; "and there she was a common woman, and took all who would come. She refused none, monk nor friar, clerk nor layman, she was so common that every man that knew her loathed her company."[82] This story too is about repentance—the woman hears a sermon, and although she dies before she can perform penance, she is saved because of her true contrition—and its assumptions about whoredom are illuminating. The proximate cause of her prostitution seems to be her degraded morals rather than financial need. The implication that she became a whore because she had no other means of support is more apparent to modern readers than it would have been to medieval ones.

Several other tales about prostitutes also depict motivations other than financial need while emphasizing the possibility of salvation. The *Alphabet of Tales* includes the story of a prostitute who travels with a great lord, servicing his retinue. She lusts after a priest until he invites her to sleep with him on a fiery bed, which does not burn him; this miracle causes her to retract a false accusation against him.[83] In a fourteenth-century Dominican miscellany, a betrothed couple separates when the man decides to become a Dominican; his fiancée then becomes a prostitute, apparently out of shame at having been repudiated (and perhaps in an allusion to Mary Magdalen, who in some medieval texts was betrothed and abandoned). Her former betrothed prays for her, and her soul is saved.[84]

All these exempla presented prostitutes not as victims but as active sinners. Exempla were intended for edification, and obviously could not be expected to depict prostitution as respectable or enjoyable. They neither sympathized with women forced into such a life nor warned away those who might be tempted into it; the point of all the tales was to contrast the depravity of the whore with the holiness of those (all of them men, except for the Virgin Mary) who bring her to salvation, and also to contrast the whore with her saved self.

Fig. 3. The Whore of Babylon. From a fourteenth-century Apocalypse manuscript. British Library, MS Additional 17333, fol. 34r. (*Reproduced by permission of the British Library.*)

Occasionally, too, we meet a whore who has not repented, as we have seen in Jacques de Vitry's story of the woman on whom a lover spends everything save his cloak. When he finally leaves her she weeps, not because she had lost him but because she has not managed to get the cloak from him too.[85] This story not only emphasizes the whore's hard-heartedness and venality but also makes her a real threat to men: she wants their money not to satisfy her own needs but in order deliberately to ruin them. This image accords well with John of Wales's derivation of *lupanar* (brothel) from *lupa* (wolf): it was the prostitute's rapacity that constituted the threat.[86]

The figure of the whore or prostitute in religious literature of course signified something more than—or different from—attitudes toward actual prostitutes in society. It could be, and often was, moralized: a whore who became a saint could symbolize the sinful soul redeemed through Christ, while a whore who remained one could be a figure of sin and temptation. Whores in the Bible, such as Rahab or the Harlot of Gaza, were interpreted allegorically.[87] The Whore of Babylon in the Book of Revelation (see fig. 3) was similarly a figure of human sin in general and a wide variety of evils in particular (including that of a corrupt clergy, an interpretation used in the Reformation and even before to apply to the pope), just as fornication could stand for a host of spiritual sins. Although these biblical figures were not understood in the same way as contemporary prostitutes, the metaphors drew their power from the whore's position as the epitome of sin.[88]

Harlot Saints and Financial Exchange

As the exempla involving converted prostitutes imply, the whore who became a saint held a fascination for medieval Christians. Christianity was a religion of repentance and forgiveness. Saints who had been sinners embodied the message that confession, contrition, and penance could wipe away the worst of sins, and saints who had been whores embodied it most dramatically.[89] Hagiography was one of the most popular literary genres of the Middle Ages, and these stories also circulated orally, in sermons and otherwise. There are four prostitute saints whose legends were widely known in England: Mary Magdalen, Mary of Egypt, Thaïs, and Pelagia.[90] These penitent whores' stories did reflect a concern with money and exchange in the market. Both motives for sin—the financial and the libidinous—appear in many of the medieval versions of their lives, which embodied the notion of the feminine in general as lustful and promiscuous.

The most important of these four saints—indeed, the most important penitent of any sort, and perhaps the most popular saint in the Middle Ages after the Virgin Mary—was Mary Magdalen.[91] Since the sixth century, theologians had identified her with three New Testament figures: Mary of Magdala, out of whom Christ cast seven devils, and who was the first to see him after his resurrection (Luke 8:2; Mark 16:9; John 20:17); Mary of Bethany, the sister of Martha and Lazarus (Luke 10:38–42); and the anonymous sinful woman who washed Christ's feet (Luke 7:37–38). Although the Bible does not specify that woman's sins, all medieval authors assumed that they were sexual. Despite the fact that Mary Magdalen became the patron saint of repentant prostitutes, she was rarely depicted as a professional, making her living from sexual acts. Her social class differentiated her from prostitutes who commonly practiced in medieval towns (muting somewhat the universality of her biography's message of repentance and salvation), yet at the same time the texts equated her with a common prostitute because of her sexual morals. She was definitely a whore if not a professional; and money did have its role to play in at least one English version of her story.

The New Testament's silence on Mary Magdalen's preconversion life gave free rein to medieval authors' imaginations. They generally followed Odo of Cluny, a tenth-century homilist, in describing her as coming from a wealthy and noble family and sinning because of the temptations of riches and youth. The Golden Legend, a popular thirteenth-century Latin compendium, attributed her sin to the combination of wealth and beauty. It repudiated the story that Mary Magdalen entered her life of sin after being jilted at the altar, but William Caxton's 1484 translation of the Golden Legend adopted it, omitting the repudiation: "Some say that S. Mary Magdalene was wedded to S. John the Evangelist when Christ called him from the wedding, and when he was called from her, she had thereof indignation that her husband was taken from her, and went and gave herself to all delight. . . ."[92] The fifteenth-century author John Mirk and the unknown author of a mid-fourteenth-century collection of metrical homilies from northern England also accepted this explanation.[93] The late medieval *Play of Mary Magdalen*, one of the few surviving English saint plays, had the death of her father send her into despair, allowing demons to tempt her into sin.[94]

Since her noble origins and her great riches were part of the explanation for her life of sin, the texts went into great detail about her family. Some of the texts, particularly the French mysteries and the German passion plays, emphasized her beauty and made her sin primarily one of pride. English versions put the emphasis more firmly on her sexual behavior, but as the *South English Legendary* has it, her neglect of her class status compounded her sin: "She became the woman of greatest folly known to memory; she did not reject even the worst wretch although she was of high family."[95] Such a stress on noble birth was by no means unusual; hagiographers generally tried to make their saints as aristocratic as possible, for high birth implied noble character and the requisite spiritual qualities for saintliness. Still, a noblewoman's failure to live up to a high standard of moral behavior was more shocking than a commoner's sin, and it may be that prostitution by a poor woman would have been considered more excusable, if not less sinful.

The Magdalen's class standing, wealth, and beauty thus made her in the medieval mind a more appropriate friend for Christ than if she were a common prostitute. Her love for him, although clearly spiritual, was described in some of the same terms used to refer to her earlier courtly dalliance. The *Lamentatyon of Mary Magdaleyne* (attributed to Chaucer but probably written later, between 1460 and 1480) uses phrases like "my own true turtledove / My life's joy" and "my most excellent paramour / Fairer than rose, sweeter than lily flower" to express her love for Christ.[96] Medieval audiences were accustomed to hearing carnal metaphors applied to spiritual relationships like God's love for humankind, so her declaration of love in physical terms would not have been shocking; nonetheless, when spoken by a former whore, the carnal language gave additional meaning to the scene. The words would have resonated with the erotic even though the audience understood them spiritually.

Although Mary Magdalen came of noble family background, in many of the texts about her early life she forfeits her claim to that background because of her immorality. The Golden Legend, and many other texts that drew on it, took the passage in Luke 7 involving the unnamed sinful woman to mean that Mary Magdalen had "lost her name." The passage does not actually say that this woman had no name, but her identification with a known character required an explanation of why her name was not used in this episode. As William Caxton put it, "[A]nd for so much as she shone in beauty greatly, and in riches, so much the more she submitted her body to delight, and therefore she lost her right name, and was called customably a sinner."[97] English texts, unlike those from the Continent, drew the specific link between the identification of her sin as sexual and the loss of her name. Osbern Bokenham's *Legends of Holy Women* says that because of her youth, wealth, and beauty,

> all her youth in wantonness
> of her body so shamelessly
> she expended, and in sinfulness
> was so common, that pitifully
> she lost her name . . .

and John Mirk wrote that she "gave herself to sin and namely to lechery, in so much that she lost the name of Magdalen, and was called the sinful woman."[98]

In some texts she loses even her given name; the sexually sinful woman thus becomes generic, no longer an individual but subsumed in the evil of her sex. According to another, however, "her family name she lost / and was called, as such a one should be / Mary the sinful."[99] That sexual misconduct should bring shame to her family accorded well with medieval views of female chastity as a commodity to be guarded and then sold not by the woman herself but by her male kin. Christianity valued female chastity in itself as a religious ideal even when it conflicted with family strategies, as biographies of female saints who remained virgins, despite their fathers' attempts to marry them off, indicate. In practice, however, such conflict between church and parents arose only rarely, for the Christian emphasis on chastity reinforced the family's need to control its daughters' sexuality.

The connection of Mary Magdalen's sexual depravity with money is problematic: To what extent was she meant to be what we would call a prostitute? Some of the German and French dramas about the Magdalen explicitly tell us that she refused money when it was offered, or that she gave her body without fee to anyone because she did not need the money. Whereas the French and German texts present Mary Magdalen merely as a lustful lady, however, the English ones either are ambiguous or explicitly make her a prostitute. In the *Play of Mary Magdalene* she does not refer to money, and takes care to distinguish herself from the lower class of women even while she searches for a lover. When a man in a tavern professes his love, she replies, "Why, sir, do you take me for a slut?" Yet immediately thereafter she proves herself a whore by allowing him to become intimate with her.[100] A lady with lovers might rank above a prostitute socially but not morally. Another text, however, is less ambiguous about her pecuniary motive: According to *The Early South-English Legendary*, "many rich men lay with her / And gave her great reward."[101] This does not necessarily mean that she was envisioned as accepting direct payment for specific acts, but it does indicate that venality was one aspect of her sexual activity, a connection apparently made in England but not elsewhere. She could be called a "common woman," which usually meant a venal one.[102]

The financial connection emerges more clearly in the lives of the other prostitute saints, especially in that of Mary of Egypt. In most versions Mary's story appears within a frame, the story of the monk Zosimus. While seeking spiritual perfection in the desert, Zosimus sees a naked figure who tries to flee from him. After he covers her with his cloak, she tells her story. Born in Egypt, she lived as a prostitute for many years in Alexandria, and then paid her passage with her body on a ship to Jerusalem. There an invisible force barred her from entering a church; only with the intercession of the Virgin Mary could she go in. In the church a voice told her to cross the Jordan and her sins would be forgiven. A charitable man gave her enough money to buy three loaves of bread, which lasted for seventeen years in the wilderness; for another thirty years she lived without eating or drinking. After Mary tells her story, Zosimus leaves. He returns the following year by arrangement to give her communion, but on his return in the second year, finding her dead, he buries her with the help of a lion.[103] The moral message of the story varied depending on the context in which it was told. Where Zosimus played the central role, the story lauded the eremitic (solitary) over the cenobitic (communal) life: she was a more perfect ascetic than he, even though she was a woman and a former sinner. The message of asceticism and repentance remained essential to all versions of the tale, but the story sometimes appeared without the Zosimus frame as a miracle of the Virgin, with a message of her intercessory power, again all the more striking because of the severity of the Egyptian woman's sin. The artistic tradition on Mary of Egypt stressed her repentant life in the desert. Illustrations of her preconversion life are rare if not nonexistent.

To the medieval reader Mary the Egyptian had sunk to the depths of sin: as she confesses to Zosimus in an agony of lamentation and self-reproach, she has committed not only fornication but also adultery (intercourse with married men or priests) and incest (intercourse with two men who were related to each other). On her voyage to Jerusalem she seduced all the men on board, even those who originally had no intention of sinning with her. She participated in all sins, particularly gluttony and other sins of the flesh, but it was the sexual that identified her and allowed her to stand as such a shining example of conversion.

Mary the Egyptian's connection with the market and financial exchange became firmer later on in the Middle Ages. In the original Latin version (a translation from an earlier Greek text), Mary tells Zosimus that she lived promiscuously for seventeen years but never accepted money for sex because she thought she would find more partners if she did not charge. This version of the story found its way into the vernacular texts; even those that told the story much more briefly, such as Adgar's Anglo-Norman collection of miracles of the Virgin from the late twelfth or early thirteenth century, included the detail of her not charging for sex: "She received everyone, and not for goods / But to fulfill her mad desire."[104] Another textual tradition emerged, however—beginning in the twelfth century with an Anglo-Norman text and spreading through France to the rest of Europe—which specifically described Mary's life of promiscuity as taking place in a brothel. In this version she does accept money.[105] The idea that she worked in a brothel, the likes of which might have been familiar to her audience, became more common in the fifteenth-century. William Caxton's late fifteenth-century translation of *The Lives of the Fathers* describes her life as follows: "[A]nd during the time of seventeen years and more she had continually made residence at the public brothel of the same town with other common women there being, in abandoning and using her proper body to all that came, and with no other thing got her living."[106] In the earlier Middle Ages, writers who translated or retold the story did not question their sources' statement about Mary's refusal to accept money for sex. But by the fifteenth century the increasing awareness and institutionalization of prostitution made such a detail unrealistic, and for Caxton and his source the need for verisimilitude outweighed the theological point. For him the whore was in it for the money.

Those versions that denied a financial motive to Mary treated her sin as aggravated by her refusal to accept payment. Although canon lawyers did not believe that financial need could ever excuse a woman's becoming a prostitute as it could a man's becoming a thief, it could at least make the sin more understandable.[107] The texts made her accept the blame for those she led into sin. When she refused payment for sex out of fear that charging money would stand in the way of her gratification, she both enticed men and made the sin easier for them: "For this deed she took from no man reward or profit / lest any should for lack of funds fail to sin with her."[108] Yet later versions that presented money as a motive were not sympathetic—they did not mention the force of financial necessity—but combined the profit motive with that of lust. Awareness of the importance of commerce did not imply an understanding of how the money economy contributed to sexual exploitation.

Except for the absence of monetary exchange, Mary of Egypt's activities could not be distinguished from prostitution. Even texts such as the Golden Legend, which gave only a very brief account of the Egyptian's life of sin, treated her as not just an immoral woman but a public one. She says: "I was born in Egypt, and when I was in the age of twelve years I went into Alexandria, and there I gave my body openly to sin by the space of seventeen years, and abandoned it to lechery and refused no man."[109] Many of the texts, both Latin and vernacular, referred to Mary as "common," "public," available to all. Such abandonment of the female body underpinned the medieval understanding of whoredom. This notion of the prostitute as the property of all men because in a sense she was the property of none was reflected in the brothel regulations that forbade prostitutes to refuse any customer or even to take a particular lover (see p. 40). The equation of whoredom with indiscriminate promiscuity may be one reason why it was considered especially shocking behavior for a woman of good family such as Mary Magdalen.

Although other prostitute saints from the desert fathers tradition never attained the popularity of Mary of Egypt, the retellings of their legends in

European vernacular traditions followed some of the same patterns. The life of Thaïs was the most widely known. The standard Latin version reports that she was so beautiful that many men sold all their goods and brought themselves to destitution for her sake, and jealousy over her caused much bloodshed. A monk by the name of Paphnutius hears of her reputation and takes it upon himself to convert her. He disguises himself as a lover and shows her his cash. When she takes him into her chamber, he asks for a more private room where they cannot be seen. Surprised at her response that no one can see them but God, he asks why, if she believes in God, she is a whore. She breaks down and repents, burns all her goods, and retires to the desert. The bulk of the story, as with that of Mary of Egypt, concerns her life in the desert and her great asceticism.[110] Most of the medieval versions of this story, including the Golden Legend, follow the original translation from Greek quite closely. They make Thaïs a woman of refinement and beauty, and keep her price high: the shilling Paphnutius gives her in Caxton's translation of the Golden Legend is far more than the typical price of a prostitute in the fifteenth century.[111] A thirteenth-century Anglo-Norman version also stresses her high price.[112] The value of the gold and other goods she burns comes to hundreds of pounds. Yet despite her riches she is still described not as a courtesan but only as "the most common strumpet in all the land," or "common of her body to all that desired her."[113] As in the stories of Mary of Egypt, the texts blame Thaïs for the sins of her customers, both their bloodshed and their sexual sins; it is she who sends them to hell, and she who must account for their souls as well as her own.[114]

Of all the lives of prostitute saints, money plays the greatest role in that of Thaïs. The texts make clear that she takes whichever lover pays her most, stress the money Paphnutius brings her, and equates her renouncing her life of prostitution with burning her gold. The ascetic life Thaïs undertakes after her conversion involves being walled up in a cell, in which she has to perform all her bodily functions. The use of excrement as an image in this story is not coincidental: it is connected with the financial aspect of her sin. The importance of money in the story did not arise from the economic changes of the High Middle Ages, however; it also appeared in much earlier versions (the excrement image figures most vividly in the work of Hrotswitha of Gandersheim in the tenth century), but later versions made the role of money much more specific. Thaïs despoils men not of their wealth generally but of a specific payment for a specific act: "[S]he was always ready to take / whoever would the first payment make."[115] She is not merely a venal whore but a prostitute in the modern sense.

The legend of Pelagia presents her as an actress, a profession notorious in antiquity and the Middle Ages for loose morals but lacking the connotation of explicit financial exchange that accompanies prostitution in the lives of the other saints. Most of the texts that describe Pelagia's life before her conversion, both the Golden Legend and vernacular versions, emphasize her beauty and riches, her gold, gems, and perfumes, but not promiscuity for pay. Pelagia happens to hear Bishop Nonnus give a sermon and writes him a letter. He ends up converting her, and she becomes a desert ascetic. During her eremitic life she disguises herself as a man; only after her death do her fellow ascetics discover her sex. Although Pelagia is clearly presented as an actress or performer by profession—Caxton's *Vitae Patrum* calls her a "juggler or dancer"—and most versions of the story describe her as promiscuous but do not mention money, once again, as with Mary Magdalen, one of the few exceptions comes from England. One Middle English version depicts her as sinning for money and as responsible for the sin of the men she tempts:

> She was a fair enough woman
> And drew many a man to sin
> For she made her body common
> In lust of the flesh and lechery.
> . . . .
> And she did a good business with her flesh.[116]

The lives of the prostitute saints in many English versions thus placed an emphasis on the element of monetary exchange, even in the case of Mary Magdalen and Pelagia where many of the Continental texts did not.[117] This is not likely to have been due to a greater awareness in England than elsewhere of commercial prostitution, for municipal brothels were certainly common in European towns. If it is more than just coincidence, the difference probably signifies a perception of feminine venality as so pervasive that it affected even wealthy women of good family, future saints. The figure of the courtesan, whose salient characteristic was charm rather than greed, was not as common in England as, for example, in Italy, or even perhaps the courts of France and Germany.[118] The English texts, then, may have had no other model than the commercial prostitute to draw on. The texts assumed that all women who engaged in nonmarital sex would take money, but it was not that which made them sinful: their sin was lust rather than greed. But the fact that they took money put them in a particular class. The distinction between the talented actress and the sought-after beauty, the noble lady and the public woman made no real difference. The need to earn a living may have provided an explanation for prostitution, but it was not an excuse.

These legends constituted the teaching about prostitution that most medieval people would have received, and what they taught was that women who enjoyed their sexuality were whores and amounted to prostitutes. By making the foremost examples of penitents women who had been completely abandoned to their sexuality, medieval culture emphasized the equation of women with lust and made the prostitute a paradigm of the feminine. The most obvious and deliberate point of the narratives dealt with conversion and repentance. The portions of the texts discussed here were merely the background against which the women's penitence stood in stark contrast. Nevertheless, the accounts of prostitution constituted a greater share of the texts' meaning than it did of their length; they linked the stories together (and medieval people did see these saints as linked together by their preconversion lives) and provided the context in which the audience understood the women's repentance.[119]

The theme of prostitution appears in the lives of several other saints as well. Saint Nicholas, who helped women avoid prostitution, and Saint Agnes, who miraculously escaped it, are the two most prominent. So many miracles involving marriage and the family surround Nicholas of Myra that he has been seen as a sort of patron saint of fertility, and indeed is sometimes connected with promiscuity.[120] In medieval times one of the most common legends was that of the three daughters.[121] A man who has become destitute plans to turn his daughters to prostitution "so that by the gain and winning of their infamy they might be sustained."[122] When Nicholas hears of this, he secretly tosses through the window three bags of gold, which become the daughters' dowries (see fig. 4). This tale was so popular that the three bags of gold became one of Nicholas's attributes; the three golden balls of pawnbrokers' shops are stylized descendants of this symbol of their patron saint. And Saint Nicholas was a popular figure in England as elsewhere in Europe. The first vernacular retelling of his legend was in Anglo-Norman, by Wace in the twelfth century, and it survives in fourteenth- and fifteenth-century English versions as well.

The Nicholas legend clearly shows an awareness of the financial constraints that forced women into prostitution. But the constraints were on the family, not on the women themselves. It was not because an unmarried woman had no other way of supporting herself that she became a prostitute, but because a man "for great need . . . ordained his daughters to be common women and get their living and his both," although one version of this legend does present it as the daughters' choice: "[T]heir decision they made all three to become loose women / and rather than be in such hunger, to live by their whoredom."[123] It was not just the destitution of the family but the fact of having three daughters who needed dowries that caused the financial hardship. The texts that included this motive for prostitution acknowledged that women were often forced into the profession by their families' plight, thus conveying the message that prostitution was undertaken out of financial need and not out of lust. This story, however, was practically alone in medieval literature in imagining the forces that might compel a woman to prostitution. The legend presented prostitution as the only alternative for the daughters (rather than, for example, domestic service) because such a fate lent the greatest emotional impact to the miracle. The fact that many women were neither married nor prostitutes was ignored in this tale.

Unlike the Nicholas story, the tales of Daria and Agnes placed no emphasis whatsoever on the financial motive for prostitution (although the brothel setting clearly implied a commercial aspect), nor indeed on lust. In the legend of Agnes, a Roman virgin who pledges herself to Christ, a prefect's son falls in love with her. When she refuses to marry him, the prefect requires her either to sacrifice to Vesta and remain a virgin or to "go to the bordel to be abandoned to all that thither come, to the great shame and blame of all thy lineage."[124] She refuses to sacrifice, and is led naked to the

Fig. 4. Saint Nicholas keeps three young women from prostitution by providing their dowries. From a late fourteenth-century English Carmelite missal. British Library, MS Additional 29204, fol. 164v. (*Reproduced by permission of the British Library.*)

brothel; but God makes her hair grow to cover her, and an angel meets her at the brothel with a shining garment. When the prefect's son and his companions come to have sex with her, the son is struck dead. In a similar story Daria, a Vestal virgin, is placed in a brothel as punishment for her conversion to Christianity, but a lion guards the door to prevent men from coming in to "deflower and corrupt" her.[125]

Sexuality and prostitution in these stories became a question of power: these women were condemned to be punished by gang rape. In its version of the Agnes story, *The Early South-English Legendary* has the prefect "cry it far and wide / that all who wished to commit wantonness should wend thither / And find there a wanton woman fair and gracious of body."[126] In Bokenham's version the men go to the brothel as a group. The son, who has previously been in love with Agnes, offered her and her family much treasure if she would marry him, and pined away at her refusal, is now quite content to rape her in a brothel: "When the prefect's son heard that Agnes was in the brothel he grew quite jolly, and with a company of young fellows he hastened there, hoping now to perform his foul fleshly lust with her."[127] As Bokenham presents him, the son makes no distinction between possessing Agnes as a wife and possessing her through rape. Agnes also fails to make the distinction. For her to be raped would truly have been a fate worse than death; martyrdom was a welcome triumph. Yet to her, marriage is no more acceptable than rape; the loss of her virginity, whether in honorable or dishonorable circumstances, is opposed to her deepest convictions.

The story of Saint Agnes reflected a fear that prostitution would lead to forcible corruption of the pure, the same motif that prompted the exaggerated publicity about the "white slave trade" in the Victorian era.[128] Medieval English court records do indicate that young women who had no intention of entering prostitution could end up in a brothel by deceit or force. The image presented there of the innocent girl corrupted by the evil bawd stands in contrast both to the image of the lustful whore and to the economic model of prostitution as a deliberately chosen survival strategy. The story of Saint Agnes made forced prostitution a deliberate act of punishment for a virtuous young woman, thus casting the brothelkeeper (conspicuously absent from the story) in the position of the agent of the evil and corrupt pagan state. The assumption that this life was the worst possible fate for a Christian woman went farther in stigmatizing the prostitute than even the descriptions of the preconversion lives of the prostitute saints.

Saint Agatha's legend also places the blame on a bawd. When the Roman official Quintinius wants to persuade Agatha to have sex with him, he hands her over to "a certain whore named Aphrodisia and her nine daughters, of the same vileness." They nonetheless fail to persuade her, either with promises of wealth or with threats.[129] When Caxton translated this text into English, he did not refer to Aphrodisia as a whore; but Osbern Bokenham called her "a woman who lived sinfully, offering her body to the uncleanness of whoever came," and The Early South-English Legendary called her "old quean . . . strong whore and bawd."[130] Aphrodisia is only a minor character here, but she serves to displace responsibility for the intended corruption of Agatha onto a woman. She also underscores the stereotype of the old and depraved woman who corrupts the young and innocent.

All the saints' lives involving prostitution shared one characteristic: they were set in the distant past.[131] The authors could take liberties with the characters and setting. There were very few penitent saints who dated from the central and late Middle Ages, and none who had been prostitutes, who devoted their lives to redeeming prostitutes, or who were miraculously saved from prostitution. Prostitution was part of everyday life, perhaps too much so to serve a symbolic function that could better be expressed at a chronological distance. The stories are not evidence for the experience of the prostitute in the Middle Ages, or even in late antiquity, when the legends were set. But the same features that make hagiography unreliable factually, including its reliance on conventions and its edifying purpose, make it valuable as evidence of the way medieval people understood sexuality. The authors of these tales could construct the social backdrop more or less as they pleased, so their choices tell us about their own cultural milieu. They connected feminine sexuality with financial exchange, depicting women as lustful and venal, and equating any and all sexual misbehavior with prostitution.

Sexuality, Money, and the Whore

The history of sexuality asks not only "What did people do and how often did they do it?" but also "How did people think about and talk about sexuality, and how did this affect the way they thought about and behaved toward women and men?" Prostitution, both in practice and in the way people viewed it, is an important component of the answers to these questions. I began this book by suggesting that we should not assume that the category of prostitute was a relevant one in the European Middle Ages. I later showed that, though it is clear enough that there were commercial prostitutes in late medieval English towns, what marked these women for their contemporaries was not the fact that they took money for sex but rather that they were generally available to men for sexual purposes. This behavior was considered both socially necessary and individually depraved. Thus, while it is possible to talk about medieval prostitution, it is the broader concept of whoredom that is more relevant to an understanding of medieval sexuality.

The evidence of the court records (particularly the way in which the term "whore" was used in everyday speech) indicates that the various terms we might translate as "prostitute" had a much wider range of meaning than "practitioner of commercial sex." The women actually prosecuted as whores were largely those who were practicing commercially, so we may assume that people did understand "whore" (or the terms I have been translating as "whore") as in some sense congruent to "prostitute." But in other areas of discourse besides the law, a whore was someone who engaged in sex in some sort of reprehensible way: either with a large number of men, or with a priest, or with a man other than her husband. This wider understanding of the term was occasionally reflected in court records, too, as there were certainly women prosecuted as whores who were not commercial prostitutes.

If late medieval English culture had no conceptual category reserved for women who engaged in sex for money, what does this reveal about that culture's understanding of sexuality? One possibility is that in this precapitalist economy it really did not matter whether or not money was involved. Today we treat an activity entirely differently depending on whether one engages in it primarily for financial or for other reasons; perhaps in the Middle Ages the remunerative status of an activity was not an important component of the way that activity was understood. Historians of sexuality have commented on the commercialization of sex that accompanied the rise of capitalism in America and Europe, whether the causes were cultural (the increasing importance of money generally), demographic (the rise in age at marriage), or economic (the prevalence of women who expected and needed to work but were unable to find jobs).[1] The lack of emphasis on money in the medieval understanding of the whore may reflect the lack of commercialization of the economy in general or the lack of a concept of profession or career.

England in the late Middle Ages, however, was hardly a natural economy. Laments might be heard even then about the good old days before everything was monetized, and about the greed of the powerful, but these only reflected the fact that commerce (if not industry) had already become the lifeblood of the country. As for the concept of a profession, the existence of guilds shows that medieval culture certainly did conceive of people according to their occupational category. Indeed, occupational categories defined people to an even greater extent than they do today. Gaining entrance into a guild was not easy, so men tended to stay in the same craft as their fathers. Many people derived their surnames from their occupation. Not everyone belonged to a guild. Casual laborers might switch from craft to craft, and women were disproportionately employed in this casual sector of the economy. But since it was still possible and indeed common for women to be identified by occupational category even if they could not join a guild (as, for example with the London silkwomen), there was no barrier in that sense to seeing prostitutes as an occupational group.[2] Nevertheless, medieval people do not seem to have conceived of them in this way, even if modern scholars who focus on their place in the economy view them in that light.

One possible reason why people did not think of prostitutes as an occupational group lies in the medieval concept of productive labor. The grounds for objections to usury (often defined as the taking of any interest on money), and to the occupation of merchant in general, as set out by twelfth-century theorists, were that money and commerce in themselves could not create value. Merchants and others who did not actually produce commodities were thus seen as suspect.[3] By the late Middle Ages, when merchants were widely accepted in England and all of Europe, dominating the towns and figuring significantly in national politics, a certain level of distrust still remained, not on the level of economic theory but in the more popular teachings of the church.[4] The merchant was a stock figure discussed under the sin of avarice and considered usurious or miserly, especially in comparison with the peasant or the craftsman.

This residue of distrust for people who did not actually produce things may have informed attitudes toward women who engaged in commercial sex. They could hardly be considered producers, as could silkwomen, spinsters, or brewsters. Canon lawyers did argue that a whore was entitled to keep her earnings; even though the transaction was sinful, that did not entitle the man to take back the money he had paid her. Nevertheless, medieval people basically conceived of the prostitute in her sexual rather than in her commercial capacity. Her income was seen not as lawful payment for services but as ill-gotten gain like that of usurers.[5] R. I. Moore has argued that the regulation of prostitution in the High Middle Ages was due to the fear of money as an instrument of social change: "[T]he relationship between a prostitute and her client could serve as a paradigm of the anxiety so widely expressed in these centuries [950–1250] that money dissolved traditional personal ties and obligations and substituted for them impersonal one-way transactions which contributed nothing to the maintenance and renewal of the social fabric."[6] This anxiety continued even though the monetary segment of the economy continued to grow in importance and to be taken for granted. Although whores were seen as demanding payment out of greed, this did not constitute their offense or distinguish them from other promiscuous women. And the fact that medieval writers accused all women of venality does not mean that they recognized financial necessity or the structure of the economy as motivations for prostitution.

Medieval people and their governmental authorities did not, of course, think of whoredom as a socially constructed category. They thought of it as a social and moral problem. Those they saw as socially disruptive were mainly the professionals, even though other women were sometimes caught in the net. When the authorities regulated "whores," rather than prosecuting them, the regulations were aimed at those who were commercially active. Although the approaches taken by different jurisdictions within England varied greatly, what all the temporal authorities' views of prostitution had in common was a desire to segregate prostitutes. Rather than incarcerating them, however, towns ordered them to leave the area bounded by the city walls, restricted them to particular streets within the town, or established official brothels. This apparent acceptance and even promotion of prostitution was accompanied by a desire to remove it from the public view. It may have been a necessary evil, but it was an offensive one to have to look at.

What was so offensive about prostitution? It certainly contradicted the teachings of the church, but so did many other activities that the secular authorities did not legislate against. Official pronouncements, as we have seen, referred to the threat prostitution posed to public order. But commercial sex is not inherently disorderly. The real reasons why the authorities felt threatened were contingent on the nature of social relations at the time.

As we have seen, one justification given for establishing official brothels, or for tolerating private ones, was the "lesser evil" argument. Masculine sexuality, particularly that of unmarried men (whether workers and apprentices, who could not afford to marry, or priests, who were not allowed to), was seen as an irrepressible force that needed some sort of outlet. If there were no prostitutes—already fallen women—to provide this outlet, these men would corrupt and cause the fall of "honest" women. This argument has the ring of familiarity to a modern audience, even if today the argument for legalizing brothels relies less on protecting respectable women from corruption and more on preventing disease and crime. The "lesser evil" argument is similar to other arguments in our society about such issues as drug use, teenage sex, and abortion. It makes the claim that if a behavior is not preventable and is going to happen anyway, the role of the authorities is to see that it happens in the least socially harmful way possible. As a tract attributed to the thirteenth-century theologian Thomas Aquinas puts it with typical medieval charm, having a sewer in one's house is not very pleasant, but it is much nicer than having one's house full of excrement.[7]

The assumption of an irrepressible male sex drive but none for the female as the basis for the "lesser evil" argument clearly indicates that it was not just social orderliness but the power of men over women that was at stake here. If people believed, as some Victorians did, that women were incapable of sexual pleasure, or at least that good women did not enjoy sex, it would make sense to argue that the male sex drive should find another outlet; even married men in this situation would be doing their wives a favor by not burdening them with sexual relations more than was necessary for conception. In the Middle Ages, however, medical theory about sexuality did not make this argument. Women were considered as lustful as men, if not more so. True, medieval culture idealized feminine chastity just as Victorian culture did, but they believed it was achieved not through innate feminine innocence but through a heroic struggle against the lusts of the body. If both men and women were subject to these same raging lusts, and according to the teachings of the church it was equally sinful for them to yield to it, female prostitution should not have been considered any more necessary as an outlet for men's lust than male prostitution for women's.

That the latter possibility would have been unthinkable indicates, again, that ensuring an outlet for male lust was not just a means of preserving order or of fulfilling the government's duty to meet the basic needs of the governed.[8] Prostitution was a question of authority, power, and property. The existence of large numbers of unmarried men threatened the property of the masters in their wives, daughters, and female servants (the women of course were not property in the legal sense, but elements of ownership were certainly present). To a male householder it did not matter if his son or a male apprentice or servant had sex, so long as he did not do it in a socially disruptive way, that is, with a woman under the master's or another householder's control. Such a man did not threaten the father or master simply by being sexually active. A sexually active wife, daughter, or female servant, however, did threaten her husband's, father's, or master's power, regardless of who her partner was.[9]

Seeking an acceptable sexual outlet was an option for men but not for women because of the traditional double standard in sexual relations.[10] An unmarried man could visit a whore, but an unmarried woman who had sex *became* a whore. Ecclesiastical tribunals did attempt to control the behavior of both sexes, but while other sexual offenses, particularly adultery and fornication, were dealt with exclusively by the ecclesiastical courts, prostitution was regulated and controlled by temporal authorities who were not so concerned with men's morals.[11] Prostitution was the only sexual offense that constituted a threat to the social order, but even so municipal authorities did not want to eradicate it completely. It was tolerated in part because it provided an outlet for men's excess sexual desire, which was privileged over women's, and in part because it allowed for an exercise of men's power over women by defining certain women as whores, common property.

Medieval English culture assumed that all women ought to belong to some man. (The exceptions were those who had taken vows of virginity and become nuns; but in late medieval England these were not numerous, and there were no groups of noncloistered religious women, Beguines or tertiaries, in England as there were elsewhere. Widows, too, could be exceptions, but they were sexually suspect if they did not remarry.)[12] Any woman who was not a wife, a daughter (directly under her father's control), or a servant (which meant any employee, but for women generally it meant a domestic servant) was suspect, and impugning her sexual morality was one way of keeping her in line. A bawd could be charged with corrupting not women generally but "men's wives and men's servants."[13] It was male control that was threatened and that had to be preserved. The fact that women who fornicated repeatedly with the same man were considered by the courts as different from whores indicates that nonmarital attachment to a particular lover, although not condoned, was not viewed as harshly as indiscriminate sexual activity. Such a woman might be called a whore in the heat of an argument, but only in the most general sense of that term.

The regulations governing the Southwark brothels indicate how central the issue of control over women was to the regulation of prostitution. Not only were no wives or nuns permitted in the brothels—these women belonged to individuals or to God, not to the public—but those women who did work in the brothels were not allowed to have their own particular lovers. If they were to be common, they must be entirely common. Control by a governmental authority, exercised by male stewholders, had replaced control by an individual man, with which it would conflict. The authorities did not want to eradicate prostitution completely; sometimes they profited from it, and surely they agreed that prostitutes' customers, if they were not allowed access to commercial sex, posed more of a threat than did the women who provided it. But they did want to control prostitution, and they did this by degrading the women. Through shame and through legislation the authorities, whether they legalized brothels or fined whores, curtailed the independence of women while at the same time keeping them available for men's sexual gratification.

The phenomenon of men in power controlling the behavior of their female subordinates more strictly than that of their male subordinates was hardly unique to medieval England. Certainly English women were not restricted to the home; they went freely about their towns and villages, and in later periods when we can more conveniently compare, their freedom was greater than that of women elsewhere in Europe, particularly in the Mediterranean countries.[14] But even if it was already true in the Middle Ages that English women were freer in terms of both physical mobility and marital choice than women elsewhere in Europe, this does not mean that men had less interest in controlling them; it may simply have been more of a losing battle in England than elsewhere, since women in England tended to marry later and thus experienced a period of relative independence. It may not even have been as much of a stain on the family honor for a daughter to be sexually active as it was, for example, in Italy; but men still saw it as their role to protect their wives' and daughters' chastity, for the sake of preserving their own authority.

The formal regulation of commercial, brothel-based prostitution differed from that elsewhere in Europe for both cultural and demographic reasons. Although there was a great deal of variation within England, and there was no single European model, municipal or municipally condoned brothels were more common on the Continent, and prostitution looms somewhat larger in descriptions of daily life in Continental towns than in English ones. Perhaps the English were less public about sex generally than the French and Italians. The lack of any works in English literature comparable to the fabliaux in sexual frankness and references to prostitution does not prove that prostitution was not as widely accepted as it was in France; but it may indicate that prostitution was not seen as commonplace in quite the same way. The regulations for the brothels of Southwark, in prohibiting the stewholders from selling food and drink, contrast with the image of brothels as houses of pleasure and relaxation, in which sex was only one of the indulgences on offer. One writer has called the Southwark brothels "sober" and "lugubrious."[15] And certainly fifteenth-century England had no renowned courtesans comparable to those of the Italian Renaissance. The greater importance of financial exchange in the English versions of the lives of the prostitute saints than in the Continental versions could be a result of the same more pragmatic, less erotic outlook. At least one thirteenth-century English writer saw lust as the quintessential French sin; envy was the English equivalent.[16]

Another reason why commercial prostitution may have been less celebrated, if not less common, in England than elsewhere is demographic. The marriage pattern in England contrasted with those found elsewhere in Europe in the Middle Ages (see pp. 49–52). A demographic regime in which marriage occurs late for both sexes is likely to entail more nonmarital sexual behavior than one in which marriage occurs early. But one would expect that this nonmarital behavior would include prostitution a good deal less where marriage is late for both sexes than where it is late for men only, as in Florence. If there were plenty of unmarried people of both sexes around, there might be opportunities for casual liaisons and not so much call for prostitution. By contrast, if all the young women were already married to older men, younger men might be more likely to turn to prostitutes (although in Florence the municipal brothel was supposedly established because the young men were turning to sodomy instead).

Another result of late marriage would be a greater degree of individual choice of marriage partner. In early modern England, where working-class women tended to marry not as adolescents but as adults already living apart from their natal families, marriages seem to have been based on mutual affection, as attested not only by diaries but also by the high incidence of bridal pregnancy.[17] It is not certain how far back into the Middle Ages this model may be read, but the sorts of marriage cases heard in the church courts indicate that men and women alike were making their own decisions. Where people make their own choices, marriage is more likely to be companionate than where it is arranged, and the husbands may have less interest in seeking sexual stimulation outside of marriage. Choice of marriage partner also implies the opportunity to meet members of the other sex. Many apprentices, journeymen, casual laborers, and domestic servants must have spent their time courting their female peers rather than visiting prostitutes. There were, of course, many women who never married, and some of them became prostitutes. Perhaps we should see the less institutional system of prostitution in England as being supply driven rather than demand driven, as municipal brothel systems were. I do not wish to paint a rosy picture of late medieval England as sexually egalitarian. It was still unswervingly patriarchal and governed by the double standard, as was the rest of Europe. But it is at least possible that marriage patterns help to explain the lack of ubiquity and glorification of prostitution (though not of prostitutes) that one finds elsewhere.

The more stringent legislation and enforcement of laws against prostitution in the sixteenth century was similar in England and elsewhere, although the changes in England, where there were fewer official brothels, may have seemed less revolutionary. Since toleration in many English towns was de facto and not de jure, it took less formal action to erode it. Prohibitions on prostitution that had previously been used to regulate and stigmatize could also be used to eradicate, at least in some more zealous jurisdictions. Fundamental attitudinal change, including increased social control and the regulation of male as well as female sexual behavior (especially among the lower classes), did not come until the late sixteenth century, a time when population pressure threatened the social order. It thus seems to have been less directly related to religious change than may have been the case on the Continent.[18]

Yet, although English patterns of legislation and regulation varied widely and differed from European ones, prostitution was still treated as a significant institution. To medieval people prostitution solved a social problem, but it also posed a threat because it created a group of women beyond male control. Adultery was a woman's repudiation of her husband's governance, but it was an individual crime; it was not a way of life independent of a man but an offense against a particular man. It was not as visible as prostitution, and it was not seen as somehow contagious. If prostitution protected "honest women" by diverting sexual attention away from them, it also had to be banned from parts of town where "honest women" went, or its practitioners had to be visually distinguished from those "honest women," lest their immorality spread. And indeed, since people believed that prostitutes entered the trade because of their lust, and enjoyed it, it was reasonable to fear that other women might "catch" the idea from them.[19]

The response to the perceived social problem of unruly whores was also a response to the unarticulated problem of feminine independence. It was not only prostitutes who posed this threat, but whatever form it took, the typical strategy would have been to sexualize it.[20] The figure of the whore was created out of the confluence of two factors: the need to derogate the sexually independent woman (or the woman who was independent in other ways that could be sexualized) and the need to regulate if not institutionalize commercial prostitution. If all women were sexually suspect, the treatment of commercial sex could become a tool to control all women.

"Public woman," a term used of prostitutes in France at this time, evokes the way women's independence and their movement outside the control of the head of household became sexualized; "common woman" in England expressed the same idea of a woman who moved into the communal realm, becoming sexually available. A whore was one who brought her sexuality out of the private and into the public arena. We can hardly say that marital sexuality in the Middle Ages was an entirely private matter. The church intervened constantly. Nevertheless, there was an attempt to restrict wives to the private sphere even when this contradicted practical economic realities. When a wife was active in commerce, it was usually (though not always) within a family business; she was criticized for dressing for the sake of her neighbors instead of her husband, or for going out too much (regardless of her contribution to the family economy by her activity in the market); and her sexual world was absolutely to revolve around her husband. Even a woman who lived with a man out of wedlock or a mistress kept by one man, did not make her sexuality public. A whore was someone who did, either by explicitly putting it on the market, or by being available to the public in general, or by making a public scandal of herself (as in the case of those known as "priest's whores").

The notion of public scandal is a key to understanding the category of whore. "Common woman" meant a woman available to all men; unlike "common man," which denoted someone of humble origins and could be used in either a derogatory or a laudatory sense, it did not convey any meaning either of nongenteel behavior or of class solidarity.[21] But "common" could also mean "by common fame." In court accusations a "common thief" did not necessarily mean a run-of-the-mill thief or one who steals from all and sundry; it could mean someone commonly reputed to be a thief. Reputation counted for a great deal in medieval society and was grounds enough for accusations to be brought in either ecclesiastical or criminal proceedings. The community's role in determining who was a whore, then, was an important one: a woman whose sexual behavior did not meet the norms of the community (and by this I mean those in positions of authority in the community, although common fame among her peers also played a role) might easily be labeled a whore. The whore was a woman out of place.

In this she resembled the scold. Although offenses of the tongue could be associated with men as well as with women, it was mainly women who were reported for scolding.[22] The court records frequently juxtaposed whores and bawds with scolds. Sometimes, although by no means always, the same people were charged. In London groups of people could be punished at the same time for "the foul and detestable sin of lechery, bawdry, and common scolding," and aldermen were asked to present "any common harlot, common bawd, common scolds, and such others."[23] The constable of the manor of East Smithfield was ordered to attach "all scolds [both the male and female forms are used], and all bawds and all disturbers of the peace."[24] In the one surviving Wardmote roll from London, the main offenses women were charged with are whoredom, bawdry, and scolding.[25] Gossiping and quarreling as well as scolding were connected with sexual immorality, as in the case of Sibyl Carpenter, a "common whore and scold and sower of quarrels and discords among her neighbors."[26]

In London and elsewhere, scolds and whores were punished with the same sort of shame rituals.[27] The clear connection of scolds with whores is apparent in a 1457 amendment to the Southwark brothel regulations: "Also, that no man's wife dwelling within the said lordship be brought into prison for scolding as the common women are, but that the constables yearly at the leets shall make their presentments of them. . . ."[28] Married scolds needed to be distinguished from prostitutes; the ordinance seems to be responding to a situation in which the two were being treated similarly.

Scolding (which probably consisted mainly in making oneself unpopular with one's neighbors through criticism; the definition was no more precise than that of a whore) was an archetypally feminine offense because words were among the few weapons women had for striking back at individual men or society in general. The scold could also be a nag, one who tried to wear the breeches in the family; Noah's wife as she appears in English mystery plays is often cited as a literary prototype, although she strikes her husband only after he hits her.[29] The woman beating her husband was a commonplace in medieval art, appearing in manuscript illumination and on misericords in a number of English churches (see fig. 5).[30] She could be a figure of fun, but she also represented the overthrow of the proper order of things.

Scolding and gossiping were not exclusive to women, though women occasioned by far the bulk of the charges. In the church courts of London, women were accused of defamation far more often than men, and not just of defaming a particular person but as "common defamers of [their] neighbors."[31] They also made up a larger percentage of those accused of scolding, although there are not as many of these as of defamers. Many of these same women were also accused of prostitution or some other sexual crime. In 1489–92, for example, of 161 women charged as whores, 45 were charged at the same time as common defamers of their neighbors, common scolds, or both.[32] When a woman was charged as a "common whore and bawd and gossip and disturber of the peace" the long list of accusations may have been merely an emphatic way of saying, "Here is a woman out of control."[33] Of course, there must have been some specific reason for the application of particular labels to particular women, since not everyone accused of being a

Fig. 5. A woman beats her husband with her distaff. From the Luttrell Psalter, English, fourteenth-century. British Library, MS Additional 42130, fol. 60r. *(Reproduced by permission of the British Library.)*

prostitute or a bawd was also accused of being a scold. The connection is common enough, though, to indicate a general concern with feminine disorderliness, of which whoredom formed an integral part. Whether it was her tongue or her body that was out of control, the independent woman had to be regulated.

Other disorderly women besides scolds can illuminate the situation of the whore. Alewives—women who brewed commercially—provide one example. In the sixteenth century there was a good deal of misogynistic literature directed against alewives, which may reflect animosities that developed earlier, the most famous work being the poem "The Tunning of Elynour Rummyng" by John Skelton.[34] Since most women brewed for their families, commercial brewing was a logical step for women interested in entering the cash economy. Alewives who did not operate directly under the authority of their husbands, however, could be seen as threatening to the social order. They undermined their husbands' position as head of household, handled money and thus challenged men's economic hegemony, and avoided regulation by male magistrates. They were seen as disrespectful not only of secular authorities but also of God and the church. Like all victualers they were suspected of cheating in their trade, but this suspicion was exacerbated by their gender and connected with the misogynist tradition. As part of that tradition the alewife could be depicted as a prostitute or a harborer of prostitutes. There were no doubt alewives who did cheat their customers and whose sexual morals were not up to the church's standards; but alewives as a group were constructed as disorderly and, like other independent women, sexualized and in some way assimilated to whores.

We have seen how the construction of the whore as one whose sexuality was out of control grew out of the gender system of late medieval England. Sexual desire and sexual behavior were attributed to the woman; sex was her raison d'être; sexual sins were the most serious for her; and chastity was her highest virtue. A woman's sexual behavior that did not conform to the norms was more shocking than a man's because a woman was defined much more entirely by her sexuality and sexual behavior. Lust was woman's archetypal sin; this was why the redeemed whore had such power as a symbol of repentance. But the whore was not only a creation of this gender system; she was also an important part of it and had her effect on the way other women—all women—were viewed and treated. Scrutiny of women's sexual behavior was a major means of social control.

The condoning, official or unofficial, of commercial prostitution fortified the notion that all women were venal. There was no sharp line between the commercial prostitute and other women. The same terms were used for prostitutes as for other sexually deviant women; whether they took money or not made no difference. The whore was lustful, like all women; she just acted on that lust indiscriminately. Prostitutes were simply the market-oriented version of a more general phenomenon. Because any woman could be considered a whore whether or not she was paid for sex, any woman could be placed in the same category of lust and venality as the commercial prostitute.

The connection of feminine sexuality with prostitution made it extremely difficult for any woman to maintain her independence. The option of chastity was open to her if she or her family could acquire the dowry for entrance into a convent; otherwise, if a woman did not marry and acquire support within the family economy, she had to find that support within another family, by working as a domestic of some sort, or else had to go it alone in a world of very limited opportunities for the never-married woman without capital.[35] At the same time that economic factors might propel her toward prostitution as a means of earning a living, cultural factors might also propel her toward whoredom: that is, a single woman was a threat, and if she did not settle down with one man—whether because she had more than one lover or because she had none—she ran a strong risk of being labeled "common," a whore.[36] Even at times when work opportunit: relatively good for women and there was less economic pressure to prostitution, independent women might for that very reason present more of a threat.

A fundamental contradiction ran through medieval England's treatment of the prostitute. As an institution prostitution was treated as a necessary evil. As individuals, however, prostitutes were stigmatized, prosecuted by various authorities, and regarded as the dregs of society. Providing a socially necessary service did not earn one society's respect. The church provided a message of hope for the repentant whore, but it also drove home the message that all women who did not completely repress their sexuality were whores. In short, the individual whore found herself devalued for her sexual behavior and feared for not fitting into the system of gender control while at the same time she was tolerated as the object of unrestrained and unreproved masculine lust.

The extent to which prostitutes themselves, women at risk for being identified as prostitutes, or other people within the prostitutes' social milieu accepted these dominant attitudes was, no doubt, less than total, but neither was it negligible. The dominant groups within the society not only controlled the production of texts but also had the opportunity to disseminate their views and to effectuate them through legal practice.

Casting certain women as whores in order to define a category of respectable, chaste womanhood under masculine control was part of a larger process by which the norms of medieval society were defined. It is in this sense that the marginal becomes central to the way a society understands itself and its members. In medieval England commercial prostitution was a small but significant part of the urban social and economic structure, but the whoredom that became conflated with it was an even more significant part of the structure of late medieval English gender relations.

Notes

BIHR	Borthwick Institute for Historical Research, York
BL	British Library
CLRO	Corporation of London Records Office
DRO	Devon Record Office
EETS	Early English Text Society
GLRO	Greater London Record Office
HMSO	His/Her Majesty's Stationery Office
HRO	Hampshire Record Office
Jour	Journal
KAO	Kent Archives Office
LAO	Lincolnshire Archives Office
L-B	Letter-Book
MCR	Mayor's Court Roll
NRO	Norfolk Record Office
NottsRO	Nottinghamshire Record Office
PMR	Plea and Memoranda Roll
PRO	Public Record Office
Rep	Repertory Book
RO	Record Office
SCRO	Southampton City Record Office
Sharpe, *Cal L-B* . . .	Reginald R. Sharpe, ed., *Calendar of Letter-Book* . . .
SP	John of Bromyard, *Summa Praedicantium*
SRO	Suffolk Record Office
Thomas, *Cal PMR*	A. H. Thomas and Philip E. Jones, eds., *Calendar of Plea and Memoranda Rolls*
WAM	Westminster Abbey Muniments
YML	York Minster Library

Introduction

1. See Monica Green, "Female Sexuality in the Medieval West," *Trends in History* 4 (1990): 130; Sarah Stanbury and Linda Lomperis, eds., *Feminist Approaches to the Body in Medieval Literature* (Philadelphia: University of Pennsylvania Press, 1993). Today gay men are often defined by their sexual identity, which implies that straight men are too, although less explicitly (since heterosexuality is presumed, it is often not labeled). Identity during the Middle Ages, however, was much less based on sexual orientation. Ruth Mazo Karras and

David Lorenzo Boyd, "*Ut Cum Muliere:* A Male Transvestite Prostitute in Fourteenth-Century London" in *The Pleasures of History: Reading Sexualities in Premodern Europe,* ed. Louise Fradenburg and Carla Freccero (London: Routledge, in press).

2. *Pace* Eve Levin, *Sex and Society in the World of the Orthodox Slavs, 900–1700* (Ithaca, N.Y.: Cornell University Press, 1989), 13, who states that "sexuality can be examined apart from family structure or the status of women" (although her analysis of sexuality among the Slavs is much more sensitive to gender issues than this programmatic statement would indicate).

3. The same might be said of male prostitutes, but there are both theoretical and practical reasons for keeping the discussion focused on female prostitution. I am here considering prostitution as an aspect of the construction of feminine sexuality, and in this regard female prostitution is most relevant. A consideration of male prostitution would be a telling point of comparison, but the practical consideration enters here: I have found only one case of male prostitution in medieval England (see p. 70). The text is given in David Lorenzo Boyd and Ruth Mazo Karras, "The Interrogation of a Male Transvestite Prostitute in Fourteenth-Century London," *GLQ: A Journal of Lesbian and Gay Studies* (1994): 459–65.

4. The most important work on the history of prostitution is Judith Walkowitz, *Prostitution and Victorian Society: Women, Class, and the State* (Cambridge: Cambridge University Press, 1980). In opposition to my claims of respectability for the history of sexuality as a field, see the essay by Catharine MacKinnon, "Does Sexuality Have a History?," in *Discourses of Sexuality: From Aristotle to AIDS,* ed. Domna C. Stanton (Ann Arbor: University of Michigan Press, 1992), 117–19, 127.

5. Those who would dispute the significance of prostitution on the grounds that there were not many prostitutes should consider the vast quantity of scholarship on medieval religious women. Nuns were not numerous either—accounting for less than 1 percent of the female population at any given time in the Middle Ages—but no one questions their importance in the history of medieval spirituality or of medieval women generally.

6. The commercial economy did not develop only in the period on which this book focuses. See R. H. Britnell, *The Commercialisation of English Society, 1000–1500* (Cambridge: Cambridge University Press, 1993), esp. 228–31.

7. For the historiography on women in medieval England, see Barbara Hanawalt, "Golden Ages for the History of Medieval English Women," in *Women in Medieval History and Historiography,* ed. Susan Mosher Stuard (Philadelphia: University of Pennsylvania Press, 1987), 1–24; see also chapter 3 in the present study.

8. Sodomy (which usually, though not always, meant sex between men) was seen not as an exclusive preference but as possible for any man, especially if access to women was denied. See Ruth Mazo Karras, "Sexuality and Marginality," paper presented at the conference "Peripheral Visions," held at the University of Oregon, April 1994.

9. I discuss here only a few works; this is not intended to be a review of the secondary literature. For a more complete bibliography, see Vern L. Bullough and Lilli Sentz, eds., *Prostitution: A Guide to Sources, 1960–1990* (New York: Garland, 1992), 81–94; Ruth Mazo Karras, "Prostitution in Medieval Europe," in

Handbook of Medieval Sexuality, ed. Vern L. Bullough and James Brundage (New York: Garland, in press).

10. Such works include Jacques LeGoff, "Licit and Illicit Trades in the Medieval West," in *Time, Work, and Culture in the Middle Ages,* trans. Arthur Goldhammer (Chicago: University of Chicago Press, 1980), 58–70; Marie-Thérèse Lorçin, "La Prostituée des fabliaux, est-elle intégrée ou exclue?," in *Exclus et systèmes d'exclusion dans la littérature et la civilisation médiévales* (Aix-en-Provence: Centre universitaire d'études et de recherches médiévales, 1978), 105–117; Bronislaw Geremek, *The Margins of Society in Late Medieval Paris,* trans. Jean Birrell (Cambridge: Cambridge University Press, 1987), 211–41; Franz Irsigler and Arnold Lassotta, *Bettler und Gaukler, Dirnen und Henker: Randgruppen und Aussenseiter in Köln, 1300–1600* (Cologne: Greven Verlag, 1984), 11–16, 179–227; Wolfgang Hartung, "Gesellschaftliche Randgruppen im Spätmittelalter. Phänomen und Begriff," in *Städtische Randgruppen und Minderheiten,* ed. Bernhard Kirchgässner and Fritz Reuter (Sigmaringen: Jan Thorbecke Verlag, 1986), 66–70. On the difference between marginality and deviance in sociological terms, see Edward Sagarin, *Deviants and Deviance: An Introduction to the Study of Disvalued People and Behavior* (New York: Praeger, 1975), 34–36.

11. See, e.g., Jill Harsin, *Policing Prostitution in Nineteenth-Century Paris* (Princeton, N.J.: Princeton University Press, 1985); Mary Gibson, *Prostitution and the State in Italy, 1860–1915* (New Brunswick, N.J.: Rutgers University Press, 1986).

12. Leah Lydia Otis, *Prostitution in Medieval Society: The History of an Urban Institution in Languedoc* (Chicago: University of Chicago Press, 1985), is the best example.

13. Walkowitz, *Prostitution and Victorian Society,* is the leading study; see also Barbara Meil Hobson, *Uneasy Virtue: The Politics of Prostitution and the American Reform Tradition* (New York: Basic Books, 1987); Carroll Smith-Rosenberg, *Disorderly Conduct* (New York: Oxford University Press, 1986), 111–13; Ruth Rosen, *The Lost Sisterhood: Prostitution in America, 1900–1918* (Baltimore, Md.: Johns Hopkins University Press, 1982), 63–68.

14. See Jacques Rossiaud, *Medieval Prostitution,* trans. Lydia G. Cochrane (Oxford: Basil Blackwell, 1988), 129–59.

15. Ibid., 38–51. Otis, *Prostitution in Medieval Society,* 100–105, discusses the historiography on this issue.

16. I dismiss out of hand sociobiological explanations which imply that prostitution is inevitable because of genetic drives, e.g., Richard Symanski, *The Immoral Landscape: Female Prostitution in Western Societies* (Toronto: Butterworths, 1981), 239–87.

17. Caroline Bynum, for example, has argued that women and men understood and used symbols differently, and that the identification of femininity with the flesh was not (at least in women's view) a negative association of women with sinful carnality but rather a positive affirmation of their connection with the humanity of Christ. See Caroline Walker Bynum, *Holy Feast and Holy Fast: The Religious Significance of Food to Medieval Women* (Berkeley: University of California Press, 1987); idem, ". . . And Woman His Humanity: Female Imagery in the Religious Writings of the Later Middle Ages," in *Gender and Religion: On the Complexity of Symbols,* ed. Caroline Walker Bynum, Stevan Harrell, and Paula Richman (Boston: Beacon Press, 1986), 257–88.

18. P. J. P. Goldberg has done this, for example, in *Women, Work, and Life Cycle in a Medieval Economy: Women in York and Yorkshire, c. 1300–1520* (Oxford: Oxford University Press, 1992).

19. This issue of agency is hotly debated today, for example, with regard to pornography and the women who participate in producing it.

20. Bonnie S. Anderson and Judith P. Zinsser, *A History of Their Own: Women in Europe from Prehistory to the Present* (New York: Harper and Row, 1988), 1:26–66.

21. Luise White, *The Comforts of Home: Prostitution in Colonial Nairobi* (Chicago: University of Chicago Press, 1990), 6–7.

22. Marilynn Wood Hill, *Their Sisters' Keepers: Prostitution in New York City, 1830–1870* (Berkeley: University of California Press, 1993), 5.

23. Valerie Jenness, *Making It Work: The Prostitutes' Rights Movement in Perspective* (New York: Aldine de Gruyter, 1993), provides a valuable account of the contemporary debate among feminists and prostitutes over the issues of agency and exploitation and over whether sex work should be treated like any other work.

24. White, *The Comforts of Home*, in particular, is based on oral interviews with former prostitutes.

25. Walkowitz, *Prostitution*.

26. Of course, anything we can know about the realities of prostitutes' lives comes to us through texts that are in their own way representations of reality. To discover how prostitutes themselves experienced their lives requires us to question the correspondence between the sources and that experience. Nevertheless, it is possible to speak of the story of what prostitutes did, where they lived, who their customers were, and so forth as being a different type of history from the story of attitudes toward prostitutes.

27. See Joan Scott, "The Evidence of Experience," *Critical Inquiry* 17 (1991): 782.

28. See Gerda Lerner, *The Creation of Patriarchy* (New York: Oxford University Press, 1986), 129–33, on the problematic notion of temple prostitution.

29. The idea of the social construction of sexuality has been most thoroughly discussed with regard to homosexuality. Although homosexuality and prostitution (in the modern understanding of the terms) are not comparable categories, the notion that the same behavior is understood differently in different cultures applies to both. For discussions of social construction (pro and con), see John Boswell, "Revolutions, Universals, and Sexual Categories," David M. Halperin, "Sex Before Sexuality: Pederasty, Politics, and Power in Classical Athens," and Robert Padgug, "Sexual Matters: Rethinking Sexuality in History," all in *Hidden from History: Reclaiming the Gay and Lesbian Past*, ed. Martin Duberman, Martha Vicinus, and George Chauncey, Jr. (New York: Penguin, 1989), 17–36, 37–53, and 54–64.

30. The *Oxford English Dictionary* attests to *prostitute* as a verb in 1530, an adjective in 1563, and a noun in 1613.

31. For example, Pennsylvania Consolidated Statues §5902 stipulates that "[a] person is guilty of prostitution; a misdemeanor of the third degree, if he or she: (1) is an inmate of a house of prostitution or otherwise engages in sexual activity as a business; or (2) loiters in or within view of any public place for the purpose of being hired to engage in sexual activity." The statute goes on to define several other terms ("inmate," "house of prostitution," "sexual activity"). See B. J. George, Jr., "Legal, Medical, and Psychiatric Considerations in the

Control of Prostitution," *Michigan Law Review* 60 (1962): 720, on the use of "common prostitute" in U.S. law.

32. Thomas of Chobham, *Thomae de Chobham Summa Confessorum*, 7.2.6a.1, ed. F. Broomfield (Louvain: Éditions Nauwelaerts, 1968), 346–47.

33. This is not meant to be a universal or "true" definition of "prostitute"; I present it merely to explain what I mean when I use the term. For formal definitions, see John H. Gagnon, "Prostitution," in *International Encyclopedia of the Social Sciences* (New York: Macmillan, 1968), 12:592; Geoffrey May, "Prostitution," in *Encyclopedia of the Social Sciences* (New York: Macmillan, 1934), 12:553. Although much of the analysis in these encyclopedia articles is outdated, the definitions still fairly reflect the way modern social scientists use the term and understand the institution. Some feminists would take a broader view of the exchange of sex for money and classify married women who are supported by their husbands as prostitutes. Joanna Russ, "Comment on 'Prostitution in Medieval Canon Law' by James Brundage," *Signs* 2 (1977): 972; Carole Pateman, *The Sexual Contract* (Stanford: Stanford University Press, 1988), 190. Emma Goldman made this point in 1917: "It is merely a question of degree whether [a woman] sells herself to one man, in or out of marriage, or to many men." Emma Goldman, *The Traffic in Women and Other Essays on Feminism* (New York: Times Change Press, 1970), 20. Yet a traditional wife provides many services to her husband other than the sexual, as analyses of the cash value of women's domestic labor have shown. Marriage in the Middle Ages, although it may in some ways have involved the purchase of a woman, was also about more than sexual access. Marital sex was important to moralists as a way of controlling concupiscence, but marriage mainly had to do with reproduction and the creation of a household economy. It is more helpful to restrict the term "prostitution" to cases where the focus was on sexual behavior rather than household formation. There were in the Middle Ages many situations other than marriage in which sexual access was exchanged for material support; the near-ubiquity of mistresses among the nobility is a case in point. These women would sometimes be labeled whores, as would mistresses of priests. Such long-term relationships, however, can easily be distinguished—by us, and also by people in the Middle Ages—from commercial sex, and we shall see that not all nonmarital liaisons were treated the same.

34. On Latin terminology, see Harry Wedek, "Synonyms for Meretrix," *Classical Weekly* 37 (1944): 116–17.

35. James A. Brundage, "Prostitution in the Medieval Canon Law," *Signs* 1 (1976): 825 n. 2, uses "synonyms for 'prostitute' such as 'harlot,' 'whore,' 'tart,' 'trollop,' and the like," on the grounds that " 'prostitute' is a relatively neutral, almost clinical term. . . . [S]ince the sources . . . employ terms which are more judgmental than neutral, it seemed appropriate to try to convey some sense of that fact by using English terms of a similar sort." Brundage is generally right that "the word *meretrix* in Latin . . . carries about as much judgmental weight as 'whore' does in English; it is certainly less neutral than 'prostitute,' " although *meretrix* can also be used in a technical legal sense. Still, I find it more useful to keep to one term for translation. "Whore" is a particularly appropriate term because it was used in much the same way in Middle English: although in the fourteenth and fifteenth centuries "hordom" included all sorts of sexual immorality and could be used to translate *adulterium*, "hore" was also given as the English equivalent of the Latin *meretrix*.

36. See Michel Foucault, *History of Sexuality,* vol. 1, *An Introduction,* trans. Robert Hurley (New York: Pantheon, 1978). Foucault argues that the medieval discourse about sex was unitary. Although this is an overstatement, it is true that it was less multiplicitous than in some later times and that there was in the Middle Ages one dominant discourse. See chapter 6 of this volume.

Chapter 1

1. Walkowitz, *Prostitution,* 69–89.

2. The central royal courts and county sessions of the peace did not deal with prostitution. Borough sessions of the peace occasionally did, as when the early sixteenth-century Quarter Sessions indictments for Norwich show an accusation of "keeping a brothel by force and arms," the formula required for a writ of trespass. NRO, Case 11, Shelf a, Parcel 1, m. 57, January 8, 1521. See, similarly, SRO, C8/1/13, m. 7: "Johanna Davy spinster committed adultery with divers men against the king's peace."

3. Richard M. Wunderli, *London Church Courts and Society on the Eve of the Reformation* (Cambridge, Mass.: Medieval Academy of America, 1981), 81; Brian Woodcock, *Medieval Ecclesiastical Courts in the Diocese of Canterbury* (London: Oxford University Press, 1952), 79; Sandra Brown, *The Medieval Courts of York Minster Peculiar* (York: St. Anthony's Press, 1984), 5. A good summary of ecclesiastical courts and the records they left is Dorothy Owen, *The Records of the Established Church in England Excluding Parochial Records* (London: British Records Association, 1970), 36–45, 47–48, 56; idem, "Ecclesiastical Jurisdiction in England, 1300–1550: The Records and Their Interpretation," in *The Materials, Sources, and Methods of Ecclesiastical History,* ed. Derek Baker (Oxford: Ecclesiastical History Society, 1975), 199–221, is slightly more detailed. See also Richard Helmholz, *Marriage Litigation in Medieval England* (London: Cambridge University Press, 1974), 6–24, which deals mainly, however, with instance cases. It is important to remember that when church officials and institutions were also landholders and hence also had manorial courts, these were distinct from the ecclesiastical courts. The same person or institution may have had both spiritual and temporal jurisdiction over an area but exercised them separately.

4. Robert C. Palmer, *English Law in the Age of the Black Death, 1348–1381: A Transformation of Governance and Law* (Chapel Hill: University of North Carolina Press, 1993), argues for an increased role for governmental power in controlling society in the second half of the fourteenth century. Although the focus is on the central government, some of the same reasons may apply on the local level as well.

5. The laws about whores and loose women thus applied to certain types of people rather than to people who committed specific acts. It is true that the phrasing of medieval legal process might imply that this was the case with most offenses—a person was punished for *being* a thief, even though this status was based on having committed a theft—but with such vague terms as "misruled" or "ill-governed," it is not particular acts but general character that is being condemned. To be affected by these laws, a woman had only to be identified by the jury of presentment; no one needed to prove that she had solicited or accepted money from a given partner.

6. CLRO, L-B A, fol. 130r (Sharpe, *Cal L-B A*, 218); CLRO, L-B D, fol. 116r (Sharpe, *Cal L-B D*, 246); Thomas Rymer, *Foedera, Conventiones, Litterae et Cujuscunque Generis Acta Publica* (London, 1818), vol. 2, pt 1, 124.

7. Henry Thomas Riley, ed., *Liber Albus*, vol. 1 of *Munimenta Gildhallae Londoniensis: Liber Albus, Liber Custumarum, et Liber Horn* (London: Longman, Brown, Green, Longmans and Roberts, 1859), 283, 332, 457–58; Henry Thomas Riley, trans., *Liber Albus: The White Book of the City of London* (London: Richard Griffin & Co., 1861), 246–47, 287, 394, except that where Riley translates *femme coursable* as "loose woman," I have substituted "whore."

8. See, e.g., CLRO, L-B K, fol. 11v (Sharpe, *Cal L-B K*, 17); L-B L, fols. 275v–276r (Sharpe, *Cal L-B L*, 269); for as late as the sixteenth century, see CLRO, L-B M, fol. 176r.

9. Riley, *Liber Albus*, 458–60; Riley, *Liber Albus: The White Book*, 394–95; also found in CLRO, L-B H, fol. 146v (see Sharpe, *Cal L-B H*, 189).

10. BL, MS Sloane 3160, fol. 84r (a fifteenth-century manuscript of the Saint Nicholas legend) has the father telling his daughters, "Tomorrow each of you take a white rod in your hands and live by your bodies." By the fourteenth century the word "yarde," one of the words used for "rod," was also being used for "penis," which might help explain the symbolism.

11. CLRO, L-B H, fol. 287r (Sharpe, *Cal L-B H*, 402), in *Memorials of London and London Life in the Thirteenth, Fourteenth, and Fifteenth Centuries*, ed. and trans. H. T. Riley (London: Longman, 1868), 535, except that I have substituted "whores" for "harlots."

12. CLRO, L-B K, fol. 179r (Sharpe, *Cal L-B K*, 230).

13. CLRO, L-B L, fol. 189v (Sharpe, *Cal L-B L*, 216).

14. CLRO, Rep 2, fol. 92v; 4, fol. 45r; 10, fol. 309v.

15. CLRO, Rep 3, fol. 33v.

16. CLRO, PMR A50, m. 5 (Thomas, *Cal PMR*, 4:124).

17. Although only one set of Wardmote presentments itself survives for the medieval period (CLRO, MS 242A for Portsoken Ward, 1465–83), the results of the Wardmote inquests were presented to the mayor and aldermen, and juries from the various wards also made presentments before the mayor and sheriffs. See, e.g., CLRO, Plea and Memoranda Rolls, A3, m. 4d, m. 14–15d; A5, m. 11 (Thomas, *Cal PMR*, 1:109, 124–27, 187–88).

18. See, e.g., CLRO, Jour 2, fols. 126r, 129v, 140v. These are occasionally accompanied by drawings of barrels or tuns, perhaps symbolizing the Tun prison where these culprits would be kept. These drawings are found occasionally with other cases but mostly with those involving incontinent priests and may indicate a particular resentment and hence gloating.

19. CLRO, L-B I, fol. 193v (Sharpe, *Cal L-B I*, 178), in Riley, *Memorials*, 647. Riley mistranscribes the amount of the fine, which is £20. See also CLRO, Jour 1, fols. 18v–19r.

20. CLRO, Jour 2, fols. 32v ff.

21. CLRO, Jour 2, fol. 106v; for bonds, see, e.g., CLRO, L-B K, fol. 54r (Sharpe, *Cal L-B K*, 75).

22. CLRO, L-B L, fol. 114r (Sharpe, *Cal L-B L*, 136).

23. CLRO, L-B I, fol. 194r (Sharpe, *Cal L-B I*, 178), 1417; quoted more fully on p. 43.

24. PRO, E13/26, m. 75d. See Michael Prestwich, trans., *York Civic Ordi-*

nances, 1301 (York: Borthwick Institute for Historical Research, 1976), 16–17.

25. Angelo Raine, ed., *York Civic Records* (York: Yorkshire Archeological Society, 1939), 1:58.

26. Francis B. Bickley, ed., *The Little Red Book of Bristol* (Bristol: W. Crofton Hemmons, 1900), 1:33–34. If such women remained, the doors of their houses were to be removed, as at York.

27. Dorothy M. Owen, *The Making of King's Lynn: A Documentary Survey* (London: British Academy, 1984), 268; Mary Bateson, ed., *Records of the Borough of Leicester* (London: C. J. Clay, 1901), 2:291; Historical Manuscripts Commission, "The Historical Manuscripts Belonging to the Mayor and Corporation of Rochester," in *Royal Commission on Historical Manuscripts, Ninth Report* (London: HMSO, 1883), 288; William Hudson, ed., *Leet Jurisdiction in the City of Norwich* (London: Bernard Quaritch, 1892), 58–59; Derek Keene, *Survey of Medieval Winchester* (Oxford: Clarendon Press, 1985), 391.

28. Historical Manuscripts Commission, "Records of the Corporation of Gloucester," in *Historical Manuscripts Commission, Twelfth Report*, pt. 9 (London: HMSO, 1891), 435.

29. DRO, Exeter Chamber Act Book, vol. 1, fols. 109r–110r.

30. Charles Henry Cooper, ed., *Annals of Cambridge* (Cambridge: Warwick & Co., 1842), 1:76, 1:85; H. E. Salter, ed., *Mediaeval Archives of the University of Oxford* (Oxford: Clarendon Press, 1920), 1:251–52; H. E. Salter, ed., *Registrum Cancellarii Oxoniensis, 1434–1469* (Oxford: Clarendon Press, 1932), 1:xviii, 332–33; Alan B. Cobban, *The Medieval English Universities: Oxford and Cambridge to c. 1500* (Berkeley: University of California Press, 1988), 364.

31. Mary Dormer Harris, ed., *The Coventry Leet Book* (London: Early English Text Society, 1909), 2:545, 2:552, 2:568.

32. In the United States, with its overcrowded prisons, prostitutes tend not to be sentenced to jail but rather are fined; similarly, in the Middle Ages prostitutes tended to be fined, as prisons were mainly for those awaiting trial rather than for punishment.

33. Riley, *Liber Albus*, 283; Riley, *Liber Albus: The White Book*, 247.

34. CLRO, L-B F, fol. 208r, in Riley, *Memorials*, 267; I have substituted "wanton" for Riley's "lewd," which in the Middle Ages had connotations of "uneducated" or "vulgar" not implied in the French *fole*.

35. CLRO, L-B H, fol. 139r, in Riley, *Memorials*, 458, except that I have substituted "whores" for his "harlots."

36. CLRO L-B A, fol. 130v (Sharpe, *Cal L-B L*, 220), I have altered Sharpe's translation, rendering *femmes* as "women" and *dames* as "ladies." For repeated parliamentary statutes limiting dress according to degree, see Frances Elizabeth Baldwin, *Sumptuary Legislation and Personal Regulation in England* (Baltimore, Md.: Johns Hopkins University Press, 1926).

37. CLRO, Rep 10, fols. 13v, 27r.

38. John Stow, *The Annales of England, faithfully collected out of the most authenticall Authors, Records, and other Monuments of Antiquitie, from the first inhabitation untill this present yeere 1592* (London: Ralfe Newbery, 1592), 392, reports a parliamentary ordinance in 1353 at the request of the Londoners, although he does not say how widely it applied. The hood was also used as an identifying mark in ritual punishment in London, Gloucester, and Exeter, and in the suburb of Westminster (WAM 50771, 50773d).

39. Bickley, *Little Red Book*, 2:229; Edward W. W. Veale, *The Great Red Book of Bristol* (Bristol: Bristol Record Society, 1933), 2:143.

40. This proclamation does not survive, and most of the cases from Great Yarmouth fined women simply for being whores. NRO, Y/C4/90, m. 12; Y/C4/94, m. 4; Y/C4/96, m. 10.

41. K. J. Allison, ed., *The City of Kingston upon Hull*, vol. 1 of *A History of the County of York: East Riding* (London: Oxford University Press, 1969), 75.

42. For East Smithfield, see PRO SC2/191/55–59; for Westminster, see WAM 50699–777; for Southwark, see Lambeth Palace Library, ED 969; for Walworth, see PRO SC2/205/29–37.

43. BL, Cotton Julius B iv, fol. 25v.

44. Maryanne Kowaleski, "Women's Work in a Market Town: Exeter in the Late Fourteenth Century," in *Women and Work in Preindustrial Europe*, ed. Barbara Hanawalt (Bloomington: Indiana University Press, 1986), 146; Ruth Mazo Karras, "The Regulation of Brothels in Later Medieval England," *Signs: Journal of Women in Culture and Society* 14 (1989): 407.

45. Keene, *Survey*, 391, although Keene feels that "the evidence is insufficient to determine whether, having abandoned the penalty of banishment, the authorities were adopting a policy of licencing brothel-keepers to operate." In both Exeter and Winchester, as elsewhere, fines for offenses such as scolding or disturbing the peace were also mixed in with commercial and sanitary fines, and it would be difficult to argue that the former were merely de facto licensing fees. The distinction between commercial offenses and offenses against the peace is not one that this type of court record made. Presentments and fines for similar activities tended to be grouped, but there was no formal division into commercial licensing fees and fines for offenses.

46. L. R. Poos, "Sex, Lies, and the Church Courts of Pre-Reformation England," *Journal of Interdisciplinary History* 25 (1995): 585–607.

47. Rape was a felony and as such was handled by the royal courts, but they treated it as a crime of violence against property rather than as a sexual offense. It is not directly relevant here. The only study for medieval England, John Marshall Carter, *Rape in Medieval England: An Historical and Sociological Study* (Lanham, Md.: University Press of America, 1985), is deeply flawed. See also John B. Post, "Ravishment of Women and the Statutes of Westminster," in *Legal Records and the Historian*, ed. J. H. Baker (London: Royal Historical Society, 1978), 150–64; James A. Brundage, "Rape and Seduction in the Medieval Canon Law," in *Sexual Practices and the Medieval Church*, ed. Vern L. Bullough and James Brundage (Buffalo: Prometheus Books, 1982), 141–48; and Kathryn Gravdal, *Ravishing Maidens: Writing Rape in Medieval French Literature and Law* (Philadelphia: University of Pennsylvania Press, 1991), 122–40, on the treatment of rape in medieval law.

48. See Judith M. Bennett, *Women in the Medieval Countryside: Gender and Household in Brigstock Before the Plague* (New York: Oxford University Press, 1987), 32–36, on the economic disadvantages of rural women.

49. Geoffrey Chaucer, *The Riverside Chaucer*, ed. Larry D. Benson (Boston: Houghton Mifflin, 1987); I have modernized the text.

50. Siegfried Wenzel, ed., *Fasciculus Morum: A Fourteenth-Century Preacher's Handbook*, bk. 6, chap. 2 (University Park: Pennsylvania State University Press,

1989), 631: "[W]hen such people are drunk they must visit the brothel and every corner of the village in search of women. . . ."

51. Marjorie McIntosh, "Finding Language for Misconduct: Jurors in Fifteenth-Century Local Courts," in *Intersections: History and Literature in the Fifteenth Century*, ed. Barbara Hanawalt and David Wallace (Minneapolis: University of Minnesota Press, in press).

52. Surrey Record Office, Kingston Manor Court Rolls, KF 1/1, m. 1d; KF 1/3, m. 1d.

53. S. C. Ratcliff, ed., *Elton Manorial Records, 1279–1351*, trans. D. M. Gregory (Cambridge: Roxburghe Club, 1946). The scribe interlined "quasi" ("sort of") before "common." Perhaps he had some notion of what a prostitute was and was trying to express that she was one.

54. Eleanor Searle, *Lordship and Community: Battle Abbey and Its Banlieu, 1066–1538* (Toronto: Pontifical Institute for Mediaeval Studies, 1974), 409.

55. Christopher Dyer, *Lords and Peasants in a Changing Society: The Estates of the Bishopric of Worcester, 680–1540* (Cambridge: Cambridge University Press, 1980), 359; Essex Record Office, D/DP M55, m. 2, D/DP M66, m. 1.

56. This is not a random sample, since some counties are far better represented in the PRO's holdings than others, and some landowners are better represented than others. Given the total absence of occurrences, however, there seems little need to be concerned with statistical techniques here. Some of the rolls, though they do not mention prostitutes, do include scolds: see, e.g., West Ham, Essex, SC2/172/18; Leyndon, Essex, SC2/173/12; Culliford, Devon, SC2/169/21; Middlewich, Chester, SC2/156/5.

57. For examples, see McIntosh, "Finding Language."

58. E. D. Jones, "The Medieval Leyrwite: A Historical Note on Female Fornication," *English Historical Review* 107 (1992): 951–52, argues that in one set of court records, large numbers of leyrwite fines are grouped together in an unusual pattern and the fines are especially high, suggesting that these women may have been brothel prostitutes. But they were not fined repeatedly, and it is difficult to imagine how one village could have supported five professional prostitutes.

59. See, e.g., Margaret Bowker, ed., *An Episcopal Court Book for the Diocese of Lincoln, 1514–1520* (Lincoln: Lincoln Record Society, 1967), 130, for a man "promoting whoredom" in his home.

60. James A. Brundage, *Law, Sex, and Christian Society in Medieval Europe* (Chicago: University of Chicago Press, 1987), is the indispensable reference on the canon law about sex.

61. Wunderli, *London Church Courts*, 99.

62. See, e.g., Guildhall MS 9064/8, fol. 147v, in which a woman is accused of being a whore "with divers persons at the Stews side." Women who lived on the London side of the river came under the London ecclesiastical courts; if they lived in the bishop of Winchester's liberty, they were also in his spiritual jurisdiction, from which records unfortunately do not survive. It would be interesting to know whether prostitutes employed at the stews sanctioned by the bishop in his temporal capacity were punished as whores by him in his spiritual capacity. Geoffrey Chaucer would indicate not: " 'By St. Peter! So women of the stews,' / Quoth the Summoner, 'are put out of our jurisdiction.' " *Riverside Chaucer*, 123, ll. 1332–33.

63. Ibid., ll. 1339–43, 1355–62.

64. Guildhall Library, MS 9064/5, fol. 159r. The defamer purged herself and was dismissed; no result survives for the other case. Cf. another pair of cases, Guildhall Library MS 9064/4 fols. 77v–78r, in which one woman was accused of defamation and another of adultery (the latter purged herself; no result survives for the former). Defamation cases were instance cases, brought by a plaintiff rather than by the court, and to bring a defamation suit the defamed plaintiff would purge herself canonically, indicating that the insult was taken as a serious accusation of illicit behavior. See, e.g., Guildhall Library, MS 9064/2, fol. 143v and passim.

65. Everston purged herself successfully, and the judge ordered that no one accuse her of the crime anymore on pain of excommunication. E. M. Elvey, ed., *The Courts of the Archdeacon of Buckingham, 1483–1523* (Aylesbury: Buckinghamshire Record Society, 1975), 202. Nash was not charged with defamation. See similarly Hereford AB 8, 140, Johanna Barrett.

66. Guildhall Library, MS 9064/4 passim. See Poos, "Sex, Lies, and the Church Courts," for related data from other jurisdictions.

67. Brundage, *Law, Sex, and Christian Society,* 248, 390, 464–65.

68. Guildhall Library, MS 9064/1, fol. 82r; 9064/4, fol. 271r; 9064/1, fol. 65v, fol. 10v.

69. The text is actually unclear on who paid whom: Guildhall Library, MS 9064/6, fol. 24v. "Joan Crompp is a common whore, and especially in adultery with a certain [blank], serving with her, by the token that he laid [supposuit] her eighteen times in one week and each time had 2d. for the work." In Latin, word order does not determine meaning, and the subject of "had" could be either Joan or the manservant. An accusation implying that a servant had three shillings to spend on sex would not be plausible, however. Supporting the idea that this accusation was based on general hostility is its conclusion citing "public voice and fame," rare in this sort of accusation. No result is given.

70. Wunderli, *London Church Courts,* 100.

71. Guildhall Library, MS 9064/6, fol. 66r. But it could also be that later information about her public reputation had come to light; this is far from the only example of interlinear additions to the charges in the London act books.

72. Guildhall Library, MS 9064/3, fol. 51v.

73. Guildhall Library, MS 9064/2, fol. 84r; 9064/1, fol. 107v.

74. Thomas of Chobham, *Summa Confessorum,* 7.2.6a.i, 346–47.

75. On the distinction between fornication and adultery, see Ruth Mazo Karras, "The Latin Vocabulary of Illicit Sex in English Ecclesiastical Court Records," *Journal of Medieval Latin* 2 (1992): 3–4.

76. If she were really a common prostitute, it is not likely that she would have been able to identify the father of her child to the satisfaction of the authorities. A. Hamilton Thompson, ed., *Visitations of Rural Deaneries by William Atwater, Bishop of Lincoln, and His Commissaries, 1517–1520,* vol. 1 of *Visitations in the Diocese of Lincoln, 1517–1531* (Hereford: Lincoln Record Society, 1940), 56.

77. Guildhall Library, MS 9064/5, fol. 59v; for "indicted whore" or "indicted bawd," see, e.g., MS 9064/1, fol. 155v and passim.

78. Guildhall Library, MS 9064/6, fol. 70r.

79. LAO, Vj/4, fol. 78r.

80. See, e.g., YML, M2(1)f, fol. 38r, in which the man confessed and did penance; BIHR D/C AB 1, fols. 37r, 111r, in which only the woman's partner, a vicar choral, was punished for scandalizing the community by bringing her into his lodgings. In none of these cases was the woman sentenced, but the same woman (Marion Scot) involved in the last two cases was sentence to penance for fornication on another occasion without being labeled a whore (BIHR D/C AB 1, fol. 77r).

81. See e.g., BIHR, D/C AB 1, fol. 215v. Joan Beecham had to find twelve compurgators, an unusually high number, in eight of the cases; in the other she confessed and was sentenced to three fustigations (penitential processions).

82. BIHR, CP.F.99.

83. Wunderli, *London Church Courts*, 76–78. These three terms occur together so often that it must be a formula. When more original phrasing is used, so that one can assume the court has recorded the actual terms, they still deal overwhelmingly with sexual offenses: for men about half the time, for women almost exclusively. (From a sample covering November 1489 to December 1490, from Guildhall Library MS 9064/4, for women defaming men there were 35 sexual insults, 25 nonsexual; for men defaming men, 21 sexual, 20 nonsexual; for women defaming women, 87 sexual, 11 nonsexual; for men defaming women, 55 sexual, 2 nonsexual). See also Poos, "Sex, Lies, and the Church Courts."

84. The Ely court records also show the defamation cases for women as being mainly sexual: see, e.g., Liber B, 5v, 14r, 18v, 34r and passim.

85. Guildhall Library, MS 9064/4, fols. 13v, 50r, 143v; 9064/2, fol. 27r.

86. Guildhall Library, MS 9064/4, fol. 66v.

87. BIHR, CP.E.72.

88. BIHR, CP.F.83; BIHR, CP.F.153; Guildhall Library, MS 9064/4, fol. 25v.

89. See Ralph Houlbrooke, *Church Courts and the People During the English Reformation, 1520–1570* (Oxford: Oxford University Press, 1979), 81, on a later period.

90. Guildhall Library, MS 9064/4, fols. 52r, 115r; 9064/1, fol. 98r. The alleged defamer in the second case was also accused of fornication with the same man, so romantic or sexual rivalry may have been involved.

91. J. A. Sharpe, *Defamation and Sexual Slander in Early Modern England: The Church Courts at York* (York: University of York, Borthwick Institute for Historical Research, 1980); C. A. Haigh, "Slander and the Church Courts in the Sixteenth Century," *Transactions of the Lancashire and Cheshire Antiquarian Society* 78 (1975): 1–13.

92. Defamation cases could also be brought in the temporal courts, both borough and manorial; here the plaintiff had to allege monetary damage, although the allegation could be purely formulaic. These also show that being called a whore was considered worth contesting. See R. H. Helmholz, ed., *Select Cases on Defamation to 1600* (London: Selden Society, 1985), for relations between the ecclesiastical and secular law on defamation, together with selected examples of court cases.

93. Gervase Rosser, "London and Westminster: The Suburb in the Urban Economy in the Late Middle Ages," in *Towns and Townspeople in the Fifteenth Century*, ed. John A. F. Thompson (Gloucester: Alan Sutton, 1988), 54–55.

94. See, e.g., Guido Ruggiero, *Binding Passions: Tales of Magic, Marriage,*

and Power at the End of the Renaissance (New York: Oxford University Press, 1993), 57–87.

Chapter 2

1. In addition to other works cited in this section, see Iwan Bloch, *Die Prostitution*, vol. 1 (Berlin: Louis Marcus Verlagsbuchhandlung, 1912), which contains a wealth of not always entirely accurate information. For a full bibliographical account, see Karras, "Prostitution in Medieval Europe."

2. Richard Trexler, "La Prostitution florentine au XVe siècle: Patronages et clientèles," *Annales: Economies, sociétés, civilisations* 36 (1980): 983; Elisabeth Pavan, "Police des moeurs, société et politique à Venise à la fin du Moyen Age," *Revue Historique* 264 (1980): 241–88; Jacques Rossiaud, "Prostitution, Youth, and Society in Towns of South Eastern France in the Fifteenth Century," trans. Elborg Forster, in *Deviants and the Abandoned in French Society*, ed. Robert Forster and Orest Ranum (Baltimore, Md.: Johns Hopkins University Press, 1978), 6–8, 12–13; Peter Schuster, *Das Frauenhaus: Städtische Bordelle in Deutschland (1350–1600)* (Paderborn: Ferdinand Schöningh, 1992), 40–51; Lyndal Roper, "Discipline and Respectability: Prostitution and the Reformation in Augsburg," *History Workshop* (1985): 4; Joseph Baader, ed., *Nürnberger Polizeiordnungen aus dem XIII bis XV Jahrhundert* (Stuttgart: Litterarische Verein, 1861), 117; Lorenz Westenrieder, *Beyträge zur vaterländischen Historie, Geographie, Staatistik, etc.* (Munich: Joseph Lindauer, 1800), 6:185; Mary Elizabeth Perry, "'Lost Women' in Early Modern Seville: The Politics of Prostitution," *Feminist Studies* 4 (1978): 196 and 204–6; idem, *Gender and Disorder in Early Modern Seville* (Princeton: Princeton University Press, 1990), 46; Otis, *Prostitution*, 103–5.

3. Hartung, "Gesellschaftliche Randgruppen," 67–68; Karras, "Sexuality and Marginality."

4. Irsigler and Lassotta, *Bettler und Gaukler*, 184; Otis, *Medieval Prostitution*, 54–56; František Graus, "Randgruppen der städtischen Gesellschaft im Spätmittelalter," *Zeitschrift für historische Forschung* 8 (1981): 408. Schuster, *Das Frauenhaus*, 45–48, argues that in German towns the brothels were generally not important sources of income.

5. Schuster, *Das Frauenhaus*, 114–21; Brigitte Rath, "Prostitution und spätmittelalterliche Gesellschaft im österreichisch-süddeutschen Raum," in *Frau und Spätmittelalterlicher Alltag. Internationaler Kongress Krems an der Donau 2. bis 5. Oktober 1984* (Vienna: Verlag der österreichischen Akademie der Wissenschaften, 1986), 567–68; Trexler, "La Prostitution florentine," 994; Roper, "Discipline and Respectability," 20.

6. Geremek, *Margins of Society*, 89–94, 214–16; see also Anne Terroine, "Le Roi de ribauds de l'Hôtel du roi et les prostituées parisiennes," *Revue historique de droit* 56 (1978): 253–67.

7. Irsigler and Lassotta, *Bettler und Gaukler*, 181–83.

8. Schuster, *Das Frauenhaus*, 145–53; Brundage, *Law, Sex, and Christian Society*, 346, 351–52. The laws prohibiting whores from wearing certain kinds of clothing also stemmed from a fear that the love of finery might otherwise cause women to prostitute themselves; see Rossiaud, "Prostitution, Youth, and Soci-

ety," 4. This does not seem to have been a concern for the towns in which whores were exempt from sumptuary legislation, where any woman wearing excessively elaborate clothing would automatically be deemed a whore.

9. Mary Elizabeth Perry, "Deviant Insiders: Legalized Prostitutes and a Consciousness of Women in Early Modern Seville," *Comparative Studies in Society and History* 27 (1985): 138–58, suggests that brothels were closed on feast days not for the sake of the prostitutes' souls but so the municipality could demonstrate that it retained control. On homes for repentant prostitutes, see Sherrill Cohen, *The Evolution of Women's Asylums Since 1500* (New York: Oxford University Press, 1992). My interpretation here differs from that in Larissa J. Taylor's "Strange Bedfellows: Preachers and Prostitutes in Late Medieval Europe" (paper presented at the Twenty-first Annual Meeting of the Western Society for French History, Missoula, Montana, October 1993), which argues for the reality and the cultural importance of the conversion of prostitutes.

10. Roper, "Discipline and Respectability," 6.

11. Schuster, *Das Frauenhaus,* 156–68.

12. Ibid., 135–58.

13. In Karras, "Regulation of Brothels," I claimed that there were only two such brothels. I now know of three and would not rule out the possibility of more.

14. William Langland, *The Vision of William Concerning Piers the Plowman,* ed. W. W. Skeat, Text C, Passus 9, ll. 71–75 (Oxford: Oxford University Press, 1886), 1:199.

15. KAO, Sa/AC1, fols. 186r, 195r. In the first of these cases a woman was called a whore for living with a married man. In the three other cases it is not clear exactly what the sexual offense was thought to be.

16. KAO, Sa/AC1, fol. 217v. The term "Galleymen" was common at the time to refer to Italian (particularly Genoese or Venetian) traders, and the name of the house may indicate whose custom was expected.

17. KAO, Sa/AC2, Sandwich Year Book 2 (White Book), fol. 32v; fols. 35r–v. For more details, see Karras, "Regulation of Brothels."

18. Annie B. Wallis Chapman, ed., *The Black Book of Southampton* (Southampton: Southampton Record Society, 1912), 1:6.

19. SCRO, SC5/3/1, fol. 44v.

20. A. L. Merson, ed., *The Third Book of Remembrance of Southampton, 1514–1602,* vol. 2 (Southampton: University of Southampton, 1955), 2.

21. SCRO, SC5/3/1, fol. 41v; H. W. Gidden, ed., *The Book of Remembrance of Southampton* (Southampton: Cox and Sharland, 1928), 2:75.

22. See, e.g., SCRO, SC5/3/1, fols. 7v, 13r, 31r, 45v.

23. SCRO, SC5/3/1, fols. 17r, 40r. Those fined for being taken at the stews may have been taken for some offense other than patronizing the prostitutes; the court records also list many foreigners arrested for getting into fights at the stews. The scribe may merely have omitted to note that these were married men, but in the case of foreigners it is hard to see how the sheriff's men would have known this.

24. SCRO, SC5/3/1, fols. 13v, 16v, 36r.

25. See, e.g., Gidden, *Book of Remembrance,* 3:4; SCRO, SC5/3/1, fol. 31v.

26. SCRO, SC5/3/1, fols. 19r, 42v, 46r.

27. David J. Johnson, *Southwark and the City* (London: Corporation of Lon-

don, 1969), 43–60. The lords of liberties, here and elsewhere, had extraordinary jurisdictional privileges.

28. *Calendar of Close Rolls Preserved in the Public Record Office: Edward III* (London: HMSO, 1904), 7:551 (1345); *Calendar of the Patent Rolls Preserved in the Public Record Office: Edward III* (London: HMSO, 1903), 9:184 (1351), 12:24 (1361); CLRO, L-B H, fol. 264v (Sharpe, *Cal L-B H*, 372); Riley, *Liber Albus*, 277; Riley, *Liber Albus: The White Book*, 242.

29. See J. B. Post, "A Fifteenth-Century Customary of the Southwark Stews," *Journal of the Society of Archivists* (1977): 418–28, for the full text of the customs; and Karras, "Regulation of Brothels," for a modern English version of Post's text.

30. *Rotuli Parliamentorum* (London: Record Commission, 1767–77), 2:282, 4:447, 4:511; CLRO, MS 39C/SCM1 (Court Leet Proceedings), fol. 2r; see Martha Carlin, "The Urban Development of Southwark, c. 1200 to 1550" (Ph.D. diss., University of Toronto, 1983), 506.

31. Karras, "Regulation of Brothels," 427; subsequent references to the regulations appear in the text, according to the paragraph numbers assigned by Post, "Fifteenth-Century Customary," and adopted by Karras, "Regulation of Brothels."

32. HRO, Eccles. I, 85/1, lists violators of the customs from the year 1505–6.

33. Carlin, "Urban Development," 487 n. 18, compares the sixty shillings eightpence paid annually by each prostitute for her room to the twenty shillings per annum for tenements owned by Sir John Fastolf in Southwark.

34. PRO, C/48/191.

35. Schuster, *Das Frauenhaus*, 109.

36. HRO, Eccles. I 85/1. This was not explicitly stated in the existing copies of the customs; but in a list of questions for the bishop's officials to ask the keepers, one query asks whether they beat any of the women (B40), and stewholders were being fined for this offense in the early sixteenth century.

37. PRO, C1/64/897, C1/363/76; Carlin, "Urban Development," 499 n. 38, 500 n. 40.

38. *Rotuli Parliamentorum*, 4:447.

39. This provision is mysterious. An apron was a garment worn over other clothing, typically by working women or craftsmen, so it is not likely to have been a sign of respectability or class status forbidden to prostitutes. An apron could also be a garment worn by a bishop; this peculiar provision could be explained if the women were signifying their employment in the stews by wearing a mockery of the bishop's robes.

40. By 1475 there were ordinances suggested for the city of London that also prohibited cooks from pulling people by their sleeves to get them to buy their goods. CLRO, L-B L, fol. 109v (Sharpe, *Cal L-B L*, 129).

41. Robert Mannyng, *Robert of Brunne's "Handlyng Synne,"* ed. Frederick J. Furnivall (London: Kegan Paul, Trench, Trübner & Co., 1901), 2:238; Danielle Jacquart and Claude Thomasset, *Sexuality and Medicine in the Middle Ages*, trans. Matthew Adamson (Princeton: Princeton University Press, 1988), 174. See Otis, *Prostitution*, 41 n. 7, on the tradition of connecting prostitutes with disease, not necessarily venereal. The penalty for violating this regulation was harsher in the later manuscript tradition, although Post, "Fifteenth-Century Customary," 422, explains that this was probably due to a copyist's error, not to a deliberate raising of the penalty as syphilis became rampant.

42. It can hardly have been the case that prostitutes would spend a whole night with each customer, since at least sometimes the women must have had more than one customer per day; from the list of questions following the regulations (B54) it seems that the problem may have arisen when a prostitute accepted money to spend the whole night and then did not do so.

43. I am indebted for this suggestion to students in the graduate seminar on fifteenth-century London taught by Sheila Lindenbaum at Indiana University in the spring of 1992.

44. This does not mean that any unmarried woman was assumed to be a prostitute; even in the Southwark stew customs (B22) "single" sometimes clearly meant just unmarried.

45. CLRO, L-B H, fol. 264v (Sharpe, Cal L-B H, 372); Riley, Liber Albus, 277; Riley, Liber Albus: The White Book, 242.

46. PRO C/16/489, m. 13d; Calendar of the Patent Rolls Preserved in the Public Record Office: Henry VI (London: HMSO, 1910), 6:610.

47. Carlin, "Urban Development," 60–69, 491–92, 487 n. 18, 496.

48. A. H. Thomas and I. D. Thornley, eds., The Great Chronicle of London (London: George W. Jones, 1938), 331.

49. Paul L. Hughes and James F. Larkin, eds., Tudor Royal Proclamations, vol. 1, The Early Tudors (New Haven: Yale University Press, 1964), 365.

50. Roper, "Discipline and Respectability." Yet Cologne, by contrast, did not establish its officially sanctioned brothel until the 1520s. Irsigler and Lassotta, Bettler und Gaukler, 181.

51. Otis, Prostitution, 40–45, 105–13; Trexler, "La Prostitution florentine," 1003ff., attributes the action in Florence to demographic changes.

52. In 1536 one Thomas Pylson was petitioning the king against a barber-surgeon who maltreated his "whore's wound caught at the Stews in Southwark." Calendar of Letters and Papers, Foreign and Domestic, of the Reign of Henry VIII, vol. 14:2 (London: HMSO, 1895), 95.

53. V. H. Galbraith, ed., The Anonimalle Chronicle, 1333–1381 (Manchester: Manchester University Press, 1927), 140.

54. CLRO, L-B I, fol. 194r (Sharpe, Cal L-B I, 178), in Riley, Memorials, 649.

55. Gervase Rosser, "Medieval Westminster: The Vill and the Urban Community, 1200–1540" (Ph.D. diss., Bedford College, 1984), 55.

56. Enforcement, in any case, was usually directed against those who ran the brothels, not those who owned the property. Patronage may also have played a role: in the sixteenth century, brothels with court clientele were often protected from prosecution. Ian Archer, The Pursuit of Stability: Social Relations in Elizabethan London (Cambridge: Cambridge University Press, 1991), 232.

57. Karras, "Regulation of Brothels," 431, regulation B22.

58. HRO, Eccles, I 85/1; PRO, SP1/18/365/5/iii, fol. 232.

59. Karras, "Regulation of Brothels," 413.

60. See, e.g., NRO Y/C4/199, m. 15.

61. P. P. A. Biller, "Marriage Patterns and Women's Lives: A Sketch of a Pastoral Geography," in Woman Is a Worthy Wight: Women in English Society, c. 1200–1500, ed. P. J. P. Goldberg (Wolfeboro Falls, N.H.: Alan Sutton, 1992), 88, citing Memoriale Presbiterum, Corpus Christi College, Cambridge, MS 148, fol. 241v.

62. Keene, Survey, 1:390–91.

63. P. J. P. Goldberg, "Women in Fifteenth-Century Town Life," in *Towns and Townspeople in the Fifteenth Century,* ed. John A. F. Thompson (Gloucester, Eng.: Alan Sutton, 1988), 119.

64. Gervase Rosser, *Medieval Westminster, 1200–1540* (Oxford: Clarendon Press, 1989), 143.

65. NottsRO, CA/1–CA/45b.

66. Kowaleski, "Women's Work," 154 n. 53, table 1.

67. See, e.g., Guildhall Library, MS 9064/4A, fol. 11r (Emmota Bellamy); BIHR D/C AB 1, fol. 119r (Medard and Agnes Leonard). On the blurriness of the line between those brothelkeepers who employed women as prostitutes and those who merely provided premises, see Archer, *Pursuit of Stability,* 211–13.

68. HRO, Eccles. I 85/1. At least some of these, however, could have been partners rather than successors.

69. CLRO, Jour 2, fols. 35r, 55v; PRO, SC2/191/56, m. 1, m. 2.

70. BIHR, D/C AB 1, fols. 95r, 100r, 119r; Guildhall Library, MS 9064/11, fol. 118r.

71. Thompson, *Visitations,* 46.

72. Guildhall Library, MS 9064/1, fol. 171r; WAM 50782, m. 1d; Guildhall Library, MS 9064/1, fol. 88r.

73. CLRO, PMR A5, m. 2 (Thomas, *Cal PMR,* 1:173); see also NRO, Y/C4/211, m. 18; Kings Lynn Borough Archives, KL/C17/4, m. 2; and NRO, Y/C4/186, m. 16d.

74. SRO, C8/1/19, m. 1; CLRO, L-B H, fol. 194v (Sharpe, *Cal L-B H,* 271).

Chapter 3

1. Nor is this a universally held modern viewpoint. Disputes broke out in the 1970s between prostitutes and feminists, the prostitutes arguing that the work they did deserved as much respect as any other sort of work, the feminists arguing that prostitutes were exploited even if they didn't realize it. See Kate Millett, *The Prostitution Papers: A Candid Dialogue* (New York: Avon, 1973), 17–27; Robin Reisig, "Sisterhood and Prostitution," *Village Voice,* December 16, 1971, 1, 72, 74. In *Backstreets: Prostitution, Money, and Love,* trans. Katherine Hanson, Nancy Sipe, and Barbara Wilson (University Park: Pennsylvania State University Press, 1992), Cecilie Høigård and Liv Finstad discuss the ugliness and exploitation of prostitution. In Gail Pheterson, ed., *A Vindication of the Rights of Whores* (Seattle: Seal Press, 1989), prostitutes argue for eliminating exploitation by guaranteeing prostitutes' rights. By contrast, some feminists object to the use of the term "sex worker" (meant to emphasize that prostitution and other work in the sex industry is labor) as an attempt to gloss over exploitation. Jenness, *Making It Work,* gives a clear account of the controversy.

2. DRO, Mayor's Court Roll 17–18 Edward II, m. 13d–15d. Kowaleski, "Women's Work," 145, estimates Exeter's population at three thousand in 1377. Even if the population was greater in 1324, the number of accused prostitutes would still be more than 2 percent of the female population. The percentage of women accused of prostitution at some point in their lives would of course be much higher. These numbers may be compared with statistics from nineteenth-century New York, where 5 to 10 percent (more during depressions) of all young

women were prostitutes at some time in their lives. Timothy J. Guilfoyle, *City of Eros: New York City, Prostitution, and the Commercialization of Sex, 1790–1920* (New York: W. W. Norton, 1992), 59.

3. See Wunderli, *London Church Courts*, 147, for a table with numbers of prostitutes; and Josiah Cox Russell, *British Medieval Population* (Albuquerque: University of New Mexico Press, 1948), 297–98, for London population in 1377 and in the sixteenth century. My estimate of proportions is very rough because there are no good population figures for the fifteenth century, and because the prostitutes came not just from the city proper but from the whole diocese.

4. The ongoing work of Robert C. Palmer concerns changes over time in the regulation of morality in late medieval England, and will no doubt bear on this issue.

5. For a discussion of the issue of continuity between the medieval and early modern periods, see Judith Bennett, "Medieval Women, Modern Women: Across the Great Divide," in *Culture and History, 1350–1600: Essays on English Communities, Identities, and Writing*, ed. David Aers (New York: Harvester Wheatsheaf, 1992), 147–75.

6. The European model was first identified by John Hajnal, "European Marriage Patterns in Perspective," in *Population in History*, ed. D. V. Glass and D. E. C. Eversley (Chicago: Aldine, 1965), 101–43, although Hajnal believed that it was a new development in the early modern period. On Italy, see David Herlihy and Christiane Klapisch-Zuber, *Tuscans and Their Families: A Study of the Florentine Catasto of 1427* (New Haven: Yale University Press, 1985), 80–81.

7. For the application to late medieval England, see Richard M. Smith, "Hypothèses sur la nuptialité en Angleterre aux XIIe–XIVe siècles," *Annales: Economies, sociétés, civilisations* 38 (1983): 107–36; idem, "Some Reflections on the Evidence for the Origins of the 'European Marriage Pattern' in England," in *The Sociology of the Family: New Directions for Britain*, ed. Chris Harris (Keele, Eng.: University of Keele, 1979), 74–112; L. R. Poos and R. M. Smith, "'Legal Windows onto Historical Populations'? Recent Research on Demography and the Manor Court in Medieval England," *Law and History Review* 2 (1984): 142–43; P. J. P. Goldberg, "Female Labour, Status, and Marriage in Late Medieval York and Other English Towns" (Ph.D. diss., Cambridge, 1987); idem, "Women in Fifteenth-Century English Town Life"; idem, "Female Labour, Service, and Marriage in the Late Medieval Urban North," *Northern History* 22 (1986): 18–38; idem, "Marriage, Migration, Servanthood, and Life Cycle in Yorkshire Towns of the Later Middle Ages: Some York Cause Paper Evidence," *Continuity and Change* 1 (1986): 141–69; L. R. Poos, *A Rural Society After the Black Death: Essex, 1350–1525* (Cambridge: Cambridge University Press, 1991), 148–58. It should be noted that these scholars are very cautious in making statements about all of medieval England; they treat their data as suggestive rather than indicative of a general pattern.

8. Goldberg, *Women, Work, and Life Cycle*, 9.

9. The evidence for prostitutes' subsequent marriage is not abundant enough to indicate whether this was the case. The life stories presented on pp. 66–70 indicate that women remained in the sex trade for the long term, but as I note there, where biographies are constructed from court records, women who left the trade tend to become invisible, so those for whom we have information may be the exceptions.

10. Luise White, "Prostitutes, Reformers, and Historians," *Criminal Justice History* 6 (1985): 207–8; White, *The Comforts of Home*, esp. 226–27.

11. Barbara Hanawalt, *Growing Up in Medieval London: The Experience of Childhood in History* (New York: Oxford University Press, 1993), 146–49, describes continuing ties between apprentices and their natal families but presents no similar evidence in her discussion of servants (173–98). Kinship networks certainly played a role in finding work for young people, but once placed they were far more closely connected with their employers' households than with their parents'.

12. Richard M. Smith, "Geographical Diversity in the Resort to Marriage in Late Medieval Europe: Work, Reputation, and Unmarried Females in the Household Formation Systems of Northern and Southern Europe," in Goldberg, *Woman Is a Worthy Wight*, 45–46.

13. Judith M. Bennett, " 'History That Stands Still': Women's Work in the European Past," *Feminist Studies* 14 (1988): 269–83; Maryanne Kowaleski and Judith M. Bennett, "Crafts, Gilds, and Women in the Middle Ages: Fifty Years After Marian K. Dale," *Signs: Journal of Women in Culture and Society* 14 (1989): 474–88; Caroline Barron, "The 'Golden Age' of Women in Medieval London," *Reading Medieval Studies* 15 (1990): 35–58; Bennett, "Medieval Women, Modern Women"; David Herlihy, *Opera Muliebria: Women and Work in Medieval Europe* (Philadelphia: Temple University Press, 1990), 154–84; Goldberg, *Women, Work, and Life Cycle*, 82–157; Heather Swanson, *Medieval Artisans: An Urban Class in Late Medieval England* (Oxford: Basil Blackwell, 1989), 35–36.

14. Swanson, *Medieval Artisans*, passim.

15. Scholars now argue that population growth was stagnant until the end of the fifteenth century or even into the 1520s. See Poos, *Rural Society*, 111ff.; John Hatcher, *Plague, Population, and the English Economy, 1348–1530* (London: Macmillan, 1977), esp. 55–73. Goldberg, *Women, Work, and Life Cycle*, 337, makes the case for the contraction of opportunities based on recession rather than population expansion.

16. Kay E. Lacey, "Women and Work in Fourteenth- and Fifteenth-Century London," in *Women and Work in Preindustrial England*, ed. Lindsey Charles and Lorna Duffin (London: Croom Helm, 1985), 25; Barron, "Golden Age," 48.

17. Judith Bennett, *Ale, Beer, and Brewsters in England: Women's Work in a Changing World, 1300–1600* (New York: Oxford University Press, forthcoming).

18. Goldberg, in *Women, Work, and Life Cycle*, 275–76, argues that there was a downturn in the age of marriage in the late fifteenth and early sixteenth centuries, which he connects to the erosion of economic opportunities, but notes that "[t]hese observations do not detract from our main findings concerning the prevailing marriage regime."

19. CLRO, Rep 5, fol. 103v; Guildhall Library, MS 9064/6, fol. 70r; CLRO, Rep 9, fol. 256v, cf. fol. 178r; John Stow, *A Survey of London*, ed. C. L. Kingsford (Oxford: Clarendon Press, 1908), 2:54; CLRO, Rep 12, fol. 27r. There are also examples of the phrase being used in other ways; it did not always mean "prostitute."

20. D. C. Coleman, *The Economy of England, 1450–1750* (London: Oxford University Press, 1977), 12–30, summarizes population estimates. E. A. Wrigley and R. S. Schofield, *The Population History of England, 1541–1871: A Recon-*

struction (Cambridge, Mass.: Harvard University Press, 1981), provides more reliable estimates, but only after 1540, which means that it does not cover the beginning of the expansion.

21. Marjorie Keniston McIntosh, "Local Change and Community Control in England, 1465–1500," *Huntington Library Quarterly* 49 (1986): 231–33, places this period of repression in England in the late fifteenth century and says that it was not so severe in the sixteenth.

22. Brothels still existed in Elizabethan London, to be sure, and were repeatedly cited as a social problem, but their clientele consisted largely of leading citizens and court figures (Archer, *Pursuit of Stability*, 211, 231–32); this does not mean, however, that there were not prostitutes outside the brothels for other clients.

23. Goldberg, *Women, Work, and Life Cycle*, xi.

24. Ibid., 152; Goldberg, "Women in Fifteenth-Century Town Life," 119; Keene, *Survey*, 392.

25. Goldberg, *Women, Work, and Life Cycle*, 119–20.

26. CLRO, MS 39C/SCM1, fol. 32r.

27. CLRO, L-B K, fols. 54r, 64r (Sharpe, *Cal. L-B K*, 75, 95; Sharpe mistakenly identifies the stew in which laundresses were prohibited as a stew for women); Kate Mertes, *The English Noble Household, 1250–1600: Good Governance and Politic Rule* (Oxford: Blackwell, 1988), 57; Karras, "Regulation of Brothels," 428; "Cock Lorell's Bote," in *Early English Poetry, Ballads, and Popular Literature of the Middle Ages*, ed. E. F. Rimbault (London: Percy Society, 1842), 1; Walter of Hemingford, *Chronicon Domini Walteri de Hemingburgh*, ed. H. C. Hamilton (London: English Historical Society, 1848), 1:248–49.

28. John of Bromyard, *Summa Praedicantium* (Venice: Domenico Nicolino, 1586), s.v. "luxuria," 1.7.25, fol. 1:461v.

29. CLRO, Coroner's Roll F, m. 7, in Reginald R. Sharpe, ed., *Calendar of Coroners Rolls of the City of London, A.D. 1300–1378* (London: Richard Clay & Sons, 1913), 197–98.

30. Guildhall Library, MS 9064/11, fol. 58r; R. C. Anderson, ed., *The Assize of Bread Book* (Southampton: Cox and Sharland, 1923), 16.

31. Percy D. Mundy, ed., *Abstracts of Star Chamber Proceedings Relating to the County of Sussex, Henry VII to Philip and Mary* (London: Mitchell Hughes and Clarke, 1913), 5–8. The girl's seducer later married her, although there was serious question about the legality of the marriage.

32. Kowaleski, "Women's Work," 154; for other towns, see, e.g., PRO SC2/191/59 m. 1; CLRO, MS 242A, passim; CLRO, Rep 5 fol. 103v; Hereford County Record Office Act Book 3, fol. 158r.

33. The regulations from the Southwark stews are cited by paragraph numbers in the text; see Post, "Fifteenth-Century Customary," and Karras, "Regulation of Brothels."

34. See, e.g., Guildhall Library, MS 9064/1, fol. 29v (John Colwell) and passim. I have found no examples of the early modern institution of wife sale, a form of unofficial divorce which was not common before the late sixteenth century; see Lawrence Stone, *The Road to Divorce: England, 1530–1987* (Oxford: Oxford University Press, 1990), 144. There is no reason to believe that such a custom lies behind any of the cases in which husbands are accused of procuring for their wives.

35. Guildhall Library, MS 9064/1, fol. 35v.

36. Guildhall Library, MS 9064/6, fol. 21v, 74v, 75r; 9064/5, fol. 56r; CLRO, PMR A3, m. 14 (Thomas, *Cal PMR*, 1:125).

37. Kowaleski, "Women's Work," 154.

38. Sylvia L. Thrupp, "Aliens in and Around London in the Fifteenth Century," in *Studies in London History*, ed. A. E. J. Hollaender and William Kellaway (London: Hodder and Stoughton, 1969), 251–72, esp. 259.

39. These women either are identified as Dutch or bear Dutch names. Karras, "Regulation of Brothels," 415–16; Lambeth Palace Library, ED 969, m. 5d, ED 1905, 4d; PRO, SC2/191/55, m. 2, m. 3; SC2/191/56, m. 2, m. 3.

40. *Anonimalle Chronicle*, 140; Stow, *Survey*, 2:54.

41. Trexler, "La Prostitution florentine," 985–86. Not only prostitutes but many male employees at the Florentine municipal brothel were Flemish.

42. PRO, C/48/191. Sometime between 1473 and 1475 Butler petitioned for a writ of habeas corpus to release her from the bishop of Winchester's prison. The result is unknown.

43. Guildhall Library, MS 9064/4, fol. 168v; 9064/9, fol. 108r; CLRO, Jour 4, fol. 134v.

44. CLRO, Rep 6, fol. 43r; Thomas and Thornley, *The Great Chronicle of London*, 258.

45. CLRO, L-B N, fol. 47v; Rep 3, fols. 157v–158r. Hanawalt, *Growing Up*, 118–20, retells Rawlyns's story in fictionalized detail, rightly suggesting that even after Rawlyns found a position in domestic service, she would still have been subject to her master's sexual advances. Hanawalt has apparently followed the reading in Repertory Book 3, "My Lady of Wyllesdon," and interprets this as referring to Rawlyns's former mistress, who hired Barton to conduct her. The text, however, does not state that Barton and Rawlyns were traveling from the same place. Letter-Book N corrects the reading to "Our Lady of Willesdon," a reference to the well-known shrine of the Virgin Mary at Willesden (Diane K. Bolton, "Willesden," in *A History of Middlesex*, ed. T. F. T. Baker [Oxford: Institute for Historical Research, 1982], 7:237), which attracted many pilgrims from London. The shrine was not far from the road between Aldenham and London, and it is more likely that the two met on the way and her previous employer had nothing to do with the incident.

46. SCRO, SC5/3/1, fols. 42v, 55v.

47. See Hanawalt, *Growing Up*, 159–60.

48. CLRO, PMR A11, m. 2d (Thomas, *Cal PMR*, 2:54).

49. CLRO, L-B H, fol. 194v (Sharpe *Cal L-B H*, 271), in Riley, *Memorials*, 484, although the translation here is mine. See Guildhall Library, MS 9064/5, fol. 182r, for the case of another embroidress. Moryng may be the same woman as the Elizabeth Brouderer who procured for the transvestite prostitute John ("Eleanor") Rykener (see p. 70 and Boyd and Karras, "Interrogation," 461–62).

50. CLRO, L-B K, fol. 11v (Sharpe, *Cal L-B K*, 17); Jour 2, fol. 19r; Guildhall Library, MS 9064/8, fol. 254v. Hanawalt, *Growing Up*, 161, suggests that apprentices would have had more protection than servants. The price mentioned for Joan Hammond was high, probably not a payment for one night but rather a sale of the girl to the barber and a group of his friends, as was certainly the case for Agnes Smith.

51. NRO, Y/C4/110 m. 5; CLRO, L-B K, fol. 169r (Sharpe, *Cal L-B K*, 216).

52. Guildhall Library, MS 9064/6, fol. 81r.

53. CLRO, Jour 2, fols. 26v–27r; CLRO, Jour 3, fol. 15v; CLRO, PMR A66, m.

5 (Thomas, *Cal PMR*, 5:13–14); CLRO, Jour 3, fol. 71v; CLRO, L-B N, fol. 21r; CLRO, Rep 3, fol. 102r; Guildhall Library, MS 9064/4, fol. 14r. For more examples of selling girls to foreigners (Easterlings and Lombards), see Guildhall Library, MS 9064/5, fols. 93v, 182r; 9064/4, fols. 87v, 276r; 9064/3, fol. 107r; 9064/2, fol. 252v. See Gravdal, *Ravishing Maidens*, 128, for some French parallels.

54. Wunderli, *London Church Courts and Society*, 93.

55. On the meaning of *pronuba*, see Karras, "Latin Vocabulary," 9–17; it did not always imply procuring.

56. See Lyndal Roper, "Mothers of Debauchery: Procuresses in Reformation Augsburg," *German History* 6 (1988): 1–19, on the parallel image in Augsburg.

57. See, e.g., Mary McLeod Banks, ed., *An Alphabet of Tales: An English Fifteenth-Century Translation of the Alphabetum Narrationum* (London: Kegan Paul, Trench, Trübner & Co., 1904), 537, 2:361; *Fasciculus Morum*, 7:6, p. 667; Nicole Bozon, *Les Contes Moralisés de Nicole Bozon, frère mineur*, ed. Lucy Toulmin Smith and Paul Meyer (Paris: Firmin Didot, 1889), no. 138, 169–70; George H. McKnight, ed., *Middle English Humorous Tales in Verse* (Boston: D. C. Heath, 1913), 1–24; [Alexander Anglicus], *Destructorium Vitiorum* (Paris: Pierre Levet, 1497), 3:10, fol. C2; see also Richard Axton, *Three Rastell Plays: "Four Elements," "Calisto and Melibea," "Gentleness and Nobility"* (Totowa, N.J.: Rowan and Littlefield, 1979), 15–17, for the literary future of this motif in English translations of *La Celestina*.

58. See Geremek, *Margins of Society*, 237; Keith Thomas, *Religion and the Decline of Magic* (New York: Scribner, 1971), 546–60.

59. This is not to say there was no understanding of adolescence as a distinct stage of life. See Hanawalt, *Growing Up*.

60. Guildhall Library, MS 9064/3, fol. 215r; 9064/6, fol. 21r; CLRO, PMR A34, m. 2; CLRO, Rep 9, fol. 147v.

61. Ann J. Kettle, "City and Close: Lichfield in the Century Before the Reformation," in *The Church in Pre-Reformation Society*, ed. Caroline M. Barron and Christopher Harper-Bill (Woodbridge, Suffolk: Boydell and Brewer, 1985), 66; see also Goldberg, "Women in Fifteenth-Century Town Life," 120; KAO, Sa/ACl, fol. 195v. Not all those accused of being bawds for their daughters had actually pressured them into commercial sex; many cases merely involved the parents' condoning the daughters' consensual sexual activities, or pushing a daughter into a nonmarital sexual relationship with one particular man (Karras, "Latin Vocabulary," 12–13; see also CLRO, L-B N, fol. 193v); but the cases cited here all allege commercial sexual activity promoted by the young women's mothers.

62. See White, "Prostitutes, Reformers, and Historians," 207–8.

63. CLRO, Rep 10, fol. 344r.

Chapter 4

1. Just because a woman was accused of being a whore does not mean that she was a prostitute or even that she had multiple sex partners. The court records, as we saw in chapter 3, do not give the outcome of many cases, and in many others the accused successfully purged herself. This chapter deals not so much with the activities of prostitutes as with the activities imputed

to those accused of prostitution, which under the circumstances is as close as we can get.

2. Ruggiero, *Binding Passions*, 33–37. On the gradations of the trade in Elizabethan London, see Archer, *Pursuit of Stability*, 213.

3. Goldberg, "Women in Fifteenth-Century Town Life," 120. See Helmholz, *Marriage Litigation*, 25–73, on this type of suit. In this case Isabella Wakefield was also called Isabella Wilson, which may have been her surname before she came to York and became known by her place of origin.

4. In York women were rarely charged with prostitution explicitly but rather were accused of repeated acts of fornication and adultery (depending on the marital status of the man). See Karras, "Latin Vocabulary."

5. Goldberg, "Women in Fifteenth-Century Town Life," 120–21; BIHR, CP.F.22; BIHR, D/C AB 1, fols. 27r, 28v, 33r, 41v, 43r, 44r, 49r, 53r, 60r, 75v, 77r, 84r; YML, H2/1 fols. 8r, 8v; YML, H1/2, fol. 23; YML, M2(1)f, fols. 36v, 39v, 42v, 45v, 49v.

6. Similarly, Joan Lawrence was active as a prostitute in 1433, when she would have been forty (in testimony in 1429 she gave her age as thirty-six). BIHR, CP.F.111; D/C AB 1 fols. 84r, 85v. Her first recorded accusation was in 1411 at age eighteen. In classifying these women as prostitutes, I am assuming that the charges of fornication were based on their practice of commercial sex. It is not necessarily valid to assume that every woman accused of repeated fornication with different men was a prostitute; indeed, one of the arguments of this book is that there was no clear distinction between those who took money for sex and those who did not. Nonetheless, when combined with charges of bawdry and brothelkeeping, these fornication accusations are likely to have been commercial in nature.

7. BIHR D/C AB 1, fols. 112v, 128r, 129r, 129v, 132r, 132v, 142r, 153r, 155v, 156v, 160v, 175v, 177r, 178r, 179r, 179v. The unnamed servant was probably the same Margaret Bugtrot.

8. For charges against Alice Dymmok, see NRO, Y/C4/191, m. 15; Y/C4/194, m. 19, m. 21; Y/C4/195, m. 13d, m. 15; Y/C4/196, m. 12; Y/C4/197, m. 9; Y/C4/198, m. 12, m. 13, m. 13d; Y/C4/199, m. 13; Y/C4/200, m. 10; Y/C4/201, m. 9, m. 10; Y/C4/202, m. 4d, m. 6; Y/C4/203, m. 7.

9. The fact that the offense was called adultery and not fornication suggests that Thomas did not die of the beating, although he does not appear in the records anymore; it may also be that it was called adultery, however, because Robbins was married. It is possible, of course, that Alice Dymmok was Thomas's daughter and not his wife.

10. Guildhall Library, MS 9065, fols. 88r–88v.

11. CLRO, PMR A34, m. 2, in Boyd and Karras, "Interrogation." Elizabeth Brouderer in 1395 lived "outside Bishopsgate"; Moryng in 1385 lived in the parish of All Hallows London Wall in Broad Street ward. For further discussion of this case, see Karras and Boyd, "'Ut cum Muliere'."

12. Boyd and Karras, "Interrogation," 91.

13. CLRO, PMR A50, m. 6d, m. 7d (Thomas, *Cal PMR*, 4:132, 138).

14. See, e.g., NRO, Y/C4/194, m. 21. Such women were not always labeled "whores" like other women in the same court records, perhaps because they were not professionals, but also perhaps because theirs was some other sort of "immorality."

15. Martin Weinbaum, ed., *The London Eyre of 1276* (London: London Record Society, 1976), 34.

16. CLRO, L-B D, fol. 131r (Sharpe, *Cal L-B D*, 263–64); BIHR, D/C AB 1, fol. 202v.

17. Guildhall Library, MS 9064/6, fol. 19.

18. CLRO, Jour 14, fol. 357.

19. Guildhall Library, MS 9064a, fol. 4v; MS 9064/8, fols. 112v, 117r.

20. Guildhall Library, MS 9064/5, fol. 43r; MS 9064/4A, fol. 18v; MS 9064/1, fol. 44v.

21. CLRO, Rep 5, fols. 52r–52v. This is not the same Bell as the one in Warwick Lane.

22. Goldberg, "Women in Fifteenth-Century English Towns," 118; Harris, *Coventry Leet Book*, 2:545; Owen, *Making of King's Lynn*, 268; CLRO, PMR A3, m. 14; WAM 50755; BIHR D/C AB 1, fol. 96v; Keene, *Survey*, 391.

23. Guildhall Library, MS 9064/6, fols. 69r, 16r.

24. CLRO, PMR A51, m. 3 (Thomas, *Cal PMR*, 4:154).

25. Norma Adams and Charles Donahue, Jr., eds., *Select Cases from the Ecclesiastical Courts of the Province of Canterbury, c. 1200–1301* (London: Selden Society, 1981), 355–59.

26. CLRO, Jour 3, fol. 34r.

27. CLRO, Jour 13, fol. 141v.

28. Guildhall Library, MS 9064/4, fols. 27r, 236v.

29. Guildhall Library, MS 9064/9, fol. 42v.

30. CLRO, PMR A66, m. 5 (Thomas, *Cal PMR*, 5:14).

31. BIHR, D/C AB 1, fol. 67r; YML, M2(1)f, fol. 43r. The women she procured are referred to as the friars' "concubines," but in this case the term does not seem to imply a long-term relationship.

32. See Karras, "Latin Vocabulary," 13–14; for examples from outside the ecclesiastical courts, see NottsRO, CA/9d, m. 5; DRO EC9/3, m. 13d.

33. Guildhall Library, MS 9064/1, fol. 105.

34. Guildhall Library, MS 9064/1, fol. 46r.

35. CLRO, MS 242A.

36. SCRO, SC5/3/1, fols. 42v, 49v.

37. Guildhall Library, MS 9064/11, fol. 15v.

38. On the logic of this position, see the conclusion to this volume.

39. The court records often do not give the marital status of men accused of visiting prostitutes. In the York records, however, we often find a number of men accused of both fornication and adultery with the same woman, presumably a commercial prostitute. The distinction between the two offenses presumably depended on the man's marital status. See Karras, "Latin Vocabulary," 4.

40. CLRO, L-B I, fol. 194r (Sharpe, *Cal L-B I*, 194), in Riley, *Memorials*, 650; CLRO, Rep 11, fol. 388v; CLRO, L-B N, fol. 88v; NottsRO, CA/20b, m. 1.

41. CLRO, L-B L, fol. 266r (Sharpe, *Cal L-B L*, 262); Maud Sellers, ed., *York Memorandum Book* (Durham: Andrews & Co., 1912), 54. Some apprenticeship agreements did leave open the possibility of visiting brothels, prohibiting the apprentice only from engaging in fornication in the master's house (East Sussex Record Office, RYE 33/7, m. 20; I am grateful to Mavis Mate for this citation); others specified the master's house or elsewhere. Sylvia Thrupp, *The Merchant Class of Medieval London* (Ann Arbor: University of Michigan Press, 1948), 169.

42. Guildhall Library, MS 9064/1, fol. 109r.

43. Thrupp, *Merchant Class*, 186, points out that in the temporal courts of London there were only forty-four arrests of priests for sexual offenses between 1401 and 1440 out of a clerical population of 690 in 1381, or 1.6 per year per thousand population. This is higher than the rate of laymen appearing in secular courts for comparable offenses.

44. Historical Manuscripts Commission, "Records of the Corporation of Gloucester," 437.

45. For such prosecutions, see CLRO, L-B I, fols. 286r–290r (Sharpe, *Cal L-B I*, 273–287).

46. CLRO, PMR A34, m. 2 (Boyd and Karras, "Interrogation," 463).

47. CLRO, PMR A51, m. 3 (Thomas, *Cal PMR*, 4:154). The term "priests' whores" was used for the domestic partners of clergymen as well as commercial prostitutes, but those who were living together would not have had to meet in a stewhouse.

48. Canterbury RO, X.10.1, fols. 50r–50v.

49. CLRO, PMR A34, m. 2 (Boyd and Karras, "Interrogation," 463). I have used male pronouns for Rykener even though the Latin does not specify gender.

50. CLRO, L-B N, fols. 21r–21v; Rep 3, fol. 103v. The name is also spelled Chebyn and Chechyn.

51. BIHR, CP.E.72/6; see Houlbrooke, *Church Courts*, 81.

52. Guildhall Library, MS 9064/2, fol. 230v.

53. Thrupp, "Aliens," 251. I use the term "foreign" here in its modern meaning—from another country, those who in the Middle Ages would have been called "aliens" or "strangers"—and not in its medieval meaning of anyone not a citizen of the town.

54. PRO, SC2/191/55, m. 2; CLRO, PMR A18, m. 3 (Thomas, *Cal PMR*, 2:151).

55. Mertes, *English Noble Household*, 57–58.

56. Kettle, "City and Close," 164–65.

57. Guildhall Library, MS 9064/4, fol. 271r; 9064/5, fol. 11v.

58. Chris Given-Wilson, *The Royal Household and the King's Affinity: Service, Politics, and Finance in England, 1360–1413* (New Haven: Yale University Press, 1986), 60.

59. Guildhall Library, MS 9064/3, fol. 174r; 9064/1, fol. 59r; 9064/3, fol. 217r; 9064/8, fol. 79v.

60. James E. Thorold Rogers, *Six Centuries of Work and Wages* (New York: Putnam's, 1884), 329; idem, *A History of Agriculture and Prices in England* (Oxford: Clarendon Press, 1882), 3:660–63. Chris Vandenbroeke, "De prijs van betaalde liefde," *Spiegel Historiael* 18:2 (1983), 90–94, argues that there has been throughout history a relatively stable equivalence between a male worker's daily wage and the cost of a visit to a prostitute. The data, however, especially for the medieval period, are not reliable enough, and the range is too great, to establish solidly such a relationship.

61. CLRO, L-B I, fol. 286v (Sharpe, *Cal L-B I*, 276–77).

62. The relinquishment was temporary; this should not be considered a wife sale.

63. CLRO, L-B H, fol. 194v (Sharpe, *Cal L-B H*, 271), in Riley, *Memorials*, 485.

64. Guildhall Library, MS 9064/5, fol. 124v.

65. Guildhall Library, MS 9064/1, fol. 82r; MS 9064/4, fol. 50r; MS 9064/1, fol. 6v; MS 9064/6, fols. 7v, 21v.

66. Rosser, "Medieval Westminster," 214; Weinbaum, *The London Eyre of 1276*, 37.

67. SCRO, SC5/3/1, fols. 57v, 62v; Anderson, *Assize of Bread Book*, 36; KAO, Sa/AC1, 195; Guildhall Library, MS 9064/6, fol. 85v.

68. Guildhall Library, MS 9064/1, fol. 35v. She ended up being excommunicated.

69. CLRO, PMR A25, m. 8d (Thomas, *Cal PMR*, 3:18).

70. W. K. Jordan, *The Charities of London, 1480–1660: The Aspirations and the Achievements of the Urban Society* (London: George Allen and Unwin, 1960), 184; Hanawalt, *Growing Up*, 213–14; P. H. Cullum, " 'And Hir Name Was Charite': Charitable Giving by and for Women in Late Medieval Yorkshire," in Goldberg, *Woman Is a Worthy Wight*, 198–99; Goldberg, "Women in Fifteenth-Century Town Life," 121; Goldberg, *Women, Work, and Life Cycle*, 156. See Cohen, *Evolution of Women's Asylums*, on houses for repentant prostitutes in Florence.

71. See Biller, "Marriage Patterns," 89, on pastoral manuals. The theme of marrying prostitutes disappears from the pastoral manuals by the late fourteenth century—the time this study begins—and it is questionable whether prostitution was a major social problem in England at the time Thomas of Chobham wrote (early thirteenth century). To the extent that his views reflected the society in which he moved, it was that of Paris. The regulations for the legally recognized brothels of Southwark and Sandwich (see chapter 2) did not require the prostitutes to attend church, as did many of those on the Continent (Otis, *Prostitution*, 86–87).

72. Jacquart and Thomasset, *Sexuality and Medicine*, 25, 63–64, 80–81. See Charles Winick and Paul M. Kinsie, *The Lively Commerce: Prostitution in the United States* (Chicago: Quadrangle, 1971), 60, for a similar modern myth.

73. See Angus McLaren, *A History of Contraception from Antiquity to the Present Day* (Oxford: Basil Blackwell, 1990), 119–30; John M. Riddle, "Oral Contraceptives and Early-Term Abortifacients During Classical Antiquity and the Middle Ages," *Past and Present*, no. 132 (August 1991): 3–32; and Riddle, *Contraception and Abortion from the Ancient World to the Renaissance* (Cambridge, Mass.: Harvard University Press, 1992), on contraceptives and abortifacients used in the Middle Ages.

74. BL, MS Harley 3407, fol. 13v, a late fourteenth- or early fifteenth-century text made in France, probably for an English owner; this, however, is the only one out of ninety MSS of this text that includes the phrase (Monica Green, personal communication, July 1992).

75. Monica Green, "Obstetrical and Gynecological Texts in Middle English," *Studies in the Age of Chaucer* 14 (1992): 65. The word I have translated as "whore" is *kelot*, the meaning of which is not entirely clear; see ibid., n. 33.

76. CLRO, PMR A34, m. 2, in Boyd and Karras, "Interrogation," 461–62. It is also possible that his partners had such a rudimentary knowledge of anatomy and of sex that they thought they were having vaginal intercourse when it was in fact anal, a possibility that is less likely but should not be dismissed. See also Joyce Wadler, "The Spy Who Fell in Love with a Shadow," *New York Times Magazine*, August 15, 1993, 54, for a description of how a man can create a false vagina out of his scrotal sac.

77. See, e.g., Guildhall Library, MS 9064/4, fol. 37r. In the two cases cited in Hanawalt, *Growing Up*, 44, the women who gave birth are not called whores;

Hanawalt apparently concludes that they were prostitutes because of the presence of a *pronuba*; but see this chapter, and Karras, "Latin Vocabulary," 9–13, on the use of that term.

78. Ruth McClure, *Coram's Children: The London Foundling Hospital in the Eighteenth Century* (New Haven: Yale University Press, 1981), 8.

79. James Gairdner, ed., *Historical Collections of a Citizen of London in the Fifteenth Century* (London: Camden Society, 1876), ix (my modernization). He also left in his will £100 dowry money for poor virgins, perhaps to prevent them from entering a life of prostitution, as well as money to prisoners in Newgate.

80. CLRO, Rep 12, fol. 499v. There is no indication of what happened to the child or the mother.

81. CLRO, Rep 10, fol. 335r.

82. See, e.g., Guildhall Library MS 9064/2, fols. 99r, 127v.

Chapter 5

1. Geremek, *Margins of Society*, 2, for example, defines those on the margins of society as those "who played no part in the processes of production, and whose life remained immune to the norms of behavior in operation." He includes criminals, prostitutes, students, jongleurs, and beggars. Irsigler and Lassotta, in *Bettler und Gaukler*, 12, define marginal groups and outsiders as those who "had no fixed abode, whose existence was considered parasitic, or whose professional activity was strongly taboo" and include vagabonds, beggars, performers, prostitutes, barbers, and executioners. Jacques LeGoff, "Les Marginaux dans l'occident médiéval," in *Les Marginaux et les exclus dans l'histoire* (Paris: Union générale d'editions, 1979), 18–28, lumps prostitutes with "the excluded" rather than "the marginal, properly so called," who include the insane, the déclassé, beggars, and usurers. On marginality, see also Graus, "Randgruppen."

2. Schuster, *Das Frauenhaus*, 17; Perry, *Gender and Disorder*, 137.

3. Hartung, "Gesellschaftliche Randgruppen," 67–69.

4. Linda Mahood, *The Magdalenes: Prostitution in the Nineteenth Century* (London: Routledge, 1990), 3–13; see also Walkowitz, *Prostitution and Victorian Society*, 192–213.

5. This question is more fully discussed, not just in relation to prostitution, in Ruth Mazo Karras, "Two Models, Two Standards: Moral Teaching and Sexual Mores," in *Intersections: Literature and History in the Fifteenth Century*, ed. Barbara Hanawalt and David Wallace (Minneapolis: University of Minnesota Press, in press).

6. On the varying views of marriage in the Middle Ages, see Christopher N. L. Brooke, *The Medieval Idea of Marriage* (Oxford: Oxford University Press, 1989), treating marriage from a Christian viewpoint.

7. Helmholz, *Marriage Litigation*, 26–31.

8. Ibid., 72. The evidence Helmholz cites would indicate that he is using "men" as a generic term rather than referring only to males.

9. See Karras, "Two Models."

10. Martin Ingram, *Church Courts, Sex, and Marriage in England, 1570–1640* (Cambridge: Cambridge University Press, 1987), 162–63.

11. Poos, *Rural Society*, 135–40 (quotation at 140); Richard M. Smith, "Marriage Processes in the English Past: Some Continuities," in *The World We Have*

Gained, ed. Richard M. Smith, Keith Wrightson, and Lloyd Bonfield (Oxford: Blackwell, 1986), 43–99. Margaret Spufford, "Puritanism and Social Control?," in *Order and Disorder in Early Modern England*, ed. Anthony Fletcher and John Stevenson (Cambridge: Cambridge University Press, 1985), 41–57, suggests that poor people may have lived together without marriage not because of different standards of morality or a different model of marriage but because they did not have money for a dowry. Michael Sheehan, "Theory and Practice: Marriage of the Unfree and the Poor in Medieval Society," *Mediaeval Studies* 50 (1988): 482–86, argues that by the fourteenth century the church was taking steps to regularize marriage among the poor by recognizing many informal relationships as clandestine marriages. Those who continued in informal relationships were made to abjure each other *sub poena nubendi:* that is, if they had sex again, they would be considered married. Of course, this does not mean that they would necessarily have regarded themselves as married. For subsequent developments, see Houlbrooke, *Church Courts*, 66; Ingram, *Church Courts*, 217–18.

12. For a discussion of this phenomenon in another society, see, e.g., John D'Emilio and Estelle B. Freedman, *Intimate Matters: A History of Sexuality in America* (New York: Harper and Row, 1988), 256–65.

13. Poos, "Sex, Lies, and the Church Courts."

14. Karras, "Two Models."

15. Brundage, "Prostitution," 835–36.

16. William Caxton, trans., *The Book of the Knight of the Tower*, ed. M. Y. Offord (London: Oxford University Press, 1971), 169.

17. GLRO, DL/C/1, fol. 55v.

18. For a discussion of this point, see Lester Little, *Religious Poverty and the Profit Economy in Medieval Europe* (Ithaca, N.Y.: Cornell University Press, 1978), 3–41; Lee Patterson, "'No Man His Reson Herde': Peasant Consciousness, Chaucer's Miller, and the Structure of the *Canterbury Tales*," in *Literary Practice and Social Change in Britain, 1380–1530*, ed. Lee Patterson (Berkeley: University of California Press, 1990), 117.

19. See Gayle Rubin, "The Traffic in Women: Notes on the 'Political Economy' of Sex," in *Toward an Anthropology of Women*, ed. Rayna R. Reiter (New York: Monthly Review Press, 1975), 157–210; and Jack Goody and S. J. Tambiah, *Bridewealth and Dowry* (Cambridge: Cambridge University Press, 1973), in general; and Diane Owen Hughes, "From Brideprice to Dowry in Mediterranean Europe," *Journal of Family History* 3 (1978): 262–96; and Herlihy and Klapisch-Zuber, *Tuscans*, 222–28, on dowry in medieval Europe.

20. See Thrupp, *Merchant Class*, 263–69.

21. Any historical "reality" against which texts can be judged is constituted by historians working from similar texts. Lee Patterson, *Negotiating the Past: The Historical Understanding of Medieval Literature* (Madison: University of Wisconsin Press, 1987), 44; and Gabrielle M. Spiegel, "History, Historicism, and the Social Logic of the Text in the Middle Ages," *Speculum* 65 (1990): 73–76, helpfully discuss the question of a text's relation to its historical context.

22. For particularly good statements of this process, see David Aers, ed., *Medieval Literature: Criticism, Ideology, and History*, (New York: St. Martin's Press, 1986), 3; and Roger Chartier, *Cultural History: Between Practices and Representations* (Ithaca, N.Y.: Cornell University Press, 1988), 4.

23. Smith-Rosenberg, *Disorderly Conduct*, 45.

24. Chaucer certainly knew and used some of the fabliaux. Since the upper

classes in England could read French well into the fourteenth century, cross-Channel cultural exchange was common, and though the fabliaux were a courtly genre, other English people probably knew them too. See William Calin, *The French Tradition in Medieval England* (Toronto: University of Toronto Press, 1994), on the influence of French literature in England. Marie-Thérèse Lorçin, *Façons de sentir et de penser: Les Fabliaux français* (Paris: Honoré Champion, 1979), 11–12, discusses the role of the English in the fabliaux, deriving them from a period when the Plantagenet kingdom spanned the Channel.

25. Sarah Melhado White, "Sexual Language and Human Conflict in Old French Fabliaux," *Comparative Studies in Society and History* 24 (1982): 185–210. On the disembodiment of bodily parts, see also R. Howard Bloch, *The Scandal of the Fabliaux* (Chicago: University of Chicago Press, 1986), 59–100.

26. See E. Jane Burns, "This Prick Which Is Not One: How Women Talk Back in Old French Literature," in *Feminist Approaches to the Body in Medieval Literature*, ed. Linda Lomperis and Sarah Stanbury (Philadelphia: University of Pennsylvania Press, 1993), 188–212.

27. Bloch, *Scandal*, 5–6.

28. Charles Muscatine, *The Old French Fabliaux* (New Haven: Yale University Press, 1986), 24–46, 152–69.

29. Lorcin, "La Prostituée," 109–10; Lorcin, *Façons*, 51–57.

30. Lorcin, "La Prostituée," 111–14; Lorcin, *Façons*, 66.

31. I. C. Lecompte, "*Richeut*, Old French Poem of the Twelfth Century, with Introduction, Notes, and Glossary," *Romanic Review* 4 (1913): 261–305.

32. Raymond Eichmann and John DuVal, eds. *The French Fabliau: B.N. MS. 837* (New York: Garland, 1984), 1:62–63, ll. 22–23.

33. Philippe Ménard, ed., "Du Preste et d'Alison," in *Fabliaux français du moyen âge* (Geneva: Droz, 1979), 1:64, ll. 192–96.

34. John DuVal and Raymond Eichmann, ed. and trans., *Cuckolds, Clerics, and Countrymen: Medieval French Fabliaux* (Fayetteville: University of Arkansas Press, 1982), 42, ll. 187–88.

35. Anatole Montaiglon and Gaston Raynaud, *Recueil général et complet des fabliaux des XIIIe et XIVe siècles imprimés ou inédits* (Paris: Librairie des Bibliophiles, 1878), 3:177.

36. Langland, *Piers the Plowman*, Text C, passus 17, ll. 91–94.

37. Langland, *Piers the Plowman*, Text C, passus 22, l. 437, 1:575; cf. Text C, passus 14, l. 75, 1:354.

38. The extant Middle English translation may be partly by Chaucer; see Russell A. Peck, *Chaucer's "Romaunt of the Rose" and "Boece," "Treatise on the Astrolabe," "Equatorie of the Planetis," Lost Works, and Chaucerian Apocrypha: An Annotated Bibliography, 1900 to 1985* (Toronto: University of Toronto Press, 1988), 1–10. The sections quoted here are not found in the Middle English *Romaunt* (Ronald Sutherland, ed., "*The Romaunt of the Rose," and "Le Roman de la Rose": A Parallel-Text Edition* [Oxford: Blackwell, 1967]). The French version, however, was widely read in England. Quotations are from Guillaume de Lorris and Jean de Meun, *The Romance of the Rose*, trans. Harry W. Robbins (New York: Dutton, 1962), cited by line in the text.

39. Joan Ferrante, *Woman as Image in Medieval Literature* (New York: Columbia University Press, 1975), 116.

40. All quotations from the *Canterbury Tales* are from *Riverside Chaucer*, cited by line in the text; modernizations of language are mine. For other discus-

sions of the role of money in Chaucer, see Virginia Schaefer Carroll, "Women and Money in 'The Miller's Tale' and 'The Reeve's Tale,'" *Medieval Perspectives* 3 (1988): 76–88; Patricia J. Eberle, "Commercial Language and the Commercial Outlook in the *General Prologue*," *Chaucer Review* 18 (1983): 161–74.

41. The use of "spend" for the male orgasm was not yet current. See Sherman Kuhn, ed., *Middle English Dictionary* (Ann Arbor: University of Michigan Press, 1956–), s.v. "spend." This meaning is not listed in the *OED*.

42. See Elizabeth M. Makowski, "The Conjugal Debt and Medieval Canon Law," *Journal of Medieval History* 3 (1977): 99–114.

43. Sheila Delany, "Sexual Economics, Chaucer's Wife of Bath, and *The Book of Margery Kempe*," in *Writing Woman: Women Writers and Women in Literature, Medieval to Modern* (New York: Schocken Books, 1983), 76–92; see also R. A. Shoaf, *Dante, Chaucer, and the Currency of the Word: Money, Images, and Reference in Late Medieval Poetry* (Norman, Okla.: Pilgrim Books, 1983), 174–77; Carolyn Dinshaw, *Chaucer's Sexual Poetics* (Madison: University of Wisconsin Press, 1989), 118; Peggy Knapp, *Chaucer and the Social Contest* (New York: Routledge, 1990), 122.

44. See Paul Strohm, *Social Chaucer* (Cambridge, Mass.: Harvard University Press, 1989), 100; Mary Flowers Braswell, "Chaucer's 'Queinte Termes of Lawe': A Legal View of the Shipman's Tale," *Chaucer Review* 22 (1988): 296; Lee Patterson, *Chaucer and the Subject of History* (Madison: University of Wisconsin Press, 1991), 349–59, esp. 352, where Patterson argues that the merchant is not satirized and all parties win (as opposed to the more standard view expressed in Albert H. Silverman, "Sex and Money in Chaucer's 'Shipman's Tale,'" *Philological Quarterly* 32 [1953]: 329–336; V. J. Scattergood, "The Originality of the 'Shipman's Tale,'" *Chaucer Review* 11 (1976): 221.

45. Priscilla Martin, *Chaucer's Women: Nuns, Wives, and Amazons* (Iowa City: University of Iowa Press, 1990), 73.

46. Paul Strohm, "Chaucer's Fifteenth-Century Audience and the Narrowing of the 'Chaucer Tradition,'" *Studies in the Age of Chaucer* 4 (1982): 3–32; Strohm, *Social Chaucer*, 175.

47. Delany, "Sexual Economics," 86. See also David Aers, *Community, Gender, and Individual Identity: English Writing, 1360–1430* (London: Routledge, 1988), 73–116.

48. *The Book of Margery Kempe*, ed. Sanford B. Meech (London: Oxford University Press, 1940), chap. 11, 24.

49. For women's right to accumulate their own money through trade, see, e.g., Shulamith Shahar, *The Fourth Estate: A History of Women in the Middle Ages*, trans. Chaya Galai (London: Methuen, 1983), 189–97.

50. Rossell Hope Robbins, ed., *Secular Lyrics of the Fourteenth and Fifteenth Centuries* (Oxford: Clarendon Press, 1956), 52.

51. Ibid., 20–21.

52. Ibid., 25.

53. PRO, SC2/191/56, m. 2, m. 2d; Owen, *Making of King's Lynn*, 428.

54. CLRO, MCR G, m. 13, m. 14d (A. H. Thomas, ed., *Calendar of Early Mayor's Court Rolls Preserved Among the Archives of the City of London at the Guildhall*, A.D. *1298–1307* [Cambridge: Cambridge University Press, 1924], 211, 218–19).

55. CLRO, PMR A11, m. 5 (Thomas, *Cal PMR*, 2:57).

56. CLRO, MCR A, m. 5d, in Thomas, *Calendar of Early Mayor's Court Rolls,* 14; CLRO, PMR A5, m. 24 (Thomas, *Cal PMR,* 1:212).

57. CLRO, Rep 3, fol. 40r. The history of this case is scattered throughout fols. 33r–42v, with its conclusion at 49v–50r. Apparently Katherine Worsley had been presented as a whore in the Wardmote on the testimony of three men. She sued them for defamation in the church court, and they complained to the Court of Aldermen. The court finally determined that each side should apologize and make a formal release to the other. The defamation case is not found in the extant church court records.

58. Colin Richmond, *John Hopton, a Fifteenth-Century Suffolk Gentleman* (Cambridge: Cambridge University Press, 1981), 180.

59. Brundage, *Law, Sex, and Christian Society,* 393.

60. I have checked the names of all the accused prostitutes I found in London city records and a sample of those in Diocese of London Commissary Court records against the names of those whose wills were recorded in the Hustings Court in London and in the Commissary Court. See Reginald R. Sharpe, ed., *Calendar of Wills Proved and Enrolled in the Court of Hustings, London,* A.D. *1258–A.D. 1688,* 2 vols. (London: J. C. Francis, 1889–90); Marc Fitch, ed., *Index to Testamentary Records in the Commissary Court of London (London Division), Now Preserved in the Guildhall Library, London,* 2 vols. (London: HMSO, 1969, 1974). Only one definite match was found, that is, a person of the same name living at the same time in the same parish: Alice Dryver of All Hallows Staining; see Guildhall Library MS 9064/2, fol. 153r, for the accusation of prostitution, MS 9168/1, fol. 77r, for the will. (This records only the administration and not the contents of the will.) The dangers of arguing from negative evidence are apparent here: the sample is not complete; the percentage of wills and testaments left by women is so small anyway that the exclusion of prostitutes may not be significant; and if a prostitute married, she might have left a will under her husband's surname. Prostitutes did move from parish to parish, and I found a number of cases in which names but not parishes coincided; but there is so much uniformity in women's names of this period that these cannot be identified as certain matches, although they are possibilities. One would not expect to find prostitutes' wills in the Hustings records, as those were limited to the enfranchised citizens of London, whose households constituted only about two thirds of the total population (Thrupp, *Merchant Class,* 50–51). Prostitutes are far more likely to have been included among the unenfranchised "foreigns." Still, their absence from or underrepresentation in the testamentary registers of the ecclesiastical courts does tend to support the unsurprising hypothesis that they were not particularly wealthy and did not make substantial charitable donations.

61. BIHR CP.F.111, in Helmholz, *Marriage Litigation,* 89; BIHR CP.F.175.

62. Goldberg, "Women in Fifteenth-Century Town Life," 119; and see, e.g., BIHR D/C AB 1, fols. 84r and 85v, and YML H2/1, fol. 4v, where Joan Lawrence, one of the witnesses in CP.F.111, was accused of multiple adultery and fornication. Jacqueline Murray, in "On the Origins and Role of the 'Wise Woman' in Causes for Annulment on the Grounds of Male Impotence," *Journal of Medieval History* 16 (1990): 235–49, discusses this sort of examination but is apparently unaware that in at least some cases the examiners were prostitutes.

63. Helmholz, *Marriage Litigation,* 88.

64. BIHR, CP.F.79 (this was something of a standard formula); CP.E.175; CP.F.104; Canterbury RO, X.10.1, fol. 16; Guildhall Library, MS 9065, fols. 178v, 180r. See the case of Margaret Morgan, pp. 69–70.

65. Guildhall Library, MS 9065, fols. 89r–92r, 99r–102r, 105r; GLRO, DL/C/205, fol. 79v.

66. Guildhall Library, MS 9065, fol. 257r. This is likely the same Togood mentioned earlier as bawd of the stews (see p. 58); he is identified here as "of the parish of St. Margaret in Southwark of Winchester."

67. Guildhall Library, MS 9064/4, fol. 38r. Another woman was accused of defamation for claiming that Margaret had made the statement (fol. 43v). The former case has "woman" instead of "ioman" (yeoman); it seems most likely that the reading "ioman" is correct, for a case of sex between women would have occasioned some comment.

68. In fact, the data from the London church courts show that in most years more accused prostitutes were acquitted by compurgation than were punished for the crime (Wunderli, *London Church Courts*, 147).

69. It is difficult to determine exactly who the compurgators were because their names are not often given. In the London church court records from 1470 to 1489, for example (Guildhall Library MSS 9064/1, 9064/2, 9064/3), there are seventeen cases (out of a total of hundreds) of women accused of whoredom or bawdry in which the compurgators are named. Of the seventy-four compurgators, eight were at one time accused in the same court of whoredom and another eight of bawdry. (On the one hand, this number may be high if there were several women of the same name, but on the other hand, it may be low because compurgators are listed by their own names, whereas many of those accused in the court records are listed by their husband's name.) This does not mean that they were guilty (in most cases the result does not survive, and most of the rest were dismissed), but it is possible that there was a network of support and compurgation within the sex trade.

70. NRO, Y/C4/143, m. 12; SRO, C8/1/5, m. 3.

71. See, e.g., CLRO, PMR A5, m. 11, in which Ellen of Evesham is accused of keeping a brothel, harboring thieves and whores, and assisting in an attack on a passer-by.

72. CLRO, L-B B, fol. 3r (Sharpe, *Cal L-B B*, 6; except that Sharpe translates *lupanaria* as "houses of ill fame").

73. DRO, EC9/3, m. 5d, 7d; NRO, KL/C17/21, m. 2d.

74. CLRO, PMR A51, m. 2 (Thomas, *Cal PMR*, 4:151).

75. Edwin Brezette DeWindt, ed., *The Court Rolls of Ramsey, Hepmangrove and Bury, 1268–1600* (Toronto: Pontifical Institute of Mediaeval Studies, 1990), fiche 1, p. 165.

76. SRO, C7/1/27, m. 1. Cf. a case from the ecclesiastical courts of Cérisy in Normandy, in Gravdal, *Ravishing Maidens*, 127.

Chapter 6

1. See Bynum, *Holy Feast*.

2. Larissa Taylor, *Soldiers of Christ: Preaching in Late Medieval and Reformation France* (New York: Oxford University Press, 1992), 170–71, gives brief examples from France.

3. Attitudes did, of course, vary within the culture. See, for example, John W. Baldwin, *The Language of Sex: Five Voices from Northern France Around 1200* (Chicago: University of Chicago Press, 1994). Some scholars have argued for a positive valuation of marital sexuality by some churchmen; see Jacqueline Murray, "The Perceptions of Sexuality, Marriage, and Family in Early English Pastoral Manuals" (Ph.D. diss., University of Toronto, 1987). Even in the case of marital sexuality, however, the best one can say is that some medieval writers were sympathetic to and understanding of the needs of the married; but, as I will show, a strong streak of disapproval, sometimes revulsion, toward sex in general ran through the teachings of the medieval church.

4. See Peter Brown, *The Body and Society: Men, Women, and Sexual Renunciation in Early Christianity* (New York: Columbia University Press, 1988), and Elaine Pagels, *Adam, Eve, and the Serpent* (New York: Random House, 1988), on origins; see Brundage, *Law, Sex, and Christian Society*, on their development throughout the Middle Ages.

5. See Katharina Wilson and Elizabeth Makowski, *Wykked Wyves and the Woes of Marriage: Misogamous Literature from Juvenal to Chaucer* (Albany: State University of New York Press, 1990), 1–2, for the distinction between misogyny and misogamy.

6. Saint Jerome had written his critique of women not to stand alone as a moral imperative but to make a theological point against Jovinian, who had argued that virgins were no better than wives in the sight of God. The argument about women, part of a longer attack, relied on biblical exegesis to refute Jovinian's arguments in favor of marriage. Indeed, the notion that women could best serve God through virginity may originally have been introduced by women themselves. See Jo Ann McNamara, *A New Song: Celibate Women in the First Christian Centuries* (New York: Haworth Press, 1983), 43–84; and Elizabeth Clark, "Devil's Gateway and Bride of Christ: Women in the Early Christian World," in *Ascetic Piety and Women's Faith: Essays on Late Ancient Christianity* (Lewiston, N.Y.: Edwin Mellen Press, 1986), 23–60, on Jerome's context.

7. Philippe Delhaye, "Le Dossier antimatrimonial de l'*Adversus Jovinianum* et son influence sur quelques écrits latins du XIIe siècle," *Mediaeval Studies* 13 (1951): 65–86; Robert Pratt, "Jankyn's Book of Wikked Wyves: Medieval Antimatrimonial Propaganda in the Universities," *Annuale medievale* 3 (1962): 5–27. For examples of such antimatrimonial writing, see Wilson and Makowski, *Wykked Wyves*; "Golias," "De coniuge non ducenda," in *The Latin Poems Commonly Attributed to Walter Mapes*, ed. Thomas Wright (1841; rpt. New York: Johnson Reprint Co., 1968), 77–85 and 295–99, for a fifteenth-century English version.

8. Banks, *Alphabet of Tales*, no. 798, 529–30; John of Wales, *Communiloquium* 2.4.1 (Augsburg: Anton Sorg, 1475), 88v–89v; see Jenny Swanson, *John of Wales: A Study of the Works and Ideas of a Thirteenth-Century Friar* (Cambridge: Cambridge University Press, 1989), 162, 201–17, for the popularity of the *Communiloquium*.

9. BL, MS Harleian 2398, fol. 161v.

10. But see Ruth Mazo Karras, "The Virgin and the Pregnant Abbess: Miracles and Gender in the Middle Ages," *Medieval Perspectives* 3 (1988): 112–32, on some of the ambiguities involved in the veneration of the Virgin Mary.

11. W. A. Pantin, *The English Church in the Fourteenth Century* (Cambridge: Cambridge University Press, 1955), 189–219; D. W. Robertson, Jr., "Fre-

quency of Preaching in Thirteenth-Century England," *Speculum* 24 (1949): 376–88; see F. M. Powicke and C. R. Cheney, eds., *Councils and Synods, with Other Documents Relating to the English Church* (Oxford: Clarendon Press, 1964), 2:886.

12. See William A. Hinnebusch, *The Early English Friars Preachers* (Rome: St. Sabina, 1951), for Dominican activities in England.

13. Many important scholars included model sermons or preaching aids among their works. Beryl Smalley, *English Friars and Antiquity in the Early Fourteenth Century* (Oxford: Blackwell, 1960). Some sermons, of course, were intended for preaching to an intellectual audience, such as a university community, but a good number also survive that were intended for the general public.

14. For example, the *Manipulus Florum*, written by Thomas of Ireland at the Sorbonne in the early fourteenth century. Richard H. Rouse and Mary A. Rouse, *Preachers, Florilegia, and Sermons: Studies on the Manipulus Florum of Thomas of Ireland* (Toronto: Pontifical Institute of Mediaeval Studies, 1979), x, 117.

15. *SP*, s.v. "audire," a.26.15, 1:75.

16. See H. Leith Spencer, *English Preaching in the late Middle Ages* (Oxford: Clarendon Press, 1993), 78–91, on the conventional nature of the material and the implications for its use by historians.

17. Some scholars argue that exempla represent a transmission of culture from the popular to the intellectual level. See Aron Gurevich, *Medieval Popular Culture: Problems of Belief and Perception*, trans. János M. Bak and Paul A. Hollingsworth (Cambridge: Cambridge University Press, 1988), 2; Bronislaw Geremek, "L'*Exemplum* et la circulation de la culture au Moyen Age," in *Rhétorique et histoire: L'"Exemplum" et le modèle de comportement dans le discours antique et médiéval* (Rome: École Française de Rome, 1980), 155–56.

18. It reached them through the confessional, too. Some handbooks for confessors are referred to later in this chapter. Explicitly misogynous teaching is not so common in this genre of text, however, since it focuses on specific acts already committed rather than on general tendencies. The extent to which the attitudes found in sermons and other texts affected the confessor's attitude toward penitents was probably substantial but also must have varied a great deal depending on the individual. The ideal was for the confessor to adapt his counsel and prescription of penance to the spiritual needs of each penitent, male or female. See Murray, *Perceptions of Sexuality*.

19. See Pantin, *English Church*, 220–43; also Vincent Gillespie, "Vernacular Books of Religion," in *Book Production and Publishing in Britain, 1375–1475*, ed. Jeremy Griffiths and Derek Pearsall (Cambridge: Cambridge University Press, 1989). Some didactic texts were cycles of related sermons intended for reading rather than preaching. Johannes Baptist Schneyer, *Repertorium der lateinischen Sermones des Mittelalters für die Zeit von 1150–1350* (Münster: Aschendorff, 1969), 1:10; T. F. Crane, "Mediaeval Sermon-Books and Stories and Their Study Since 1883," *Proceedings of the American Philosophical Society* 56 (1917): 380.

20. D. W. Robertson, "The Cultural Tradition of *Handlyng Synne*," *Speculum* 22 (1947): 164; Richard Newhauser, *The Treatise on Vices and Virtues in Latin and the Vernacular* (Turnhout: Brepols, 1993), 142–50.

21. J.-Th. Welter, *L'Exemplum dans la littérature religieuse et didactique du moyen âge* (Paris: Occitania, 1927), 425–27; G. R. Owst, *The Destructorium*

Viciorum of Alexander Carpenter (London: Society for the Propagation of Christian Knowledge, 1952).

22. Janet Coleman, *Medieval Readers and Writers, 1350-1400* (New York: Columbia University Press, 1981), 23; Robert E. Lewis and Angus McIntosh, *A Descriptive Guide to the Manuscripts of the Prick of Conscience* (Oxford: Society for the Study of Medieval Languages and Literatures, 1982), 1-2. Some of the devotional treatises circulating in the fifteenth century were the work of Lollards, but the Lollard texts did not place as much emphasis on outward morality as the orthodox preachers and tracts. This was not because the Lollards had different standards of morality, but because they were largely preaching to the converted and did not have to be concerned with the sexual behavior of the masses. The Lollards, in common with other fringe religious movements, also allowed women a much greater role than did the orthodox church, including in preaching and teaching, which may have accounted to some degree for their lesser misogyny. See Claire Cross, " 'Great Reasoners in Scripture': The Activities of Women Lollards, 1380-1530," in *Medieval Women*, ed. Derek Baker (Oxford: Basil Blackwell, 1978), 359-80; Margaret Aston, "Lollard Women Priests?," *Journal of Ecclesiastical History* 31 (1980): 441-61.

23. Gurevich, *Medieval Popular Culture*, 6.

24. Coleman, *Medieval English Readers*, 176-77. Examples of the use of preaching aids include the fourteenth-century monk and bishop of Rochester John Sheppey (who used the sermons of the Dominicans Robert Holcot and Thomas Walleys as well as Bromyard's *Summa Praedicantium*) and the several identifiable preachers who used the manual *Fasciculus Morum*. Jean Longère, *La Prédication médiévale* (Paris: Études Augustiniennes, 1983), 127; see 102, 118, 123 on other English preachers. For fifteenth-century sermons using exempla, see Welter, *L'Exemplum*, 410ff. For the *Fasciculus Morum* and its use, see Siegfried Wenzel, *Verses in Sermons: Fasciculus Morum and Its Middle English Poems* (Cambridge, Mass.: Medieval Academy of America, 1978), 42-45.

25. G. R. Owst, *Literature and Pulpit in Medieval England* (Cambridge: Cambridge University Press, 1933), 377; see also Robert A. Pratt, "Chaucer and the Hand That Fed Him," *Speculum* 41 (1968): 641.

26. Hermann Oesterley, ed., *Gesta Romanorum* (Berlin: Weidmann, 1872). Nor does this use of allegory mean that women were identified with the spiritual side of humanity; women may have been used as an allegory for the soul simply because the word *anima* is feminine in gender.

27. See Hjälmar Crohns, *Legenden och medeltidens latinska predikan och "exempla" i deras värdesättning av kvinnan* (Helsinki: Helsingfors Centraltryckeri och Bokbinderi Aktiebolag, 1915), 35; Ferrante, *Woman as Image*, 1-2. Some scholars argue that literature and art use representations of women symbolically, and therefore we should not read these texts or images as conveying information about women. See, e.g. Veronica Sekules, "Women and Art in England in the Thirteenth and Fourteenth Century," in *The Age of Chivalry: Art in Plantagenet England, 1200-1400*, ed. Jonathan Alexander and Paul Binski (London: Royal Academy of Arts, 1987), 41-48. A symbol can still have a literal meaning, too, however, and we may legitimately ask what it would have meant to medieval people that women were used to represent negative traits that were often connected with femininity.

28. J.-Th. Welter, ed., *Le Speculum laicorum: Edition d'une collection d'ex-*

empla composée en Angleterre à la fin du XIIIe siècle (Paris: Picard, 1914), 194–95, 203–5, 209; Nicole Bozon, *Metaphors of Brother Bozon, a Friar Minor*, trans. J[ohn]. R[ose]. (London: Constable & Co., 1913).

29. Latin distinguishes between *homines*, "human beings" (often translated as "men" by those who use "men" as generic) and *viri*, "men" in the sense of male adults. Some sins are common to all *homines*, but very rarely is any specifically noted as common to all *viri*. See, e.g., Priscilla Heath Barnum, ed., *Dives and Pauper*, 2 vols. (Oxford: EETS, 1980), book 6 chap. 10, 80.

30. On the sins in general and as they developed in England, see Hanno Fink, *Die sieben Todsünden in der mittelenglischen erbaulichen Literatur* (Hamburg: Cram, De Gruyter & Co., 1969); Morton W. Bloomfield, *The Seven Deadly Sins: An Introduction to the History of a Religious Concept, with Special Reference to Medieval English Literature* (East Lansing, Mi.: State College Press, 1952). On the sins as organizing principle for preaching aids, see Siegfried Wenzel, "Vices, Virtues, and Popular Preaching," in *Medieval and Renaissance Studies: Proceedings of the Southeastern Institute of Medieval and Renaissance Studies, Summer 1974*, ed. Dale B. J. Randall (Durham, N.C.: Duke University Press, 1976), 28–54; Wenzel, *Verses in Sermons*.

31. *SP*, s.v. "abusionis," a.6.3, 1:8; see also Siegfried Wenzel, *Preachers, Poets, and the Early English Lyric* (Princeton: Princeton University Press, 1986), 177.

32. See Ellen Kosmer, "The 'Noyous Humoure of Lecherie,'" *Art Bulletin* 57 (1975): 1–8; Adolf Katzenellenbogen, *Allegories of the Virtues and Vices in Mediaeval Art* (London: Warburg Institute, 1939); Anthony Weir and James Jerman, *Images of Lust: Sexual Carvings on Medieval Churches* (London: B. T. Batsford, 1986), 58–79; Emile Male, *Religious Art in France, the Twelfth Century: A Study of the Origins of Medieval Iconography* (Princeton: Princeton University Press, 1982), 373–74. When sins themselves were personified rather than represented by examples, of course, all were depicted as female because abstract nouns in Latin all have feminine gender.

33. Ruth Mazo Karras, "Gendered Sin and Misogyny in John of Bromyard's 'Summa Predicantium,'" *Traditio* 47 (1992): 237. Not all the exempla, of course, dealt with these seven sins, which were not an important organizing principle for this particular work. On the use of this text, see Longère, *La Prédication*, 127; Coleman, *Medieval Readers*, 178–79; Christina Von Nolcken, "Some Alphabetical *Compendia* and How Preachers Used Them in Fourteenth-Century England," *Viator* 12 (1981): 279; Siegfried Wenzel, "Chaucer and the Language of Contemporary Preaching," *Studies in Philology* 73 (1976): 145; for the date, see Leonard E. Boyle, "The Date of the *Summa Praedicantium* of John Bromyard," *Speculum* 48 (1973): 533–37.

34. For details on the counting method and the statistics, see Karras, "Gendered Sin," 241–42.

35. See Donald Weinstein and Rudolph M. Bell, *Saints and Society: The Two Worlds of Western Christendom* (Chicago: University of Chicago Press, 1982), 83 and 87, for male saints tempted by women and for the connection of sexual problems with even saintly women.

36. *SP*, s.v. "adulterium," a.17.1 (female stork commits adultery), a.17.9 (husband suspects wife and tests her), a.17.12 (ghosts of adulterers chase each other eternally), fols. 1:43v–45r; s.v. "filiatio," f.5.18 (wife informs husband that only one son is actually his), fol. 1:301v; s.v. "ebrietas," e.1.3 (man chooses drunkenness as lesser evil but commits adultery when drunk), fols. 1:218r–218v. For an

example of the last-mentioned story in a fourteenth-century sermon, see sermon of John Richesdale, Balliol 149, fol. 95v.

37. *SP*, s.v. "adulterium," a.17.14, fol. 1:45r; BL, MS Harl 1288, fol. 35v. For other examples, see, e.g., in BL, MS Royal 7.D.i, fol. 72r; used in sermon in BL, MS Harl 505, fol. 84r.

38. *SP*, s.v. "ordo clericalis," o.6.61, 2:152v; Oxford, Bodleian Library, MS Lat.Th.d.1, fol. 88r; BL, MS Harl 4894, fol. 95r. Clerical concubinage was a particular preoccupation of monks and friars, as shown, e.g., by the tales in BL, MS Royal 7.D.i, 132v–135v. See Stephen L. Forte, "A Cambridge Dominican Collector of Exempla in the Thirteenth Century," *Archivum Fratrum Praedicatorum* 28 (1958): 115–48. Some of the same tales are also assembled in BL, MS Add 33956, 85–85v.

39. Edward N. Weatherly, ed., *Speculum Sacerdotale* (London: Oxford University Press, 1936), 89.

40. *SP*, s.v. "luxuria," 1.7.35, fol. 1:463v.

41. *SP*, s.v. "luxuria," 1.7.37, fol. 1:462v; Étienne de Bourbon, *Anecdotes historiques, légendes et apologues tirés du recueil inédit d'Étienne de Bourbon, Dominicain du XIIIe siècle*, ed. A. Lecoy de la Marche (Paris: Société de l'histoire de France, 1877), no. 502, 432. It is clear that the story is not classified under lust because of the man's lust; the man is only an incidental character.

42. Sermons of Robert Rypon (fourteenth century), BL, MS Harl 4894, fol. 176v. See also a fifteenth-century homilist, BL, MS Add 21253, fols. 106r–106v; *Riverside Chaucer*, "Parson's Tale," ll. 422–25; Owst, *Literature and Pulpit*, 391–406; for later examples, see J. W. Blench, *Preaching in England in the Late Fifteenth and Sixteenth Centuries* (New York: Barnes and Noble, 1964), 241–43.

43. Karras, "Gendered Sin," 248–50.

44. See discussion in Owst, *Literature and Pulpit*, 404–411; Blench, *Preaching in England*, 241. For more actual sermon examples, see Oxford, Pembroke College Library, MS 199, fol. 67r (fifteenth century), sermon 63; Oxford, Bodleian Library, Laud Misc 706 (fifteenth century), fol. 73r; Oxford, Bodleian Library, MS Bodley 649 (fifteenth century), fol. 156v; John Felton, University of Pennsylvania Library, MS Lat 35, fol. 140v; Nicole Bozon, *Nine Verse Sermons by Nicole Bozon: The Art of an Anglo-Norman Poet and Preacher*, ed. Barton J. Ley (Oxford: Society for the Study of Medieval Languages and Literatures, 1981), 49, 67–68.

45. Woodburn O. Ross, ed. *Middle English Sermons* (London: Oxford University Press, 1940), 234–35.

46. BL, MS Royal 8.C.i, fol. 13r; see Owst, *Literature and Pulpit*, 392; and Margaret J. Morin, "John Waldeby, O.S.A., Preacher, with a Critical Edition of his Tract on the Ave Maria," *Analecta Augustiniana* 35 (1972): 24. Cf. *SP*, s.v. "luxuria," 1.7.20, fol. 1:460v.

47. *SP*, s.v. "ornatus," o.7.1–10, fols. 2:158v–160v.

48. *SP*, s.v. "pulchritudo," p.14.5, fol. 2:281r; s.v. "luxuria," 1.7.39, fol. 1:464v.

49. Wenzel, *Fasciculus Morum*, book 1 chap. 5, 51, and book 7 chap. 17, 704–5; Alexander Anglicus, *Destructorium Vitiorum* 6:69, fol. F4r. See also BL, MS Harl 1197, fol. 1v.

50. There is no indication in women's writings that they saw themselves as responsible for tempting men. This does not, of course, mean that women did

not come to accept this view. Those exceptional women who did write are not likely to have been the ones most susceptible to this sort of self-hatred.

51. Karl Inge Sandred, ed., *A Middle English Version of the Gesta Romanorum Edited from Gloucester Cathedral MS 22* (Uppsala: Almqvist and Wiksell, 1971), no. 21, 71. The Latin version has a different interpretation (Oesterley, *Gesta Romanorum,* no. 166, 552). There the queen represents the soul.

52. Étienne de Bourbon, *Recueil,* no. 276, 230; no. 285, 238.

53. "Golias," "De Coniuge non Ducenda," 80.

54. BL, MS Add 21253, fol. 54v (see Owst, *Literature and Pulpit,* 386); *SP,* s.v. "castitas," c.3.1, fol. 1:108v.

55. Margaret Jennings, "Tutivillus: The Literary Career of the Recording Demon," *Studies in Philology: Texts and Studies* 74 (1977): 1–96.

56. See the connection between prostitution and scolding, pp. 138–40; McIntosh, "Finding Language." And see Sharon Farmer, "Persuasive Voices: Clerical Images of Medieval Wives," *Speculum* 61 (1986): 539–41, on the positive aspects of women's speech.

57. Bozon, *Metaphors,* no. 53, 82; see also Odo of Cheriton, *The Fables of Odo of Cheriton,* trans. John C. Jacobs (Syracuse: Syracuse University Press, 1985), no. 95, 143. Other versions of this tale cited in Owst, *Literature and Pulpit,* 389 n. 4. It is used in a sermon in BL, MS Arundel 231, fol. 205r (fourteenth century).

58. *SP,* s.v. "luxuria," 1.7.1–3, fol. 1:457r; Johannes Hubertus Lodewijk Kengen, "Memoriale Credencium: A Late Middle English Manual of Theology for Lay People, Edited from Bodley MS Tanner 201" (Ph.D. diss., Nijmegen, 1979), 138ff.; John of Wales, *Monoloquium,* BL, MS Harl 632, fols. 312r–312v; Rypon, BL, MS Harl 4894, fol. 16r; John Wyclif, "On the Seven Deadly Sins," in *Select English Works of John Wyclif,* ed. Thomas Arnold (Oxford: Clarendon Press, 1871), 3:119–67; BL, MS Add 11579, fol. 128r. Another version of this schema added the branch of "abuse," meaning wrongful sex with one's wife. BL, MS Harl 1197, fol. 28r; MS Sloane 3160, fol. 17r.

59. John Myrc, *Instructions for Parish Priests,* ed. Edward Peacock (London: Kegan Paul, Trench, Trübner & Co., 1902), 40.

60. Wenzel, *Fasciculus Morum,* book 7 chap. 7, 669; I have substituted "whore" for "prostitute" as a translation for *meretrix.*

61. See Karras, "Two Models."

62. BL, MS Harl 665, fol. 69r (fifteenth century); MS Add 11579, fol. 18v (fourteenth century).

63. John W. Smeltz, "*Speculum Vitae:* An Edition of British Museum Manuscript Royal 17.C.viii" (Ph.D. diss., Duquesne University, 1977), 441. The reasons why sex with a prostitute is particularly sinful are taken from the tradition of confessors' manuals. See Murray, "Perceptions of Sexuality," 109, 196–97; Robert of Flamborough, *Liber Poenitentialis,* ed. J. J. Francis Firth (Toronto: Pontifical Institute of Mediaeval Studies, 1971), book 4 chap. 228, 198.

64. Smeltz, "*Speculum Vitae,*" 354–55.

65. See Hope Emily Allen, "The *Speculum Vitae:* Addendum," *PMLA* 32 (1917): 161–62. The textual tradition includes the fourteenth-century *Ayenbite of Inwit,* the fifteenth-century allegorical devotional handbook *Jacob's Well,* and a fifteenth-century prose reworking of the *Speculum.*

66. *Handlyng Synne,* if we are to judge from the manuscript tradition, was not as widely read as the French version. See Charlton Laird, "Character and Growth of the *Manuel des Pechiez," Traditio* 4 (1946): 253–306; Fritz Kemmler, *"Exempla" in Context: A Historical and Critical Study of Robert Mannyng of Brunne's "Handlyng Synne,"* (Tübingen: Gunter Narr Verlag, 1984), 13–14.

67. Mannyng, *Handlyng Synne,* 237–38, ll. 7435–38, 7443–56.

68. Peter Idley, *Peter Idley's Instructions to His Son,* ed. Charlotte d'Evelyn (Boston: Modern Language Association, 1935), 203.

69. Weatherly, *Speculum Sacerdotale,* 69.

70. BL, MS Harl 4894, fol. 68v.

71. Barnum, *Dives and Pauper,* 2:58.

72. BL, MS Harl 2398, fol. 162v.

73. *Abundancia Exemplorum in Usum Praedicatorum,* BL, MS Add 28682, fol. 274v.

74. Banks, *Alphabet of Tales,* no. 468, 2:320; see also [Wynkyn de Worde], *The Myracles of Oure Blessyd Lady* [London, Wynkyn de Worde, 1496], fol. E1v, using the word "strumpet."

75. Hilding Kjellman, ed., *La Deuxième Collection anglo-normande des miracles de la sainte vierge* (Paris: Edouard Champion, 1922), 70, ll. 102–19; Adgar, *Marienlegenden,* ed. Carl Neuhaus (Heilbronn: Gebr. Henninger, 1886), 230, ll. 244–47. For a stemma of versions of this tale, see Robert Guiette, *La Légende de la sacristine* (Paris: Librairie Honoré Champion, 1927), 489–502.

76. On the relation of the Virgin Mary to Beatrice and other sexual sinners, see Karras, "The Virgin," 116.

77. Carl Horstmann, ed., *The Minor Poems of the Vernon MS* (London: Kegan Paul, Trench, Trübner & Co., 1892), 1:145–49.

78. BL, MS Harl 2371, fols. 33r–33v. See also John Myrc, *Mirk's Festial: A Collection of Homilies,* ed. Theodor Erbe (London: EETS, 1905), 132.

79. *Henri d'Arci's Vitas Patrum,* ed. Basilides A. O'Connor (Washington, D.C.: Catholic University of America Press, 1949), 221, ll. 6852–53; BL, MS Harl 1288, fol. 59v; Ross, *Middle English Sermons,* 148.

80. BL, MS Royal 7.D.i, fol. 96v. This manuscript comes from near Cambridge and was compiled by a Dominican in the thirteenth century. See also BL, MS Add 33956, fols. 21v–22r (a fourteenth-century Franciscan collection), for a tale of a priest who converts a prostitute and finds her a husband.

81. Jacques de Vitry, *The Exempla, or Illustrative Stories from the Sermones Vulgares of Jacques de Vitry,* ed. Thomas Frederick Crane (1890; rpt. Nendeln: Kraus Reprint, 1967), 108. Jacques de Vitry's works were used extensively in England; for other collections in which this tale appears, see Frederic C. Tubach, *Index Exemplorum: A Handbook of Medieval Religious Tales* (Helsinki: Suomalainen Tiedeakatemia, 1969), no. 2440.

82. Sandred, *Middle English Version,* no. 72, 390.

83. Banks, *Alphabet of Tales,* no. 487, 2:330–31.

84. BL, MS Harl 2316, fols. 1r–1v. For other converted prostitutes, see BL, MS Add 33956, fols. 21v–22r; Ross, *Middle English Sermons,* no. 31, 160.

85. Jacques de Vitry, *Exempla,* 83–84. This story is told elsewhere of women who have sex with priests; but Jacques's numerous stories of priests' partners are clearly labeled as such, and this is not one of them. In a fourteenth-century English Franciscan version the woman is also a whore rather than a more perma-

nent partner, though her lover is specified as a priest or cleric; see BL, MS Add 33956, fol. 125r. In other versions he gives her the cloak when she weeps; see Tubach, *Index*, no. 2463.

86. John of Wales, *Monoloquium*, BL, MS Harl 632, fol. 310v, citing Augustine and Isidore of Seville. This etymology is in fact correct, although given the often fanciful nature of medieval etymology, its accuracy must be seen as accidental and irrelevant. *Lupa* was Roman slang for a prostitute, and the word for "brothel" derived from it; but *lupa* as a term for "prostitute" was no longer current in the Middle Ages.

87. See Jean Leclerq, *Monks on Marriage: A Twelfth-Century View* (New York: Seabury Press, 1982), 88–89; H. U. von Balthasar, "Casta Meretrix," in *Sponsa Verbi* (Einsiedeln: Johannes Verlag, 1961), 203–305.

88. For the prostitute as metaphor, see, e.g., BL, MS Arundel 231 (fourteenth-century sermons), sermon 33, fol. 208r.

89. See Erhard Dorn, *Der sündige Heilige in der Legende des Mittelalters* (Munich: Wilhelm Fink Verlag, 1967), on this general theme. I discuss some texts, like the Golden Legend (a thirteenth-century Latin compendium), that were not written in English but were known and/or translated in England.

90. This section draws heavily on Ruth Mazo Karras, "Holy Harlots: Prostitute Saints in Medieval Legend," *Journal of the History of Sexuality* 1 (1990): 3–32, where more detailed references can be found. The article also discusses Saint Mary the Niece of Abraham (Mary the Harlot) and Saint Afra, who are not included in any of the English collections or in most texts of the Golden Legend.

91. Victor Saxer, *Le Culte de Marie Madeleine en occident des origines à la fin du moyen âge* (Auxerre: Société des Fouilles Archéologiques et des Monuments Historiques de l'Yonne, 1959), discusses the widespread popularity of her cult.

92. *The Golden Legend or Lives of the Saints as Englished by William Caxton*, ed. F. S. Ellis (1900; rpt. New York: AMS Press, 1973), 4:87; for the Latin, see Jacobus a Voragine, *Legenda Aurea*, ed. Theodor Graesse (Dresden: Libraria Arnoldiana, 1846), 416.

93. Myrc, *Festial*, 203; Carl Horstmann, ed., *Altenglische Legenden, neue folge* (Heilbronn: Gebr. Henninger, 1881), 81.

94. Donald C. Baker, John L. Murphy, and Louis B. Hall, Jr., eds., *The Late Medieval Religious Plays of Bodleian MSS Digby 133 and E Museo 160* (Oxford: Oxford University Press, 1982), 39, ll. 454–55. See Clifford Davidson, "The Middle English Saint Play and Its Iconography," in *The Saint Play in Medieval Europe*, ed. Clifford Davidson (Kalamazoo, Mich.: Medieval Institute Publications, 1986), 31–122.

95. Charlotte D'Evelyn and Anna J. Mill, ed., *The South English Legendary* (London: Oxford University Press, 1956), 1:303, ll. 19–20.

96. Bertha Skeat, ed., *The Lamentatyon of Mary Magdaleyne* (Cambridge: Fabb and Tyler, 1897), 36, ll. 41–42; 51, ll. 678–79.

97. Caxton, *Golden Legend*, 4:74; Latin text in Jacobus a Voragine, *Legenda Aurea*, 408.

98. Osbern Bokenham, *Legendys of Hooly Wummen*, ed. Mary S. Serjeantson (London: EETS, 1938), 148; Myrc, *Mirk's Festial*, 203. Osbern Bokenham, *A Legend of Holy Women*, trans. Sheila Delany (South Bend, Ind.: University of Notre Dame Press, 1992), 108, translates the Bokenham passage as "she lost her

good name," which is certainly the implication (not that she became anonymous but that she lost her honor).

99. Carl Horstmann, ed., *Sammlung altenglischer Legenden* (Heilbronn: Gebr. Henninger, 1878), 163, ll. 8–10.

100. Baker, Murphy, and Hall, *Late Medieval Religious Plays*, 41, l. 520. The editors translate the word *kelle* as "prostitute" (251), but they derive this meaning entirely from context. They note that it means "clearly a 'loose woman.'" I find no warrant to be more specific than that and translate it as "prostitute." See Kuhn, *Middle English Dictionary*, s.v. "kelis." The clear implication is that she does not want to be taken for someone of low status.

101. Carl Horstmann, ed., *The Early South-English Legendary or Lives of Saints* (London: N. Trübner & Co., 1887), 463, l. 54.

102. Richard Morris, ed., *Cursor Mundi, or the Cours of the Worlde* (London: Oxford University Press, 1874), 3:800–801, ll. 13971–5.

103. For an English translation from the Latin text in the *Patrologia Latina,* itself a translation from the Greek text attributed to the seventh-century author Sophronius, see Benedicta Ward, *Harlots of the Desert: A Study of Repentance in Early Monastic Source* (Kalamazoo, Mich.: Cistercian Publications, 1987), 35–56.

104. Adgar, *Marienlegenden*, 194, ll. 9–10.

105. A. T. Baker, "La Vie de Sainte Marie l'Égyptienne," *Revue des langues romanes* 59 (1916): 145–400; Peter F. Dembowski, ed., *La Vie de sainte Marie l'Égyptienne: Versions en ancien et en moyen français* (Geneva: Droz, 1977), 16–17, 37.

106. William Caxton, trans., *Vitas Patrum* (London: Caxton, 1495), fol. 68r. His use of sources is discussed in Constance Rosenthal, "The *Vitae Patrum* in Old and Middle English Literature" (Ph.D. diss., University of Pennsylvania, 1936), 134. Caxton used a French version (*Vie des anciens Saintz peres hermites* [Lyon: Nicolaus Philippi and Jean Dupré, 1486], 57), and in this passage he followed the French directly. The passage found in the Lyon edition differs from the Latin edition on which the French translation was based, which includes the traditional statement about her refusal to accept money. See *Vitae Sanctorum Patrum* (Nuremberg: Anton Koberger, 1478), 50.

107. Brundage, "Prostitution," 835–36.

108. Horstmann, *Early South-English Legendary*, 261, ll. 15–16; see also W. M. Metcalfe, ed., *Legends of the Saints in Scottish Dialect of the Fourteenth Century* (Edinburgh: William Blackwood & Sons, 1896), 1:309, ll. 455–60. This story assumed that cost was an obstacle to having sex with prostitutes; modern authors (see, e.g., Millett, *The Prostitution Papers*, 93; Harry Benjamin and R. E. L. Masters, *Prostitution and Morality* [New York: Julian Press, 1964], 101) have noted that men often seek out prostitutes precisely because they do charge, which makes the relationship with a prostitute different from that with another woman.

109. Caxton, *Golden Legend*, 3:107; Jacobus a Voragine, *Legenda Aurea*, 248.

110. For an English translation from the Latin of the *Patrologia Latina*, see Ward, *Harlots*, 83–84.

111. Caxton, *Golden Legend*, 5:241.

112. Henri d'Arci, *Vitas Patrum*, 147, l. 2.

113. Banks, *Alphabet of Tales*, 1:3; Arthur Brandeis, ed., *Jacob's Well* (London: Kegan Paul, Trench, Trübner & Co., 1900), 22.

114. Henri d'Arci, *Vitas Patrum*, 147, l. 4; see also Banks, *Alphabet of Tales*, 1:3; and Carl Horstmann, ed., "Die Evangelien-Geschichten der Homiliensammlung des Ms. Vernon," *Archiv für die Erforschung der neueren Sprachen* 57 (1877): 279, l. 4.

115. Metcalfe, *Legends of the Saints*, 2:215, ll. 11–12.

116. Horstmann, "Evangelien-Geschichten," 300, ll. 5–8, 16; see also Metcalfe, *Legends*, 2:205.

117. See Karras, "Holy Harlots," 29, for a discussion of these differences.

118. On Italian courtesans, see Lynne Lawner, *Lives of the Courtesans: Portraits of the Renaissance* (New York: Rizzoli, 1987); Cathy Santore, "Julia Lombardo, 'Somtuosa Meretrize': A Portrait by Property," *Renaissance Quarterly* 41 (1988): 44–83.

119. Taylor, "Strange Bedfellows," places more stress on the conversion aspect of these narratives, especially in fifteenth- and sixteenth-century Italian versions, and suggests that the conversion stories as used in preaching are evidence of a generally tolerant societal attitude toward prostitution. My reading of the English material does not support this idea. When Mary Magdalen's repentance is the focus, the point is the possibility of redemption not for prostitutes but for people in general.

120. Charles W. Jones, *Saint Nicholas of Myra, Bari, and Manhattan: Biography of a Legend* (Chicago: University of Chicago Press, 1978), 318–19.

121. On this legend and its popularity in both literature and art, see Karl Meisen, *Nikolauskult und Nikolausbrauch im Abendlande. Eine kultgeographisch-volkskundliche Untersuchung* (Düsseldorf: L. Schwann, 1931), 232–45.

122. Caxton, *Golden Legend*, 2:110; Jacobus a Voragine, *Legenda Aurea*, 23. The *Speculum Sacerdotale* adds that they were to go to a brothel; BL, MS Add 36791, fol. 138v.

123. BL, MS Harl 2371, fol. 54v; see also Horstmann, *Altenglische Legenden, neue folge*, 12, ll. 111–20; Myrc, *Mirk's Festial*, chap. 3, 12; Horstmann, *Early South-English Legendary*, 24, ll. 28–29.

124. Caxton, *Golden Legend*, 2:247; Jacobus a Voragine, *Legenda Aurea*, 114.

125. Caxton, *Golden Legend*, 6:61; Jacobus a Voragine, *Legenda Aurea*, 701.

126. D'Evelyn and Mill, *South English Legendary*, 21, ll. 52–54.

127. Bokenham, *A Legend*, 88; Bokenham, *Legendys*, 121, ll. 4407–13.

128. See Rosen, *Lost Sisterhood*, 112–35.

129. Jacobus a Voragine, *Legenda Aurea*, 170.

130. Caxton, *Golden Legend*, 3:33; Bokenham, *A Legend*, 159; Bokenham, *Legendys*, 229, ll. 8398–8400; D'Evelyn and Mill, *South English Legendary* 1:54, l. 7. "Strong" was used as an emphatic adjective, much as a speaker today might say, "She's the biggest whore"; the phrase "strong whore" is often found in defamation cases.

131. Perhaps this reflects a late antique urban society in which prostitution was more common than in the Middle Ages, but what is important here is that it was not a society with which the authors were familiar.

Conclusion

1. See, e.g., D'Emilio and Freedman, *Intimate Matters*, 130–38, 181–83, 208–15; Walkowitz, *Prostitution*, 13–31.

2. See Kowaleski and Bennett, "Crafts, Gilds, and Women."

3. See LeGoff, "Licit and Illicit Trades."

4. On economic theory, see Joel B. Kaye, "Quantification of Quality: The Impact of Money and Monetization on the Development of Scientific Thought in the Fourteenth Century" (Ph.D. diss., University of Pennsylvania, 1991).

5. Brundage, "Prostitution," 837–39. Although the prostitute was entitled to her wage, however, if part of the sum promised was based on deception (that is, if the man agreed to pay a large sum because she was particularly beautiful, when in fact her beauty came from cosmetics), she was entitled only to what he would have paid if he had seen her as she actually appeared.

6. R. I. Moore, *The Formation of a Persecuting Society: Power and Deviance in Western Europe, 950–1250* (New York: Basil Blackwell, 1987), 95.

7. "Remove the sewer and you will fill the palace with ordure; similarly with the bilge from a ship; remove whores from the world and you will fill it with sodomy." Thomas Aquinas, "De Regimine Principium ad Regem Cypri," 4.14, in *Opera Omnia* (Parma: Pietro Fiaccadori, 1864), 16:281. Scholars question the authenticity of book 4; see James A. Weisheipl, *Friar Thomas D'Aquino: His Life, Thought, and Work* (Garden City, N.Y.: Doubleday, 1974), 189–91. Nevertheless, whether Aquinas wrote these words or not, they were repeated by other authors during the late Middle Ages and early modern period.

8. The possibility of providing brothels for women was raised in the sixteenth century, but only as a reductio ad absurdum to criticize the provision of brothels for men. Lyndal Roper, *The Holy Household: Women and Morals in Reformation Augsburg* (Oxford: Clarendon Press, 1989), 107–8. See Pateman, *Sexual Contract*, 189–209, on the structural reasons why male prostitution (with female customers) is not prevalent today.

9. This discussion applies only to women's heterosexual behavior. There is extremely little evidence for sexual relations between women in the Middle Ages, in England or elsewhere. This may be because it was not common, but it may also be that nonpenetrative sex was simply not recognized as significant sexual behavior. E. Ann Matter, "My Sister, My Spouse: Women-Identified Women in Medieval Christianity," *Journal of Feminist Studies in Religion* 2 (1986): 81–93. See John Boswell, *Christianity, Social Tolerance, and Homosexuality: Gay People in Western Europe from the Beginning of the Christian Era to the Fourteenth Century* (Chicago: University of Chicago Press, 1980), 290, on punishments for lesbian sex; and Judith Brown, *Immodest Acts: The Life of a Lesbian Nun in Renaissance Italy* (New York: Oxford University Press, 1986), 6–20, on the general issue. See chapter 5, n. 67, for the only shred of evidence I have found from this period that might possibly refer to women's same-sex relations.

10. See Keith Thomas, "The Double Standard," *Journal of the History of Ideas* 20 (1959): 195–216; Karras, "Two Models."

11. The temporal courts in London occasionally heard cases of adultery, but these all involved priests, and this in a very anticlerical era in that city.

12. For nuns, see Eileen E. Power, *Medieval English Nunneries, c. 1275 to*

1535 (Cambridge: Cambridge University Press, 1922), 4. For widows, see Joel Rosenthal, "Fifteenth-Century Widows and Widowhood: Bereavement, Reintegration, and Life Choices," and Barbara Hanawalt, "Remarriage as an Option for Urban and Rural Widows in Late Medieval England," both in *Wife and Widow in Medieval England*, ed. Sue Sheridan Walker (Ann Arbor: University of Michigan Press, 1993), 33–58 and 141–64.

13. Guildhall Library, MS 9064/3, fol. 6v.

14. See, e.g., Keith Wrightson, *English Society, 1580–1680* (New Brunswick, N.J.: Rutgers University Press, 1982), 73–74.

15. Andrew McCall, *The Medieval Underworld* (London: Hamish Hamilton, 1979), 184–85. Of course, the prohibitions on the sale of refreshments may not have been observed. But in Southwark there is less evidence than elsewhere of men visiting brothels in groups.

16. Mannyng, *Handlyng Synne*, 140. This national distinction is not found in the French text Mannyng was paraphrasing.

17. Alan Macfarlane, *Marriage and Love in England: Modes of Reproduction, 1300–1840* (Oxford: Basil Blackwell, 1986), 119–47, 174–208; Ralph A. Houlbrooke, *The English Family, 1450–1700* (New York: Longman, 1984), 68–78; Wrightson, *English Society*, 66–88.

18. Ingram, *Church Courts*, 155–57; Archer, *Pursuit of Stability*, 251–54. This stricter morality is coincident with the rise of Puritanism, which may have been less a cause of changing moral attitudes than a concomitant in the religious sphere of those changing attitudes.

19. More realistically, the way in which the existence of prostitutes would have affected other women is that men would have learned that women were available for the asking, resulting in nonprostitutes' suffering the same sort of harassment and objectification that prostitutes endured. But this was hardly a concern for medieval authorities; and even medieval women would not have expressed the problem in anything resembling these terms.

20. See Paul Strohm, *Hochon's Arrow: The Social Imagination of Fourteenth-Century Texts* (Princeton: Princeton University Press, 1992), 137–39.

21. See Lyndal Roper, "'The Common Man,' 'the Common Good,' 'Common Women': Gender and Meaning in the German Reformation Commune," *Social History* 12 (1987): 1–21, on the parallel term in Germany; also George, "Legal, Medical, and Psychiatric Considerations," 720; and Symanski, *Immoral Landscape*, 96, on the term as used in the twentieth century.

22. McIntosh, "Finding Language." For early modern England, see David Underdown, "The Taming of the Scold," in *Order and Disorder in Early Modern England*, ed. Anthony Fletcher and John Stevenson (Cambridge: Cambridge University Press, 1985), 116–36; Susan Dwyer Amussen, *An Ordered Society: Gender and Class in Early Modern England* (Oxford: Basil Blackwell, 1988), 22–23.

23. CLRO, L-B N, fols. 193v, 233r–233v, 260v; L-B P, fol. 4r; Rep 4, fol. 45r; Rep 6, fol. 16v.

24. PRO, SC2/191/55, m. 1; see also m. 3 for keeping prostitutes juxtaposed with keeping dice games.

25. CLRO, MS 242A.

26. See, e.g., WAM, 50734, 50711; NRO Y/C4/90, m. 12. See also Kettle, "City and Close," 141.

27. See, e.g., W. H. Black and G. M. Hills, "The Hereford Municipal Records

and the Customs of Hereford," *Journal of the British Archaeological Association* 27 (1871): 486.

28. Karras, "Regulation of Brothels," 433.

29. V. A. Kolve, *The Play Called Corpus Christi* (Stanford: Stanford University Press, 1966), 146–49; George England and Alfred W. Pollard, eds., *The Towneley Plays* (London: Oxford University Press, 1897), 29–30, ll. 218–34, and 35, ll. 406–14.

30. G. L. Remnant, *A Catalogue of Misericords in Great Britain* (Oxford: Clarendon Press, 1969), 24, 27, 49, 52, 98, 167, 176.

31. Wunderli, *London Church Courts*, 75–76.

32. Guildhall Library, MS 9064/4 and 5 passim. This does not include women who were charged with the two sorts of offenses on different occasions.

33. See WAM 50740 for a list of women charged in this manner.

34. See Judith Bennett, "Misogyny, Popular Culture, and Women's Work," *History Workshop* 21 (1991), esp. 177–179, from which the argument here is taken; and see *The Complete Poems of John Skelton, Laureate*, ed. Philip Henderson (London: J. M. Dent, 1946), 112–30, for the poem.

35. Widows were in a different position; see, e.g., Barron, "Golden Age," 41–44.

36. Cf. Geremek, *Margins*, 221.

Bibliography

Manuscript Sources

Canterbury, Cathedral, City, and Diocesan Record Office
  Deposition Book
    X.10.1, 1410–21

Chelmsford, Essex Record Office
  Ingatestone Manorial Court Rolls
    D/DP/M1–D/DP/M74, 1279–1510

Cambridge, Cambridge University Library
  Ely Diocesan Records: Act Books (consulted in microform publication): *Eccle-siastical Authority in England: Church Court Records, c. 1400–c. 1660*, ser. 1, *The Church Court Records of Ely*, pt. 2, *Office Act Books and Formularies, 1469–1639* (Brighton: Harvester Microforms, 1986)
    Liber B

Exeter, Devon Record Office
  Mayor's Court Rolls
    17–18 Edward II to 40–41 Edward III, 1323–67
  Rolls of Mayor's Tourn
    EC9/2–E9/15, 1378–1444
  Exeter City Corporation, Chamber Act Books
    1, 1509–1538

Hereford, County Record Office
  Hereford Diocesan Records, Consistory Court Books, Acts of Office (consulted on microfilm at Family History Library, Church of Jesus Christ of Latter-Day Saints, Broomall, Pa.)
    3, 1445–46
    8, 1468–69

Ipswich, Suffolk Record Office
  Ipswich Borough Court Rolls
    C8/1/5–CB/1/44, 1459–1544
  Ipswich Courts Leet
    C7/1/1–C7/1/27, 1359–1508

King's Lynn, King's Lynn Borough Archives
  Leet Rolls
    KL/C17/1–KL/C17/22, 1309–1434

Kingston-upon-Thames, Surrey Record Office
  Kingston Manorial Court Rolls (consulted on microfilm at Family History
  Library, Church of Jesus Christ of Latter-Day Saints, Broomall, Pa.)
    KF1/1–KF1/8, 1434–1498

Lincoln, Lincolnshire Archives Office
  Visitation Records
    Vj4, Lincoln and Stow, 1473

London, British Library
  Additional MSS
    11579
    21253
    28682
    33956
    36791
  Arundel MSS
    231
  Cotton MSS
    Julius B iv
  Harleian MSS
    505
    632
    665
    1197
    1288
    2316
    2371
    2398
    4894
  Royal MSS
    7.D.i
    8.C.i
  Sloane MSS
    3160

London, Corporation of London Records Office
  Coroner's Rolls
    F, 1336–37
  Journals of Court of Common Council
    1, 1416–21
    2, 1425–29
    3, 1436–42
    13, 1527–36
    14, 1536–43
  Letter-Books
    A, 1275–98
    B, 1275–1312
    D, 1309–14
    F, 1337–52
    H, 1375–99
    I, 1400–22

K, 1422–61
L, 1461–97
M, 1497–1515
N, 1515–26
P, 1532–48
Mayor's Court Rolls
A, 1298
G, 1305
Plea and Memoranda Rolls
A3, 1338–41
A5, 1338–45
A11, 1366
A18, 1372–73
A25, 1382–85
A34, 1394–95
A50, 1421–22
A51, 1422–23
A66, 1439
Repertory Books of the Council of Aldermen
2, 1506–15
3, 1515–19
4, 1519–24
5, 1518–21
6, 1522–24
9, 1533–37
10, 1537–43
11, 1543–48
12, 1548–52
Southwark Court Leet Records
MS 39C/SCM1, 1543
Wardmote Records
242A, Portsoken Ward, 1465–81

London, Greater London Record Office
Consistory Court Instance Act Books
DL/C/1, 1496–1505
Deposition Books
DL/C/205, 1467–76

London, Guildhall Library, Department of Manuscripts
Acta Probacionem Testamentorum (Commissary Court Wills)
9168/1, 1496–1500
Acta quoad correctionem delinquentium (Commissary Court Act Books)
9064a, 1485
9064/1, 1470–73
9064/2, 1483–89
9064/3, 1480–83, 1475–77
9064/4, 1489–91
9064/4A, 1491–92
9064/5, 1492–94
9064/6, 1494–96

9064/8, 1496–1501
9064/9, 1502–3
9064/11, 1511–1516
Liber Examinationum (Consistory Court Deposition Book)
9065, 1486–96

London, Lambeth Palace Library
Archbishopric Estate Court Rolls
ED 969 (Southwark), 1504–11
ED 1905 (Lambeth), 1442–60

London, Public Record Office
Chancery Proceedings (Early)
C1/48/191, 1473–75
C1/64/897, 1475–85
C1/363/76, 1504–15
Exchequer of Pleas, Plea Rolls
E13/26, 1302–3
Manorial Court Records
SC2/156/5 (Middlewich), 1415–16
SC2/169/21 (Culliford), 1476–77
SC2/172/18 (West Ham), 1463–75
SC2/173/12 (Leyndon), 1462–82
SC2/191/55–SC2/191/59 (East Smithfield), 1421–1534
SC2/205/29–SC2/205/37 (Walworth), 1413–1509
Patent Rolls
C/16/489, 1460
State Papers
SP1/18/365/5/iii, 1519

London, Westminster Abbey Muniments Room
Court Rolls, Manor of Westminster
50699–50782, 1364–*temp.* Henry VIII

Maidstone, Kent Archives Office
Sandwich Year Books
Sa/AC1, 1432–87 (Old Black Book)
Sa/AC2, 1488–1526 (White Book)

Norwich, Norfolk Record Office
Norwich City Records, Sessions Indictments and Recognizances
Case 11, Shelf a, Parcel 1, *temp.* Henry 8
Great Yarmouth Borough Records, Borough Court Rolls
Y/C4/81–Y/C4/226, 1367–1524

Nottingham, Nottinghamshire Record Office
Borough Quarter Sessions
CA/1–CA/45b, 1452–1550

Oxford, Balliol College Library
MS 149

Oxford, Bodleian Library
MS Bodley 649
MS Laud. Misc. 706
MS Lat.Th.d.1

Oxford, Pembroke College Library
  MS 199
Philadelphia, University of Pennsylvania Library
  MS Lat. 35
Southhampton, Southhampton City Record Office
  Mayor's Book of Fines
    SC5/3/1, 1488–1594
Winchester, Hampshire Record Office
  Southwark Manorial Court Records
    Eccles I 85/1, 1505–6
York, Borthwick Institute for Historical Research
  Cause Papers, Fourteenth Century
    CP.E.72, 1356
    CP.E.79, 1358
    CP.E.175, 1390
  Cause Papers, Fifteenth Century
    CP.F.22, 1402
    CP.F.83, 1417
    CP.F.99, 1430
    CP.F.104, 1432
    CP.F.111, 1432
    CP.F.153, 1422
    CP.F.175, 1432
  Dean and Chapter Act Books
    D/C AB 1, 1387–1494
York, York Minster Library
  Dean and Chapter Act Books
    H1/2, 1343–70
    H2/1, 1410–20
    M2(1)f, 1357–1485

Published Primary Sources

Adams, Norma, and Charles Donahue, Jr., eds. *Select Cases from the Ecclesiastical Courts of the Province of Canterbury, c. 1200–1301.* Selden Society, vol. 95. London: Selden Society, 1981.

Adgar. *Marienlegenden.* Ed. Carl Neuhaus. Altfranzösische Bibliothek, 9. Heilbronn: Gebr. Henninger, 1886.

[Alexander Anglicus.] *Destructorium Vitiorum.* Paris: Pierre Levet, 1497.

Anderson, R. C., ed. *The Assize of Bread Book.* Publications of the Southampton Record Society. Southampton: Cox and Sharland, 1923.

Axton, Richard, ed. *Three Rastell Plays: "Four Elements," "Calisto and Melibea," "Gentleness and Nobility."* Totowa, N.J.: Rowan and Littlefield, 1979.

Baader, Joseph, ed. *Nürnberger Polizeiordnungen aus dem XIII bis XV Jahrhundert.* Bibliothek des litterarischen Vereins in Stuttgart, 63. Stuttgart: Litterarische Verein, 1861.

Baker, A. T. "La Vie de Sainte Marie l'Égyptienne." *Revue des langues romanes* 59 (1916): 145–400.

Baker, Donald C., John L. Murphy, and Louis B. Hall, Jr., eds. *The Late Medieval Religious Plays of Bodleian MSS Digby 133 and E Museo 160.* EETS, 283. Oxford: Oxford University Press, 1982.

Banks, Mary McLeod, ed. *An Alphabet of Tales: An English Fifteenth-Century Translation of the Alphabetum Narrationum.* 2 vols. EETS, 126–27. London: Kegan Paul, Trench, Trübner & Co., 1904.

Barnum, Priscilla Heath, ed. *Dives and Pauper.* 2 vols. EETS, 275, 280. Oxford: EETS, 1980.

Bateson, Mary, ed. *Records of the Borough of Leicester.* Vols. 1–3. London: C. J. Clay, 1899–1905.

Bickley, Francis B., ed. *The Little Red Book of Bristol.* 2 vols. Bristol: W. Crofton Hemmons, 1900.

Bokenham, Osbern. *Legendys of Hooly Wummen.* Ed. Mary S. Serjeantson. EETS, 206. London: EETS, 1938.

———. *A Legend of Holy Women.* Trans. Sheila Delany. South Bend, Ind.: University of Notre Dame Press, 1992.

Bowker, Margaret, ed. *An Episcopal Court Book for the Diocese of Lincoln, 1514–1520.* Publications of the Lincoln Record Society, 61. Lincoln: Lincoln Record Society, 1967.

Boyd, David Lorenzo, and Ruth Mazo Karras. "The Interrogation of a Male Transvestite Prostitute in Fourteenth-Century London." *GLQ: A Journal of Lesbian and Gay Studies,* 1 (1994): 459–65.

Bozon, Nicole. *Les Contes moralisés de Nicole Bozon, frère mineur.* Ed. Lucy Toulmin Smith and Paul Meyer. Paris: Firmin Didot, 1889.

———. *Metaphors of Brother Bozon, a Friar Minor.* Trans. J[ohn]. R[ose]. London: Constable & Co., 1913.

———. *Nine Verse Sermons by Nicole Bozon: The Art of an Anglo-Norman Poet and Preacher.* Ed. Barton J. Ley. Medium Aevum Monographs, n.s., 11. Oxford: Society for the Study of Medieval Languages and Literatures, 1981.

Brandeis, Arthur. *Jacob's Well.* EETS, 115. London: Kegan Paul Trench Trübner & Co., 1900.

Calendar of Close Rolls Preserved in the Public Record Office: Edward III. 14 vols. London: HMSO, 1896–1913.

Calendar of Letters and Papers, Foreign and Domestic, of the Reign of Henry VIII. 21 vols. London: HMSO, 1862–1910.

Calendar of the Patent Rolls Preserved in the Public Record Office: Edward III. 16 vols. London: HMSO, 1891–1916.

Calendar of the Patent Rolls Preserved in the Public Record Office: Henry VI. 6 vols. London: HMSO, 1901–10.

Caxton, William, trans. *The Book of the Knight of the Tower.* Ed. M. Y. Offord. EETS Supplemental Series, 2. London: Oxford University Press, 1971.

———, trans. *The Golden Legend or Lives of the Saints as Englished by William Caxton.* Ed. F. S. Ellis. 7 vols. London: J. M. Dent & Sons, 1900. Reprint. New York: AMS Press, 1973.

———, trans. *Vitas Patrum.* London: Caxton, 1495.

Chapman, Annie B. Wallis, ed. *The Black Book of Southampton.* 2 vols. Southampton: Southampton Record Society, 1912.

Chaucer, Geoffrey. *The Riverside Chaucer.* Ed. Larry P. Benson. Boston: Houghton Mifflin, 1987.

Cooper, Charles Henry, ed. *Annals of Cambridge*. 5 vols. Cambridge: Warwick & Co., 1842–52, 1908.

Dembowski, Peter F. *La Vie de sainte Marie l'Égyptienne: Versions en ancien et en moyen français*. Publications romanes et françaises, 144. Geneva: Droz, 1977.

D'Evelyn, Charlotte, and Anna J. Mill, eds. *The South English Legendary*. 3 vols. EETS, 235, 236, 244. London: Oxford University Press, 1956–59.

DeWindt, Edwin Brezette, ed. *The Court Rolls of Ramsey, Hepmangrove and Bury, 1268–1600*. Toronto: Pontifical Institute of Mediaeval Studies, 1990.

DuVal, John, and Raymond Eichmann, ed. and trans. *Cuckolds, Clerics, and Countrymen: Medieval French Fabliaux*. Fayetteville: University of Arkansas Press, 1982.

Eichmann, Raymond, and John DuVal, eds. *The French Fabliau: B.N. MS 837*. 2 vols. Garland Library of Medieval Literature, 16, ser. A. New York: Garland, 1984.

Elvey, E. M., ed. *The Courts of the Archdeacon of Buckingham, 1483–1523*. Buckinghamshire Record Society, 19. Aylesbury: Buckinghamshire Record Society, 1975.

England, George, and Alfred W. Pollard, eds. *The Towneley Plays*. EETS, Extra Series, 71. London: Oxford University Press, 1897.

Étienne de Bourbon. *Anecdotes historiques, légendes et apologues tirés du recueil inédit d'Étienne de Bourbon, Dominicain du XIIIe siècle*. Ed. A. Lecoy de la Marche. Paris: Société de l'histoire de France, 1877.

Fitch, Marc, ed. *Index to Testamentary Records in the Commissary Court of London (London Division) Now Preserved in the Guildhall Library, London*. 2 vols. British Record Society Index Library, 82, 86. London: HMSO, 1969, 1974.

Gairdner, James, ed. *Historical Collections of a Citizen of London in the Fifteenth Century*. Camden Society, n.s., 17. London: Camden Society, 1876.

Galbraith, V. H., ed. *The Anonimalle Chronicle, 1333–1381*. Publications of the University of Manchester, Historical Series, 45. Manchester: Manchester University Press, 1927.

Gidden, H. W., ed. *The Book of Remembrance of Southampton*. 3 vols. Publications of the Southampton Record Society, 27, 28, 30. Southampton: Cox and Sharland, 1927–30.

"Golias." "De Coniuge non Ducenda." In *The Latin Poems Commonly Attributed to Walter Mapes*. Ed. Thomas Wright. London: Camden Society, 1841. Reprint. New York: Johnson Reprint Co., 1968.

Guillaume de Lorris and Jean de Meun. *The Romance of the Rose*. Trans. Harry W. Robbins. New York: Dutton, 1962.

Harris, Mary Dormer, ed. *The Coventry Leet Book*. 4 vols. EETS, 134, 135, 138, 146. London: Early English Text Society, 1907–13.

Helmholz, R. H., ed. *Select Cases on Defamation to 1600*. Selden Society, 101. London: Selden Society, 1985.

Henri d'Arci. *Henri d'Arci's Vitas Patrum*. Ed. Basilides A. O'Connor. Washington, D.C.: Catholic University of America Press, 1949.

Historical Manuscripts Commission. "Records of the Corporation of Gloucester." In *Historical Manuscripts Commission, Twelfth Report*. Pt. 9. London: HMSO, 1891.

————. "The Historical Manuscripts Belonging to the Mayor and Corporation of Rochester." In *Royal Commission on Historical Manuscripts, Ninth Report*. London: HMSO, 1883.

Horstmann, Carl, ed. *Altenglische Legenden, neue folge*. Heilbronn: Gebr. Henninger, 1881.

————, ed. *The Early South-English Legendary or Lives of Saints*. EETS, 87. London: N. Trübner & Co., 1887.

————, ed. "Die Evangelien-Geschichten der Homiliensammlung des Ms. Vernon." *Archiv für die Erforschung der neueren Sprachen* 57 (1877): 241–316.

————, ed. *The Minor Poems of the Vernon MS*. 2 vols. EETS, 98, 117. London: Kegan Paul, Trench, Trübner & Co., 1892–1901.

————, ed. *Sammlung altenglischer Legenden*. Heilbronn: Gebr. Henninger, 1878.

Hudson, William, ed. *Leet Jurisdiction in the City of Norwich*. Selden Society, 5. London: Bernard Quaritch, 1892.

Hughes, Paul L., and James F. Larkin, eds. *Tudor Royal Proclamations*. Vol. 1. *The Early Tudors*. New Haven: Yale University Press, 1964.

Idley, Peter. *Peter Idley's Instructions to His Son*. Ed. Charlotte d'Evelyn. Boston: Modern Language Association, 1935.

Jacobus a Voragine. *Legenda Aurea*. Ed. Theodor Graesse. Dresden: Libraria Arnoldiana, 1846.

Jacques de Vitry. *The Exempla, or Illustrative Stories from the Sermones Vulgares of Jacques de Vitry*. Ed. Thomas Frederick Crane. Folk-Lore Society Publications, 26. London: D. Nutt, 1890. Reprint. Nendeln: Kraus Reprint, 1967.

John of Bromyard. *Summa Praedicantium*. 2 vols. Venice: Domenico Nicolino, 1586.

John of Wales. *Communiloquium*. Augsburg: Anton Sorg, 1475.

Kempe, Margery. *The Book of Margery Kempe*. Ed. Sanford B. Meech. EETS, 212. London: Oxford University Press, 1940.

Kengen, Johannes Hubertus Lodewijk. "Memoriale Credencium. A Late Middle English Manual of Theology for Lay People, Edited from Bodley MS Tanner 201." Ph.D. diss., Nijmegen, 1979.

Kjellman, Hilding, ed. *La Deuxième Collection anglo-normande des miracles de la sainte vierge*. Paris: Edouard Champion, 1922.

Langland, William. *The Vision of William Concerning Piers the Plowman*. Ed. W. W. Skeat. 2 vols. Oxford: Oxford University Press, 1886.

Lecompte, I. C. "*Richeut*, Old French Poem of the Twelfth Century, with Introduction, Notes, and Glossary." *Romanic Review* 4 (1913): 261–305.

McKnight, George H., ed. *Middle English Humorous Tales in Verse*. Boston: D. C. Heath, 1913.

Mannyng, Robert. *Robert of Brunne's "Handlyng Synne."* Ed. Frederick J. Furnivall. EETS, 119. London: Kegan Paul, Trench, Trübner & Co., 1901.

Merson, A. L., ed. *The Third Book of Remembrance of Southampton, 1514–1602*. 4 vols. Southampton Records Series, 2–3, 8, 22. Southampton: University of Southampton, 1952–79.

Ménard, Philippe, ed. "Du Preste et d'Alison." In *Fabliaux français du moyen âge*. Vol. 1. Textes littéraires français, 193. Geneva: Droz, 1979.

Metcalfe, W. M., ed. *Legends of the Saints in Scottish Dialect of the Fourteenth*

Century. 3 vols. Scottish Text Society, 13, 23, 35. Edinburgh: William Black-wood & Sons, 1896.

Montaiglon, Anatole, and Gaston Raynaud. *Recueil général et complet des fa-bliaux des XIIIe et XIVe siècles imprimés ou inédits.* 6 vols. Paris: Librairie des Bibliophiles, 1872–1890.

Morris, Richard, ed. *Cursor Mundi, or the Cours of the Worlde.* 7 vols. EETS, 57, 59, 62, 66, 68, 99, 101. London: Oxford University Press, 1874–93.

Mundy, Percy D., ed. *Abstracts of Star Chamber Proceedings Relating to the County of Sussex, Henry VII to Philip and Mary.* Sussex Record Society, 16. London: Mitchell Hughes and Clarke, 1913.

Myrc, John. *Instructions for Parish Priests.* Ed. Edward Peacock. EETS, 31. Lon-don: Kegan Paul, Trench, Trübner & Co., 1902.

———. *Mirk's Festial: A Collection of Homilies.* Ed Theodor Erbe. EETS Extra Series, 96. London: Early English Text Society, 1905.

Odo of Cheriton. *The Fables of Odo of Cheriton.* Trans. John C. Jacobs. Syracuse: Syracuse University Press, 1985.

Oesterley, Hermann, ed. *Gesta Romanorum.* Berlin: Weidmann, 1872.

Owen, Dorothy M., ed. *The Making of King's Lynn: A Documentary Survey.* Records of Social and Economic History, n.s., 9. London: British Academy, 1984.

Post, J. B. "A Fifteenth-Century Customary of the Southwark Stews." *Journal of the Society of Archivists* (1977): 418–28.

Powicke, F. M., and C. R. Cheney, eds. *Councils and Synods, with Other Docu-ments Relating to the English Church.* 2 vols. Oxford: Clarendon Press, 1964.

Prestwich, Michael, trans. *York Civic Ordinances, 1301.* Borthwick Papers, 49. York: Borthwick Institute for Historical Research, 1976.

Raine, Angelo, ed. *York Civic Records.* Vol. 1. Yorkshire Archaeological Society Record Series, 98. York: Yorkshire Archaeological Society, 1939.

Ratcliff, S. C., ed. *Elton Manorial Records, 1279–1351.* Trans. D. M. Gregory. Cambridge: Roxburghe Club, 1946.

Riley, H. T., ed. *Memorials of London and London Life in the Thirteenth, Four-teenth, and Fifteenth Centuries.* London: Longman, 1868.

———, ed. *Liber Albus.* Vol. 1 of *Munimenta Gildhallae Londoniensis: Liber Albus, Liber Custumarum, et Liber Horn.* London: Longman, Brown, Green, Longmans and Roberts, 1859.

———, trans. *Liber Albus: The White Book of the City of London.* London: Richard Griffin & Co., 1861.

Rimbault, E. F., ed. *Early English Poetry, Ballads, and Popular Literature of the Middle Ages.* London: Percy Society, 1842.

Robbins, Rossell Hope, ed. *Secular Lyrics of the Fourteenth and Fifteenth Cen-turies.* Oxford: Clarendon Press, 1956.

Robert of Flamborough. *Liber Poenitentialis.* Ed. J. J. Francis Firth. PIMS Texts and Studies, 18. Toronto: Pontifical Institute for Mediaeval Studies, 1971.

Ross, Woodburn O., ed. *Middle English Sermons.* EETS, 209. London: Oxford University Press, 1940.

Rotuli Parliamentorum. 6 vols. London: Record Commission, 1767–77.

Rymer, Thomas. *Foedera, Conventiones, Litterae et Cujuscunque Generis Acta Publica.* London, 1818.

Salter, H. E., ed. *Mediaeval Archives of the University of Oxford.* 2 vols. Oxford Historical Society, 70, 73. Oxford: Clarendon Press, 1920–21.

———, ed. *Registrum Cancellarii Oxoniensis, 1434–1469.* 2 vols. Oxford Historical Society, 93–94. Oxford: Clarendon Press, 1932.

Sandred, Karl Inge, ed. *A Middle English Version of the Gesta Romanorum Edited from Gloucester Cathedral MS 22.* Studia Anglica Upsaliensia, 8. Uppsala: Almqvist and Wiksell, 1971.

Sellers, Maud, ed. *York Memorandum Book.* Surtees Society, 120. Durham: Andrews & Co., 1912.

Sharpe, Reginald R., ed. *Calendar of Letter-Books Preserved Among the Archives of the City of London at the Guildhall.* 11 vols. London: Corporation of the City of London, 1899–1911.

———, ed. *Calendar of Coroners Rolls of the City of London, A.D. 1300–1378.* London: Richard Clay & Sons, 1913.

———, ed. *Calendar of Wills Proved and Enrolled in the Court of Hustings, London, A.D. 1258–A.D. 1688.* 2 vols. London: J. C. Francis, 1889–90.

Skeat, Bertha. *The Lamentatyon of Mary Magdaleyne.* Cambridge: Fabb and Tyler, 1897.

Skelton, John. *The Complete Poems of John Skelton, Laureate.* Ed. Philip Henderson. London: J. M. Dent, 1946.

Smeltz, John W., ed. *"Speculum Vitae:* An Edition of British Museum Manuscript Royal 17.C.viii." Ph.D. diss., Duquesne University, 1977.

Stow, John. *The Annales of England, faithfully collected out of the most authenticall Authors, Records, and other Monuments of Antiquitie, from the first inhabitation untill this present yeere 1592.* London: Ralfe Newbery, 1592.

———. *A Survey of London.* Ed. C. L. Kingsford. 2 vols. Oxford: Clarendon Press, 1908.

Sutherland, Ronald, ed. *The Romaunt of the Rose, and Le Roman de la Rose: A Parallel-Text Edition.* Oxford: Blackwell, 1967.

Thomas Aquinas. "De Regimine Principium ad Regem Cypri." In *Opera Omnia,* vol. 16. Parma: Pietro Fiaccadori, 1864.

Thomas of Chobham. *Thomae de Chobham Summa Confessorum.* Ed. F. Broomfield. Analecta Mediaevalia Namurcensia, 25. Louvain: Éditions Nauwelaerts, 1968.

Thomas, A. H., ed. *Calendar of Early Mayor's Court Rolls Preserved Among the Archives of the City of London at the Guildhall, A.D. 1298–1307.* Cambridge: Cambridge University Press, 1924.

Thomas, A. H., and Philip E. Jones, eds. *Calendar of Plea and Memoranda Rolls Preserved Among the Archives of the City of London at the Guildhall.* 6 vols. Cambridge: Cambridge University Press, 1926–61.

Thomas, A. H., and I. D. Thornley, eds. *The Great Chronicle of London.* London: George W. Jones, 1938.

Thompson, A. Hamilton, ed. *Visitations of Rural Deaneries by William Atwater, Bishop of Lincoln, and His Commissaries, 1517–1520.* Vol. 1 of *Visitations in the Diocese of Lincoln, 1517–1531.* Publications of the Lincoln Record Society, 33. Hereford: Lincoln Record Society, 1940.

Veale, Edward W. *The Great Red Book of Bristol.* 5 vols. Bristol Record Society, 2, 4, 8, 16, 18. Bristol: Bristol Record Society, 1931–53.

Vie des anciens Saintz peres hermites. Lyons: Nicolaus Philippi and Jean Dupré, 1486.

Vitae Sanctorum Patrum. Nuremberg: Anton Koberger, 1478.

Walter of Hemingford. *Chronicon Domini Walteri de Hemingburgh.* Ed. H. C. Hamilton. 2 vols. London: English Historical Society, 1848–49.

Weatherly, Edward N., ed. *Speculum Sacerdotale.* EETS, 200. London: Oxford University Press, 1936.

Weinbaum, Martin, ed. *The London Eyre of 1276.* London: London Record Society, 1976.

Welter, J.-Th. *Le Speculum laicorum. Edition d'une collection d'exempla composée en Angleterre à la fin du XIIIe siècle.* Thesaurus Exemplorum, 5. Paris: Picard, 1914.

Wenzel, Siegfried, ed. *Fasciculus Morum: A Fourteenth-Century Preacher's Handbook.* University Park: Pennsylvania State University Press, 1989.

Wyclif, John. "On the Seven Deadly Sins." In *Select Works of John Wyclif.* Ed. Thomas Arnold. 3 vols. Oxford: Clarendon Press, 1869–71.

[Wynkyn de Worde]. *The Myracles of Oure Blessyd Lady.* [London: Wynkyn de Worde, 1496].

Secondary Works

Aers, David. *Community, Gender, and Individual Identity: English Writing, 1360–1430.* London: Routledge, 1988.

———, ed. *Medieval Literature: Criticism, Ideology, and History.* New York: St. Martin's Press, 1986.

Allen, Hope Emily. "The *Speculum Vitae:* Addendum." *PMLA* 32 (1917): 133–62.

Allison, K. J., ed. *The City of Kingston upon Hull.* Vol. 1 of *A History of the County of York: East Riding.* Victoria History of the Counties of England. London: Oxford University Press, 1969.

Amussen, Susan Dwyer. *An Ordered Society: Gender and Class in Early Modern England.* Oxford: Basil Blackwell, 1988.

Anderson, Bonnie S., and Judith P. Zinsser. *A History of Their Own: Women in Europe from Prehistory to the Present.* 2 vols. New York: Harper and Row, 1988.

Archer, Ian. *The Pursuit of Stability: Social Relations in Elizabethan London.* Cambridge: Cambridge University Press, 1991.

Aston, Margaret. "Lollard Women Priests?" *Journal of Ecclesiastical History* 31 (1980): 441–61.

Atkinson, Clarissa. *Mystic and Pilgrim: The Book and the Life of Margery Kempe.* Ithaca, N.Y.: Cornell University Press, 1983.

Baldwin, Frances Elizabeth. *Sumptuary Legislation and Personal Regulation in England.* Johns Hopkins University Studies in Historical and Political Science, ser. 44, 1. Baltimore: Johns Hopkins University Press, 1926.

Baldwin, John W. *The Language of Sex: Five Voices from Northern France Around 1200.* Chicago: University of Chicago Press, 1994.

Barron, Caroline. "The 'Golden Age' of Women in Medieval London." *Reading Medieval Studies* 15 (1990): 35–58.

Benjamin, Harry, and R. E. L. Masters. *Prostitution and Morality.* New York: Julian Press, 1964.

Bennett, Judith. *Ale, Beer, and Brewsters in England: Women's Work in a*

Changing World, 1300–1600. New York: Oxford University Press. Forthcoming.

———. "'History That Stands Still': Women's Work in the European Past." *Feminist Studies* 14 (1988): 269–83.

———. "Medieval Women, Modern Women: Across the Great Divide." In *Culture and History, 1350–1600: Essays on English Communities, Identities, and Writing.* Ed. David Aers. New York: Harvester Wheatsheaf, 1992.

———. "Misogyny, Popular Culture, and Women's Work." *History Workshop* 31 (1991): 166–88.

———. *Women in the Medieval Countryside: Gender and Household in Brigstock Before the Plague.* New York: Oxford University Press, 1987.

Biller, P. P. A. "Marriage Patterns and Women's Lives: A Sketch of a Pastoral Geography." In *Woman Is a Worthy Wight: Women in English Society, c. 1200–1500.* Ed. P. J. P. Goldberg. Wolfeboro Falls, N.H.: Alan Sutton, 1992.

Black, W. H., and G. M. Hills. "The Hereford Municipal Records and the Customs of Hereford." *Journal of the British Archaeological Association* 27 (1871): 453–88.

Blench, J. W. *Preaching in England in the Late Fifteenth and Sixteenth Centuries.* New York: Barnes and Noble, 1964.

Bloch, Iwan. *Die Prostitution.* Vol. 1. Handbuch der gesamten Sexualwissenschaft in Einzeldarstellungen, 1. Berlin: Louis Marcus Verlagsbuchhandlung, 1912.

Bloch, R. Howard. *The Scandal of the Fabliaux.* Chicago: University of Chicago Press, 1986.

Bloomfield, Morton W. *The Seven Deadly Sins: An Introduction to the History of a Religious Concept, with Special Reference to Medieval English Literature.* East Lansing, Mich.: State College Press, 1952.

Bolton, Diane K. "Willesden." In *A History of Middlesex.* Ed. T. F. T. Baker. Victoria History of the Counties of England. Oxford: Institute for Historical Research, 1982.

Boswell, John. *Christianity, Social Tolerance, and Homosexuality: Gay People in Western Europe from the Beginning of the Christian Era to the Fourteenth Century.* Chicago: University of Chicago Press, 1980.

———. "Revolutions, Universals, and Sexual Categories." In *Hidden From History: Reclaiming the Gay and Lesbian Past.* Ed. Martin Duberman, Martha Vicinus, and George Chauncey, Jr. New York: Penguin, 1989.

Boyle, Leonard E. "The Date of the *Summa Praedicantium* of John Bromyard." *Speculum* 48 (1973): 533–37.

Braswell, Mary Flowers. "Chaucer's 'Queinte Termes of Lawe': A Legal View of 'The Shipman's Tale.'" *Chaucer Review* 22 (1988): 295–304.

Britnell, R. H. *The Commercialisation of English Society, 1000–1500.* Cambridge: Cambridge University Press, 1993.

Brooke, Christopher N. L. *The Medieval Idea of Marriage.* Oxford: Oxford University Press, 1989.

Brown, Judith. *Immodest Acts: The Life of a Lesbian Nun in Renaissance Italy.* New York: Oxford University Press, 1986.

Brown, Peter. *The Body and Society: Men, Women, and Sexual Renunciation in Early Christianity.* New York: Columbia University Press, 1988.

Brown, Sandra. *The Medieval Courts of York Minster Peculiar.* Borthwick Papers, 66. York: St. Anthony's Press, 1984.

Brundage, James A. *Law, Sex, and Christian Society in Medieval Europe.* Chicago: University of Chicago Press, 1987.

———. "Prostitution in the Medieval Canon Law." *Signs* 1 (1976): 825–45.

———. "Rape and Seduction in the Medieval Canon Law." In *Sexual Practices and the Medieval Church.* Ed. Vern L. Bullough and James Brundage. Buffalo, N.Y.: Prometheus Books, 1982.

Bullough, Vern L., and Lilli Sentz, eds. *Prostitution: A Guide to Sources, 1960–1990.* New York: Garland, 1992.

Burns, E. Jane. "This Prick Which Is Not One: How Women Talk Back in Old French Fabliaux." In *Feminist Approaches to the Body in Medieval Literature.* Ed. Linda Lomperis and Sarah Stanbury. Philadelphia: University of Pennsylvania Press, 1993.

Bynum, Caroline Walker. ". . . And Woman His Humanity: Female Imagery in the Religious Writings of the Later Middle Ages." In *Gender and Religion: On the Complexity of Symbols.* Ed. Caroline Walker Bynum, Stevan Harrell, and Paula Richman. Boston: Beacon Press, 1986.

———. *Holy Feast and Holy Fast: The Religious Significance of Food to Medieval Women.* Berkeley: University of California Press, 1987.

Calin, William. *The French Tradition and Medieval England.* Toronto: University of Toronto Press, 1994.

Camille, Michael. *Image on the Edge.* Cambridge, Mass.: Harvard University Press, 1992.

Carlin, Martha. "The Urban Development of Southwark, c. 1200 to 1550." Ph.D. diss., University of Toronto, 1983.

Carroll, Virginia Schaefer. "Women and Money in 'The Miller's Tale' and 'The Reeve's Tale,'" *Medieval Perspectives* 3 (1988): 76–88.

Carter, John Marshall. *Rape in Medieval England: An Historical and Sociological Study.* Lanham, Md.: University Press of America, 1985.

Chartier, Roger. *Cultural History: Between Practices and Representations.* Ithaca, N.Y.: Cornell University Press, 1988.

Clark, Elizabeth. "Devil's Gateway and Bride of Christ: Women in the Early Christian World." In *Ascetic Piety and Women's Faith: Essays on Late Ancient Christianity.* Lewiston, N.Y.: Edwin Mellen Press, 1986.

Cobban, Alan B. *The Medieval English Universities: Oxford and Cambridge to c. 1500.* Berkeley: University of California Press, 1988.

Cohen, Sherrill. *The Evolution of Women's Asylums Since 1500.* New York: Oxford University Press, 1992.

Coleman, D. C. *The Economy of England, 1450–1750.* London: Oxford University Press, 1977.

Coleman, Janet. *Medieval Readers and Writers, 1350–1400.* New York: Columbia University Press, 1981.

Crane, T. F. "Mediaeval Sermon-Books and Stories and Their Study Since 1883." *Proceedings of the American Philosophical Society* 56 (1917): 369–402.

Crohns, Hjälmar. *Legenden och medeltidens latinska predikan och "exempla" i deras värdesättning av kvinnen.* Helsinki: Helsingfors Centraltryckeri och Bokbinderi Aktiebolag, 1915.

Cross, Claire. "'Great Reasoners in Scripture': The Activities of Women Lollards, 1380–1530." In *Medieval Women.* Ed. Derek Baker. Studies in Church History Subsidia, 1. Oxford: Basil Blackwell, 1978.

Cullum, P. H. "'And Hir Name Was Charite': Charitable Giving by and for

Women in Late Medieval Yorkshire." In *Woman Is a Worthy Wight: Women in English Society, c. 1200–1500*. Ed. P. J. P. Goldberg. Wolfeboro Falls, N.H.: Alan Sutton, 1992.

Davidson, Clifford. "The Middle English Saint Play and Its Iconography." In *The Saint Play in Medieval Europe*. Ed. Clifford Davidson. Kalamazoo, Mich.: Medieval Institute Publications, 1986.

Delany, Sheila. "Sexual Economics, Chaucer's Wife of Bath, and *The Book of Margery Kempe*." In *Writing Woman: Women Writers and Women in Literature, Medieval to Modern*. New York: Schocken Books, 1983.

Delhaye, Philippe. "Le Dossier antimatrimonial de l'*Adversus Jovinianum* et son influence sur quelques écrits latins du XIIe siècle." *Mediaeval Studies* 13 (1951): 65–86.

D'Emilio, John, and Estelle B. Freedman. *Intimate Matters: A History of Sexuality in America*. New York: Harper and Row, 1988.

Dinshaw, Carolyn. *Chaucer's Sexual Poetics*. Madison: University of Wisconsin Press, 1989.

Dorn, Erhard. *Der sündige Heilige in der Legende des Mittelalters*. Medium Aevum Philologische Studien, 10. Munich: Wilhelm Fink Verlag, 1967.

Duberman, Martin, Martha Vicinus, and George Chauncey, Jr., eds. *Hidden from History: Reclaiming the Gay and Lesbian Past*. New York: Penguin, 1989.

Dyer, Christopher. *Lords and Peasants in a Changing Society: The Estates of the Bishopric of Worcester, 680–1540*. Cambridge: Cambridge University Press, 1980.

Eberle, Patricia J. "Commercial Language and the Commercial Outlook in the *General Prologue*." *Chaucer Review* 18 (1983): 161–74.

Farmer, Sharon. "Persuasive Voices: Clerical Images of Medieval Wives." *Speculum* 61 (1986): 517–43.

Ferrante, Joan. *Woman as Image in Medieval Literature*. New York: Columbia University Press, 1975.

Fink, Hanno. *Die sieben Todsünden in der mittelenglischen erbaulichen Literatur*. Britannica et Americana, 17. Hamburg: Cram, De Gruyter & Co., 1969.

Forte, Stephen L. "A Cambridge Dominican Collector of Exempla in the Thirteenth Century." *Archivum Fratrum Praedicatorum* 28 (1958): 115–48.

Foucault, Michel. *The History of Sexuality*. Vol. 1. *An Introduction*. Trans. Robert Hurley. New York: Pantheon, 1978.

Gagnon, John H. "Prostitution." In vol. 12 of *International Encyclopedia of the Social Sciences*. New York: Macmillan, 1968.

George, B. J., Jr. "Legal, Medical, and Psychiatric Considerations in the Control of Prostitution." *Michigan Law Review* 60 (1962): 717–60.

Geremek, Bronislaw. "L'*Exemplum* et la circulation de la culture au Moyen Age." In *Rhétorique et histoire. L'"Exemplum" et le modèle de comportement dans le discours antique et médiéval*. Mélanges de l'École française de Rome, Moyen âge–temps modernes, 92. Rome: École française de Rome, 1980.

———. *The Margins of Society in Late Medieval Paris*. Trans. Jean Birrell. Cambridge: Cambridge University Press, 1987.

Gibson, Mary. *Prostitution and the State in Italy, 1860–1915*. New Brunswick, N.J.: Rutgers University Press, 1986.

Gillespie, Vincent. "Vernacular Books of Religion." In *Book Production and*

Publishing in Britain, 1375–1475. Ed. Jeremy Griffiths and Derek Pearsall. Cambridge: Cambridge University Press, 1989.

Given-Wilson, Chris. *The Royal Household and the King's Affinity: Service, Politics, and Finance in England, 1360–1413.* New Haven: Yale University Press, 1986.

Goldberg, P. J. P. "Female Labour, Service, and Marriage in the Late Medieval Urban North." *Northern History* 22 (1986): 18–38.

———. "Female Labour, Status, and Marriage in Late Medieval York and Other English Towns." Ph.D. diss., Cambridge, 1987.

———. "Marriage, Migration, Servanthood, and Life Cycle in Yorkshire Towns of the Later Middle Ages: Some York Cause Paper Evidence." *Continuity and Change* 1 (1986): 141–69.

———. "Women in Fifteenth-Century Town Life." In *Towns and Townspeople in the Fifteenth Century.* Ed. John A. F. Thompson. Gloucester: Alan Sutton, 1988.

———. *Women, Work, and Life Cycle in a Medieval Economy: Women in York and Yorkshire, c. 1300–1520.* Oxford: Oxford University Press, 1992.

Goldberg, P. J. P., ed. *Woman Is a Worthy Wight: Women in English Society, c. 1200–1500.* Wolfeboro Falls, N.H.: Alan Sutton, 1992.

Goldman, Emma. *The Traffic in Women and Other Essays on Feminism.* New York: Times Change Press, 1970.

Goody, Jack, and S. J. Tambiah. *Bridewealth and Dowry.* Cambridge Papers in Social Anthropology, 7. Cambridge: Cambridge University Press, 1973.

Graus, František. "Randgruppen der städtischen Gesellschaft im Spätmittelalter." *Zeitschrift für historische Forschung* 8 (1981): 385–437.

Gravdal, Kathryn. *Ravishing Maidens: Writing Rape in Medieval French Literature and Law.* Philadelphia: University of Pennsylvania Press, 1991.

Green, Monica. "Female Sexuality in the Medieval West." *Trends in History* 4 (1990): 127–58.

———. "Obstetrical and Gynecological Texts in Middle English." *Studies in the Age of Chaucer* 14 (1992): 53–88.

Guiette, Robert. *La Légende de la sacristine.* Bibliothèque de la Revue de Littérature Comparée, 43. Paris: Librairie Honoré Champion, 1927.

Guilfoyle, Timothy J. *City of Eros: New York City, Prostitution, and the Commercialization of Sex, 1790–1920.* New York: W. W. Norton, 1992.

Gurevich, Aron. *Medieval Popular Culture: Problems of Belief and Perception.* Trans. János M. Bak and Paul A. Hollingsworth. Cambridge Studies in Oral and Literate Culture, 14. Cambridge: Cambridge University Press, 1988.

Haigh, C. A. "Slander and the Church Courts in the Sixteenth Century." *Transactions of the Lancashire and Cheshire Antiquarian Society* 78 (1975): 1–13.

Hajnal, John. "European Marriage Patterns in Perspective." In *Population in History.* Ed. D. V. Glass and D. E. C. Eversley. Chicago: Aldine, 1965.

Halperin, David M. "Sex Before Sexuality: Pederasty, Politics, and Power in Classical Athens." In *Hidden from History: Reclaiming the Gay and Lesbian Past.* Ed. Martin Duberman, Martha Vicinus, and George Chauncey, Jr. New York: Penguin, 1989.

Hanawalt, Barbara. "Golden Ages for the History of Medieval English Women." In *Women in Medieval History and Historiography.* Ed. Susan Mosher Stuard. Philadelphia: University of Pennsylvania Press, 1987.

————. *Growing Up in Medieval London: The Experience of Childhood in History.* New York: Oxford University Press, 1993.

————. "Remarriage as an Option for Urban and Rural Widows in Late Medieval England." In *Wife and Widow in Medieval England.* Ed. Sue Sheridan Walker. Ann Arbor: University of Michigan Press, 1993.

Harsin, Jill. *Policing Prostitution in Nineteenth-Century Paris.* Princeton: Princeton University Press, 1985.

Hartung, Wolfgang. "Gesellschaftliche Randgruppen im Spätmittelalter. Phänomen und Begriff." In *Städtische Randgruppen und Minderheiten.* Ed. Bernhard Kirchgässner and Fritz Reuter. Stadt in der Geschichte, 13. Sigmaringen: Jan Thorbecke Verlag, 1986.

Hatcher, John. *Plague, Population, and the English Economy, 1348–1530.* London: Macmillan, 1977.

Helmholz, R. H. *Marriage Litigation in Medieval England.* London: Cambridge University Press, 1974.

Herlihy, David. *Opera Muliebria: Women and Work in Medieval Europe.* Philadelphia: Temple University Press, 1990.

Herlihy, David, and Christiane Klapisch-Zuber. *Tuscans and Their Families: A Study of the Florentine Catasto of 1427.* New Haven: Yale University Press, 1985.

Hill, Marilynn Wood. *Their Sisters' Keepers: Prostitution in New York City, 1830–1870.* Berkeley: University of California Press, 1993.

Hinnebusch, William A. *The Early English Friars Preachers.* Institutum Historicum FF. Praedicatorum Romae ad S. Sabinae, Dissertationes Historicae, 14. Rome: St. Sabina, 1951.

Hobson, Barbara Meil. *Uneasy Virtue: The Politics of Prostitution and the American Reform Tradition.* New York: Basic Books, 1987.

Høigård, Cecilie, and Liv Finstad. *Backstreets: Prostitution, Money, and Love.* Trans. Katherine Hanson, Nancy Sipe, and Barbara Wilson. University Park: Pennsylvania State University Press, 1992.

Houlbrooke, Ralph. *Church Courts and the People During the English Reformation, 1520–1570.* Oxford: Oxford University Press, 1979.

————. *The English Family, 1450–1700.* New York: Longman, 1984.

Hughes, Diane Owen. "From Brideprice to Dowry in Mediterranean Europe." *Journal of Family History* 3 (1978): 262–96.

Ingram, Martin. *Church Courts, Sex, and Marriage in England, 1570–1640.* Cambridge: Cambridge University Press, 1987.

Irsigler, Franz, and Arnold Lassotta. *Bettler und Gaukler, Dirnen und Henker: Randgruppen und Aussenseiter in Köln, 1300–1600.* Cologne: Greven Verlag, 1984.

Jacquart, Danielle, and Claude Thomasset. *Sexuality and Medicine in the Middle Ages.* Trans. Matthew Adamson. Princeton: Princeton University Press, 1988.

Jenness, Valerie. *Making It Work: The Prostitutes' Rights Movement in Perspective.* New York: Aldine de Gruyter, 1993.

Jennings, Margaret. "Tutivillus: The Literary Career of the Recording Demon." *Studies in Philology: Texts and Studies* 74 (1977): 1–96.

Johnson, David J. *Southwark and the City.* London: Corporation of London, 1969.

Jones, Charles W. *Saint Nicholas of Myra, Bari, and Manhattan: Biography of a Legend.* Chicago: University of Chicago Press, 1978.

Jones, E. D. "The Medieval Leyrwite: A Historical Note on Female Fornication." *English Historical Review* 107 (1992): 945–53.

Jordan, W. K. *The Charities of London, 1480–1660: The Aspirations and the Achievements of the Urban Society.* London: George Allen and Unwin, 1960.

Karras, Ruth Mazo. "Gendered Sin and Misogyny in John of Bromyard's 'Summa Predicantium.'" *Traditio* 47 (1992): 233–57.

———. "Holy Harlots: Prostitute Saints in Medieval Legend." *Journal of the History of Sexuality* 1 (1990): 3–32.

———. "The Latin Vocabulary of Illicit Sex in English Ecclesiastical Court Records." *Journal of Medieval Latin* 2 (1992): 1–17.

———. "Prostitution in Medieval Europe." In *Handbook of Medieval Sexuality.* Ed. Vern L. Bullough and James Brundage. New York: Garland, in press.

———. "The Regulation of Brothels in Later Medieval England." *Signs: Journal of Women in Culture and Society* 14 (1989): 399–433.

———. "Sexuality and Marginality." Paper presented at "Peripheral Visions" conference, University of Oregon, April 1994.

———. "Two Models, Two Standards: Moral Teaching and Sexual Mores." In *Intersections: Literature and History in the Fifteenth Century.* Ed. Barbara Hanawalt and David Wallace. Minneapolis: University of Minnesota Press, in press.

———. "The Virgin and the Pregnant Abbess: Miracles and Gender in the Middle Ages." *Medieval Perspectives* 3 (1988): 112–32.

Karras, Ruth Mazo, and David Lorenzo Boyd. "'*Ut cum Muliere*': A Male Transvestite Prostitute in Fourteenth-Century London." In *The Pleasures of History: Reading Sexualities in Premodern Europe.* Ed. Louise Fradenburg and Carla Freccero. London: Routledge, in press.

Katzenellenbogen, Adolf. *Allegories of the Virtues and Vices in Mediaeval Art.* London: Warburg Institute, 1939.

Kaye, Joel B. "Quantification of Quality: The Impact of Money and Monetization on the Development of Scientific Thought in the Fourteenth Century." Ph.D. diss., University of Pennsylvania, 1991.

Keene, Derek. *Survey of Medieval Winchester.* Winchester Studies, vol. 2. Oxford: Clarendon Press, 1985.

Kemmler, Fritz. *"Exempla" in Context: A Historical and Critical Study of Robert Mannyng of Brunne's "Handlyng Synne."* Studies and Texts in English, 6. Tübingen: Gunter Narr Verlag, 1984.

Kettle, Ann J. "City and Close; Lichfield in the Century Before the Reformation." In *The Church in Pre-Reformation Society.* Ed. Caroline M. Barron and Christopher Harper-Bill. Woodbridge, Suffolk: Boydell and Brewer, 1985.

Knapp, Peggy. *Chaucer and the Social Contest.* New York: Routledge, 1990.

Kolve, V. A. *The Play Called Corpus Christi.* Stanford: Stanford University Press, 1966.

Kosmer, Ellen. "The 'Noyous Humoure of Lecherie.'" *Art Bulletin* 57 (1975): 1–8.

Kowaleski, Maryanne. "Women's Work in a Market Town: Exeter in the Late Fourteenth Century." In *Women and Work in Preindustrial Europe.* Ed. Barbara Hanawalt. Bloomington: Indiana University Press, 1986.

Kowaleski, Maryanne, and Judith M. Bennett. "Crafts, Gilds, and Women in the Middle Ages: Fifty Years After Marian K. Dale." *Signs: Journal of Women in Culture and Society* 14 (1989): 474–88.

Kuhn, Sherman, ed. *Middle English Dictionary.* Ann Arbor: University of Michigan Press, 1956–.

Lacey, Kay E. "Women and Work in Fourteenth- and Fifteenth-Century London." In *Women and Work in Preindustrial England.* Ed. Lindsey Charles and Lorna Duffin. London: Croom Helm, 1985.

Laird, Charlton. "Character and Growth of the *Manuel des Pechiez.*" *Traditio* 4 (1946): 253–306.

Lawner, Lynne. *Lives of the Courtesans: Portraits of the Renaissance.* New York: Rizzoli, 1987.

Leclerq, Jean. *Monks on Marriage: A Twelfth-Century View.* New York: Seabury Press, 1982.

LeGoff, Jacques. "Licit and Illicit Trades in the Medieval West." In *Time, Work, and Culture in the Middle Ages.* Trans. Arthur Goldhammer. Chicago: University of Chicago Press, 1980.

———. "Les Marginaux dans l'occident médiéval." In *Les Marginaux et les exclus dans l'histoire.* Cahiers Jussieu, 5. Paris: Union générale d'éditions, 1979.

Lerner, Gerda. *The Creation of Patriarchy.* New York: Oxford University Press, 1986.

Levin, Eve. *Sex and Society in the World of the Orthodox Slavs, 900–1700.* Ithaca, N.Y.: Cornell University Press, 1989.

Lewis, Robert E., and Angus McIntosh. *A Descriptive Guide to the Manuscripts of the Prick of Conscience.* Medium Aevum Monographs, n.s., 12. Oxford: Society for the Study of Medieval Languages and Literatures, 1982.

Little, Lester. *Religious Poverty and the Profit Economy in Medieval Europe.* Ithaca, N.Y.: Cornell University Press, 1978.

Longère, Jean. *La Prédication médiévale.* Paris: Études Augustiniennes, 1983.

Lorcin, Marie-Thérèse. *Façons de sentir et de penser: Les Fabliaux français.* Paris: Honoré Champion, 1979.

———. "La Prostituée des fabliaux, est-elle intégrée ou exclue?" In *Exclus et systèmes d'exclusion dans la littérature et la civilisation médiévales.* Sénéfiance, 5. Aix-en-Provence: Centre universitaire d'études et de recherches médiévales, 1978.

McCall, Andrew. *The Medieval Underworld.* London: Hamish Hamilton, 1979.

McClure, Ruth. *Coram's Children: The London Foundling Hospital in the Eighteenth Century.* New Haven: Yale, 1981.

Macfarlane, Alan. *Marriage and Love in England: Modes of Reproduction, 1300–1840.* Oxford: Basil Blackwell, 1986.

McIntosh, Marjorie Keniston. "Finding Language for Misconduct: Jurors in Fifteenth-Century Local Courts." In *Intersections: History and Literature in the Fifteenth Century.* Ed. Barbara Hanawalt and David Wallace. Minneapolis: University of Minnesota Press, in press.

———. "Local Change and Community Control in England, 1465–1500." *Huntington Library Quarterly* 49 (1986): 219–42.

MacKinnon, Catharine A. "Does Sexuality Have a History?" In *Discourses of Sexuality: From Aristotle to AIDS.* Ed. Domna C. Stanton. Ann Arbor: University of Michigan Press, 1992.

McLaren, Angus. *A History of Contraception from Antiquity to the Present Day.* Oxford: Basil Blackwell, 1990.

McNamara, Jo Ann. *A New Song: Celibate Women in the First Christian Centuries.* New York: Haworth Press, 1983.

Mahood, Linda. *The Magdalenes: Prostitution in the Nineteenth Century.* London: Routledge, 1990.

Makowski, Elizabeth M. "The Conjugal Debt and Medieval Canon Law." *Journal of Medieval History* 3 (1977): 99–114.

Mâle, Emile. *Religious Art in France, the Twelfth Century: A Study of the Origins of Medieval Iconography.* Princeton: Princeton University Press, 1982.

Martin, Priscilla. *Chaucer's Women: Nuns, Wives, and Amazons.* Iowa City: University of Iowa Press, 1990.

Matter, E. Ann. "My Sister, My Spouse: Women-Identified Women in Medieval Christianity," *Journal of Feminist Studies in Religion* 2 (1986): 81–93.

May, Geoffrey. "Prostitution." In *Encyclopedia of the Social Sciences.* New York: Macmillan, 1934.

Meisen, Karl. *Nikolauskult und Nikolausbrauch im Abendlande. Eine kultgeographisch-volkskundliche Untersuchung.* Forschungen zur Volkskunde, 9–12. Düsseldorf: L. Schwann, 1931.

Mertes, Kate. *The English Noble Household, 1250–1600: Good Governance and Politic Rule.* Oxford: Blackwell, 1988.

Millett, Kate. *The Prostitution Papers: A Candid Dialogue.* New York: Avon, 1973.

Moore, R. I. *The Formation of a Persecuting Society: Power and Deviance in Western Europe, 950–1250.* New York: Basil Blackwell, 1987.

Morin, Margaret J. "John Waldeby, O.S.A., Preacher, with a Critical Edition of His Tract on the Ave Maria." *Analecta Augustiniana* 35 (1972): 7–80, 36 (1973): 5–79, 37 (1974): 5–41.

Murray, Jacqueline. "On the Origins and Role of the 'Wise Woman' in Causes for Annulment on the Grounds of Male Impotence," *Journal of Medieval History* 16 (1990): 235–49.

——. "The Perceptions of Sexuality, Marriage, and Family in Early English Pastoral Manuals." Ph.D. diss., University of Toronto, 1987.

Muscatine, Charles. *The Old French Fabliaux.* New Haven: Yale University Press, 1986.

Newhauser, Richard. *The Treatise on Vices and Virtues in Latin and the Vernacular.* Typologie des sources du moyen âge occidental, fasc. 68. Turnhout: Brepols, 1993.

Otis, Leah Lydia. *Prostitution in Medieval Society: The History of an Urban Institution in Languedoc.* Chicago: University of Chicago Press, 1985.

Owen, Dorothy. "Ecclesiastical Jurisdiction in England, 1300–1550: The Records and Their Interpretation." In *The Materials, Sources, and Methods of Ecclesiastical History.* Ed. Derek Baker. Studies in Church History, 11. Oxford: Ecclesiastical History Society, 1975.

——. *The Records of the Established Church in England Excluding Parochial Records.* Archives and the User, 1. London: British Records Association, 1970.

Owst, G. R. *The Destructorium Viciorum of Alexander Carpenter.* London: Society for the Promotion of Christian Knowledge, 1952.

——. *Literature and Pulpit in Medieval England.* Cambridge: Cambridge University Press, 1933.

Padgug, Robert. "Sexual Matters: Rethinking Sexuality in History." In *Hidden from History: Reclaiming the Gay and Lesbian Past.* Ed. Martin Duberman, Martha Vicinus, and George Chauncey, Jr. New York: Penguin, 1989.

Pagels, Elaine. *Adam, Eve, and the Serpent.* New York: Random House, 1988.

Palmer, Robert C. *English Law in the Age of the Black Death, 1348–1381: A Transformation of Governance and Law.* Chapel Hill: University of North Carolina Press, 1993.

Pantin, W. A. *The English Church in the Fourteenth Century.* Cambridge: Cambridge University Press, 1955.

Pateman, Carole. *The Sexual Contract.* Stanford: Stanford University Press, 1988.

Patterson, Lee. *Chaucer and the Subject of History.* Madison: University of Wisconsin Press, 1991.

———. *Negotiating the Past: The Historical Understanding of Medieval Literature.* Madison: University of Wisconsin Press, 1987.

———. "'No Man His Reson Herde': Peasant Consciousness, Chaucer's Miller, and the Structure of the *Canterbury Tales.*" In *Literary Practice and Social Change in Britain, 1380–1530.* Ed. Lee Patterson. Berkeley: University of California Press, 1990.

Pavan, Elisabeth. "Police des moeurs, société et politique à Venise à la fin du Moyen Age." *Revue Historique* 264 (1980): 241–88.

Peck, Russell A. *Chaucer's "Romaunt of the Rose" and "Boece," "Treatise on the Astrolabe," "Equatorie of the Planetis," Lost Works, and Chaucerian Apocrypha: An Annotated Bibliography, 1900 to 1985.* Chaucer Bibliographies, 2. Toronto: University of Toronto Press, 1988.

Perry, Mary Elizabeth. "Deviant Insiders: Legalized Prostitutes and a Consciousness of Women in Early Modern Seville." *Comparative Studies in Society and History* 27 (1985): 138–58.

———. *Gender and Disorder in Early Modern Seville.* Princeton: Princeton University Press, 1990.

———. "'Lost Women' in Early Modern Seville: The Politics of Prostitution." *Feminist Studies* 4 (1978): 195–214.

Pheterson, Gail, ed. *A Vindication of the Rights of Whores.* Seattle: Seal Press, 1989.

Poos, L. R. *A Rural Society After the Black Death: Essex. 1350–1525.* Cambridge: Cambridge University Press, 1991.

———. "Sex, Lies, and the Church Courts of Pre-Reformation England." *Journal of Interdisciplinary History* 25 (1995): 585–607.

Poos, L. R., and R. M. Smith. "'Legal Windows onto Historical Populations'? Recent Research on Demography and the Manor Court in Medieval England." *Law and History Review* 2 (1984): 128–52.

Post, J. B. "Ravishment of Women and the Statutes of Westminster." In *Legal Records and the Historian.* Ed. J. H. Baker. London: Royal Historical Society, 1978.

Power, Eileen E. *Medieval English Nunneries, c. 1275 to 1535.* Cambridge: Cambridge University Press, 1922.

Pratt, Robert A. "Chaucer and the Hand That Fed Him." *Speculum* 41 (1968): 619–42.

———. "Jankyn's Book of Wikked Wyves: Medieval Antimatrimonial Propaganda in the Universities." *Annuale Medievale* 3 (1962): 5–27.

Rath, Brigitte. "Prostitution und spätmittelalterliche Gesellschaft im österreichisch-süddeutschen Raum." In *Frau und Spätmittelalterlicher Alltag. Internationaler Kongress Krems an der Donau 2. bis 5. Oktober 1984.* Österreichische Akademie der Wissenschaften, Philosophisch-historische Klasse, Sitzungsberichte, 473. Vienna: Verlag der österreichischen Akademie der Wissenschaften, 1986.

Reisig, Robin. "Sisterhood and Prostitution." *Village Voice*, December 16, 1971.

Remnant, G. L. *A Catalogue of Misericords in Great Britain.* Oxford: Clarendon Press, 1969.

Richmond, Colin. *John Hopton, a Fifteenth-Century Suffolk Gentleman.* Cambridge: Cambridge University Press, 1981.

Riddle, John M. *Contraception and Abortion from the Ancient World to the Renaissance.* Cambridge, Mass.: Harvard University Press, 1992.

_____. "Oral Contraceptives and Early-Term Abortifacients During Classical Antiquity and the Middle Ages." *Past and Present*, no. 132 (August 1991): 3–32.

Robertson, D. W., Jr. "The Cultural Tradition of *Handlyng Synne.*" *Speculum* 22 (1947): 162–85.

_____. "Frequency of Preaching in Thirteenth-Century England." *Speculum* 24 (1949): 376–88.

Roper, Lyndal. " 'The Common Man,' 'The Common Good,' 'Common Women': Gender and Meaning in the German Reformation Commune." *Social History* 12 (1987): 1–21.

_____. "Discipline and Respectability: Prostitution and the Reformation in Augsburg." *History Workshop* (1985): 3–28.

_____. *The Holy Household: Women and Morals in Reformation Augsburg.* Oxford: Clarendon Press, 1989.

_____. "Mothers of Debauchery: Procuresses in Reformation Augsburg." *German History* 6 (1988): 1–19.

Rosen, Ruth. *The Lost Sisterhood: Prostitution in America, 1900–1918.* Baltimore, Md.: Johns Hopkins University Press, 1982.

Rosenthal, Constance L. "The *Vitae Patrum* in Old and Middle English Literature." Ph.D. diss., University of Pennsylvania, 1936.

Rosenthal, Joel. "Fifteenth-Century Widows and Widowhood: Bereavement, Reintegration, and Life Choices." In *Wife and Widow in Medieval England.* Ed. Sue Sheridan Walker. Ann Arbor: University of Michigan Press, 1993.

Rosser, G. A. "London and Westminster: The Suburb in the Urban Economy in the Late Middle Ages." In *Towns and Townspeople in the Fifteenth Century.* Ed. John A. F. Thompson. Gloucester: Alan Sutton, 1988.

_____. *Medieval Westminster, 1200–1540.* Oxford: Clarendon Press, 1989.

_____. "Medieval Westminster: The Vill and the Urban Community, 1200–1540." Ph.D. diss., Bedford College, 1984.

Rossiaud, Jacques. *Medieval Prostitution.* Trans. Lydia G. Cochrane. Oxford: Basil Blackwell, 1988.

_____. "Prostitution, Youth, and Society in Towns of South Eastern France in the Fifteenth Century." Trans. Elborg Forster. In *Deviants and the Abandoned in French Society.* Ed. Robert Forster and Orest Ranum. Baltimore, Md.: Johns Hopkins University Press, 1978.

Rouse, Richard H., and Mary A. Rouse. *Preachers, Florilegia, and Sermons: Studies on the Manipulus Florum of Thomas of Ireland.* Toronto: Pontifical Institute for Mediaeval Studies, 1979.

Rubin, Gayle. "The Traffic in Women: Notes on the 'Political Economy' of Sex."

In *Toward an Anthropology of Women*. Ed. Rayna R. Reiter. New York: Monthly Review Press, 1975.

Ruggiero, Guido. *Binding Passions: Tales of Magic, Marriage, and Power at the End of the Renaissance*. New York: Oxford University Press, 1993.

Russ, Joanna. "Comment on 'Prostitution in Medieval Canon Law' by James Brundage." *Signs* 2 (1977): 922–23.

Russell, Josiah Cox. *British Medieval Population*. Albuquerque: University of New Mexico Press, 1948.

Sagarin, Edward. *Deviants and Deviance: An Introduction to the Study of Disvalued People and Behavior*. New York: Praeger, 1975.

Santore, Cathy. "Julia Lombardo, 'Somtuosa Meretrize': A Portrait by Property." *Renaissance Quarterly* 41 (1988): 44–83.

Saxer, Victor. *Le Culte de Marie Madeleine en occident des origines à la fin du moyen âge*. Cahiers d'archéologie et d'histoire, 3. Auxerre: Société des Fouilles archéologiques et des Monuments historiques de l'Yonne, 1959.

Scattergood, V. J. "The Originality of 'The Shipman's Tale.'" *Chaucer Review* 11 (1976): 210–31.

Schneyer, Johannes Baptist. *Repertorium der lateinischen Sermones des Mittelalters für die Zeit von 1150–1350*. 9 vols. Beiträge zur Geschichte der Philosophie und Theologie des Mittelalters, 43. Münster: Aschendorff, 1969.

Schuster, Peter. *Das Frauenhaus: Städtische Bordelle in Deutschland (1350–1600)*. Paderborn: Ferdinand Schöningh, 1992.

Scott, Joan. "The Evidence of Experience." *Critical Inquiry* 17 (1991): 773–97.

Searle, Eleanor. *Lordship and Community: Battle Abbey and Its Banlieu, 1066–1538*. Studies and Texts, 26. Toronto: Pontifical Institute for Mediaeval Studies, 1974.

Sekules, Veronica. "Women and Art in England in the Thirteenth and Fourteenth Century." In *The Age of Chivalry: Art in Plantagenet England, 1200–1400*. Ed. Jonathan Alexander and Paul Binski. London: Royal Academy of Arts, 1987.

Shahar, Shulamith. *The Fourth Estate: A History of Women in the Middle Ages*. Trans. Chaya Galai. London: Methuen, 1983.

Sharpe, J. A. *Defamation and Sexual Slander in Early Modern England: The Church Courts at York*. Borthwick Papers, 58. York: University of York, Borthwick Institute for Historical Research, 1980.

Sheehan, Michael. "Theory and Practice: Marriage of the Unfree and the Poor in Medieval Society." *Mediaeval Studies* 50 (1988): 457–87.

Shoaf, R. A. *Dante, Chaucer, and the Currency of the Word: Money, Images, and Reference in Late Medieval Poetry*. Norman, Okla.: Pilgrim Books, 1983.

Silverman, Albert H. "Sex and Money in Chaucer's 'Shipman's Tale.'" *Philological Quarterly* 32 (1953): 329–36.

Smalley, Beryl. *English Friars and Antiquity in the Early Fourteenth Century*. Oxford: Blackwell, 1960.

Smith, Richard M. "Geographical Diversity in the Resort to Marriage in Late Medieval Europe: Work, Reputation, and Unmarried Females in the Household Formation Systems of Northern and Southern Europe." In *Woman Is a Worthy Wight: Women in English Society, c. 1200–1500*. Ed. P. J. P. Goldberg. Wolfeboro Falls, N.H.: Alan Sutton, 1992.

_____. "Hypothèses sur la nuptialité en Angleterre aux XIIe–XIVe siècles." *Annales: Economies, sociétés, civilisations* 38 (1983): 107–36.

_____. "Marriage Processes in the English Past: Some Continuities." In *The World We Have Gained*. Ed. Richard M. Smith, Keith Wrightson, and Lloyd Bonfield. Oxford: Blackwell, 1986.

_____. "Some Reflections on the Evidence for the Origins of the 'European Marriage Pattern' in England." In *The Sociology of the Family: New Directions for Britain*. Ed. Chris Harris. Sociological Review Monograph, 28. Keele, Eng.: University of Keele, 1979.

Smith-Rosenberg, Carroll. *Disorderly Conduct*. New York: Oxford University Press, 1986.

Spencer, H. Leith. *English Preaching in the Late Middle Ages*. Oxford: Clarendon Press, 1993.

Spiegel, Gabrielle M. "History, Historicism, and the Social Logic of the Text in the Middle Ages." *Speculum* 65 (1990): 59–86.

Spufford, Margaret. "Puritanism and Social Control?" In *Order and Disorder in Early Modern England*. Ed. Anthony Fletcher and John Stevenson. Cambridge: Cambridge University Press, 1985.

Stanbury, Sarah, and Linda Lomperis, eds. *Feminist Approaches to the Body in Medieval Literature*. Philadelphia: University of Pennsylvania Press, 1993.

Stone, Lawrence. *The Road to Divorce: England, 1530–1987*. Oxford: Oxford University Press, 1990.

Strohm, Paul. "Chaucer's Fifteenth-Century Audience and the Narrowing of the 'Chaucer Tradition.'" *Studies in the Age of Chaucer* 4 (1982): 3–32.

_____. *Hochon's Arrow: The Social Imagination of Fourteenth-Century Texts*. Princeton: Princeton University Press, 1992.

_____. *Social Chaucer*. Cambridge, Mass.: Harvard University Press, 1989.

Swanson, Heather. *Medieval Artisans: An Urban Class in Late Medieval England*. Oxford: Basil Blackwell, 1989.

Swanson, Jenny. *John of Wales: A Study of the Works and Ideas of a Thirteenth-Century Friar*. Cambridge: Cambridge University Press, 1989.

Symanski, Richard. *The Immoral Landscape: Female Prostitution in Western Societies*. Toronto: Butterworths, 1981.

Taylor, Larissa J. *Soldiers of Christ: Preaching in Late Medieval and Reformation France*. New York: Oxford University Press, 1992.

_____. "Strange Bedfellows: Preachers and Prostitutes in Late Medieval Europe." Paper presented at the Twenty-first Annual Meeting of the Western Society for French History, Missoula, Mont., October 1993.

Terroine, Anne. "Le Roi de ribauds de l'Hôtel du roi et les prostituées parisiennes." *Revue historique de droit* 56 (1978): 253–67.

Thomas, Keith. "The Double Standard." *Journal of the History of Ideas* 20 (1959): 195–216.

_____. *Religion and the Decline of Magic*. New York: Scribner, 1971.

Thorold Rogers, James E. *A History of Agriculture and Prices in England*. 7 vols. Oxford: Clarendon Press, 1866–1902.

_____. *Six Centuries of Work and Wages*. New York: Putnam's, 1884.

Thrupp, Sylvia L. "Aliens in and Around London in the Fifteenth Century." In *Studies in London History*. Ed. A. E. J. Hollaender and William Kellaway. London: Hodder and Stoughton, 1969.

———. *The Merchant Class of Medieval London.* Ann Arbor: University of Michigan Press, 1948.

Trexler, Richard. "La Prostitution florentine au XVe siècle: Patronages et clientèles." *Annales: Economies, sociétés, civilisations* 36 (1981): 983–1015.

Tubach, Frederic C. *Index Exemplorum: A Handbook of Medieval Religious Tales.* Folklore Fellows Communications, 204. Helsinki: Suomalainen Tiedeakatemia, 1969.

Underdown, David. "The Taming of the Scold." In *Order and Disorder in Early Modern England.* Ed. Anthony Fletcher and John Stevenson. Cambridge: Cambridge University Press, 1985.

Vandenbroeke, Chr. "De prijs van betaalde liefde." *Spiegel Historiael* 18, no. 2 (1983): 90–94.

von Balthasar, H. U. "Casta Meretrix." In *Sponsa Verbi.* Skizzen zur Theologie, 2. Einsiedeln: Johannes Verlag, 1961.

Von Nolcken, Christina. "Some Alphabetical *Compendia* and How Preachers Used Them in Fourteenth-Century England." *Viator* 12 (1981): 271–88.

Wadler, Joyce. "The Spy Who Fell in Love with a Shadow." *New York Times Magazine.* August 15, 1993.

Walkowitz, Judith R. *Prostitution and Victorian Society: Women, Class, and the State.* Cambridge: Cambridge University Press, 1980.

Ward, Benedicta. *Harlots of the Desert: A Study of Repentance in Early Monastic Sources.* Kalamazoo, Mich.: Cistercian Publications, 1987.

Wedek, Harry. "Synonyms for Meretrix." *Classical Weekly* 37 (1944): 116–17.

Weinstein, Donald, and Rudolph M. Bell. *Saints and Society: The Two Worlds of Western Christendom.* Chicago: University of Chicago Press, 1982.

Weir, Anthony, and James Jerman. *Images of Lust: Sexual Carvings on Medieval Churches.* London: B. T. Batsford, 1986.

Weisheipl, James A. *Friar Thomas D'Aquino: His Life, Thought, and Work.* Garden City, N.Y.: Doubleday & Co., 1974.

Welter, J.-Th. *L'Exemplum dans la littérature religieuse et didactique du moyen âge.* Paris: Occitania, 1927.

Wenzel, Siegfried. "Chaucer and the Language of Contemporary Preaching." *Studies in Philology* 73 (1976): 138–61.

———. *Preachers, Poets, and the Early English Lyric.* Princeton: Princeton University Press, 1986.

———. *Verses in Sermons: Fasciculus Morum and Its Middle English Poems.* Cambridge, Mass.: Medieval Academy of America, 1978.

———. "Vices, Virtues, and Popular Preaching." In *Medieval and Renaissance Studies: Proceedings of the Southeastern Institute of Medieval and Renaissance Studies, Summer 1974.* Ed. Dale B. J. Randall. Durham, N.C.: Duke University Press, 1976.

Westenrieder, Lorenz. *Beyträge zur vaterländischen Historie, Geographie, Staatistik, etc.* Vol. 6. Munich: Joseph Lindauer, 1800.

White, Luise. *The Comforts of Home: Prostitution in Colonial Nairobi.* Chicago: University of Chicago Press, 1990.

———. "Prostitutes, Reformers, and Historians." *Criminal Justice History* 6 (1985): 201–27.

White, Sarah Melhado. "Sexual Language and Human Conflict in Old French Fabliaux." *Comparative Studies in Society and History* 24 (1982): 185–210.

Wilson, Katharina, and Elizabeth Makowski. *Wykked Wyves and the Woes of*

Marriage: Misogamous Literature from Juvenal to Chaucer. Albany: State University of New York Press, 1990.

Winick, Charles, and Paul M. Kinsie. *The Lively Commerce: Prostitution in the United States.* Chicago: Quadrangle, 1971.

Woodcock, Brian. *Medieval Ecclesiastical Courts in the Diocese of Canterbury.* London: Oxford University Press, 1952.

Wrightson, Keith. *English Society, 1580–1680.* New Brunswick, N.J.: Rutgers University Press, 1982.

Wrigley, E. A., and R. S. Schofield. *The Population History of England, 1541–1871: A Reconstruction.* Cambridge, Mass.: Harvard University Press, 1981.

Wunderli, Richard M. *London Church Courts and Society on the Eve of the Reformation.* Speculum Anniversary Monographs, 7. Cambridge, Mass.: Medieval Academy of America, 1981.

Index